MEANINGS OF MAPLE

FOOD AND FOODWAYS
SERIES EDITORS:
JENNIFER JENSEN WALLACH
AND MICHAEL WISE

OTHER TITLES IN THIS SERIES

*The Taste of Art: Food, Cooking, and Counterculture
in Contemporary Art*

*Devouring Cultures: Perspectives on Food, Power, and Identity
from the Zombie Apocalypse to Downton Abbey*

*Latin@s' Presence in the Food Industry:
Changing How We Think about Food*

*Dethroning the Deceitful Pork Chop:
Rethinking African AmericanFoodways from Slavery to Obama*

American Appetites: A Documentary Reader

Meanings of Maple

AN ETHNOGRAPHY OF SUGARING

MICHAEL A. LANGE

The University of Arkansas Press
Fayetteville
2017

ISBN: 9781682260357 (cloth)
ISBN: 9781682260371 (paper)
e-ISBN: 9781610756174

∞ The paper used in this publication meets the minimum requirements of the American National Standard for Permanence of Paper for Printed Library Materials Z39.48-1984.

Library of Congress Control Number: 2017934989

Dedicated to the GoE—you know who you are

CONTENTS

SERIES EDITORS' PREFACE

The University of Arkansas Press Series on Food and Foodways explores historical and contemporary issues in global food studies. We are committed to representing a diverse set of voices that tell lesser known food stories and to provoking new avenues of interdisciplinary research. Our strengths are works in the humanities and social sciences that use food as a critical lens to examine broader cultural, environmental, and ethical issues.

In *Meanings of Maple*, Michael A. Lange offers readers a sustained cultural analysis of maple sugarmaking. Built upon Lange's extensive ethnographic research and written in a voice that is both accessible and precise, the book at once communicates the technical worlds inhabited by maple sugarmakers and expresses sugarmakers' diverse understandings of the changing places and identities of maple sugar within the food cultures of the twenty-first century. Lange takes readers deep into a Vermont sugarbush webbed from tree to tree and tap to tap by a maze of plastic tubes, mainline valves, and collection tanks. He reveals the interior of the sugarhouse, crammed with gas evaporators and reverse osmosis machines; often no piles of wood nor red-checkered jackets in sight. With characteristic humor and empathy, Lange describes encounters between sugarmakers and their foodie-tourist admirers from southern New England and elsewhere, who are bent on experiencing the sights, smells, and tastes of syrups cooked over a wood fire, overeager to invest Vermont sugarmaking with mythological fantasies of rural simplicity.

Lange accomplishes much more than just narrating these bittersweet tales of modern-day maple, however. For food studies scholars, Lange also demonstrates how the unique technical steps of maple sugar production complicate our understandings of what constitute differences between foraging and farming. He explores, as well, how boiling maple falls within an intermediary shade of cooking. From studying seasonal flows of sap to considering controversies over the grading and marketing process, Lange thoughtfully traces the many ways that this staple ingredient, rendered from the liquid guts of trees, transcends many of the agricultural, economic, and cultural assumptions that the so-called food movement have taken for granted. So much more than just another commodity study, *Meanings of Maple* frames a new approach for evaluating the broader cultural and ecological contexts of iconic foodways, like Vermont maple sugar, as tastes rooted as much in the terroirs of historical memory and geographical imagination as in the technical stages of their production and consumption. The first book of its kind, *Meanings of Maple* will animate conversations in food studies for years to come.

JENNIFER JENSEN WALLACH
AND MICHAEL WISE, SERIES EDITORS

ACKNOWLEDGMENTS

First, of course, I want to acknowledge the contributions of all the sugarmakers and others associated with sugaring who shared their time and thoughts with me. I have found sugarmakers mostly to be a kind, generous lot, and their generosity has made this book possible. My thanks go to all sugarmakers who have spoken with me, formally or informally, but I would like to thank two in particular: Burr Morse of East Montpelier and Jon Branon of Fairfield. These two sugarmakers take different approaches to sugaring as a business and a way of life, and they both represent the very best of Vermont sugaring in their own ways. Jon and Burr have each spoken with me several times, and both have been particularly kind and open with their knowledge, analysis, wisdom, and expertise. Burr and Jon also agreed to give me permission to use their names in this book, for which I am very grateful. Amy Trubek permitted me to use her name in connection with some quotations from a conversation we had, too. While I chose to keep the vast majority of the people who spoke with me anonymous, using these three names roots my discussion firmly in Vermont and in a larger intellectual context, and my book is better for it.

I would also like to thank the faculty and students in the Folklore Department at Memorial University of Newfoundland, Canada, where I had a sabbatical position in the spring term of 2015. Their warm and friendly welcome to the office down the hall made my sabbatical there comfortable, enjoyable, and stimulating. The manuscript for *Meanings of Maple* was written entirely in that office, with the dbj watching over me. Everyone in the department was wonderful and I appreciate them all, but I would like to thank three colleagues there especially for reading drafts and giving me feedback on my writing: Diane Tye, Philip Hiscock, and Jillian Gould. Earlier, from the fieldwork stage, I want to acknowledge Katie Wynn and Mabel Agozzino, who acted as my research assistants on some of my interviews.

I would like to thank Michael Wise and Deena Owens at the University of Arkansas Press, and copyeditor Debbie Upton, who helped me get my manuscript into fighting shape. Several entities have granted me permission to reprint text or graphics. The Vermont Maple Sugar Makers Association granted permission to reprint their explanatory graphic of the new Vermont syrup grading system, and the University of Vermont's Department of Nutrition and Food Science gave permission to reprint their descriptions of tasting notes and off-flavors for maple syrup. Portions of the economic chapter appear in my contribution to *Folklorist in the Marketplace* (Utah State University Press). I also thank Chuck Mitchell for making the piece of artwork that graces the front cover of this book, and Judd Lamphere for photographing it.

On the home front, the organizers and attendees of the George "Honeyboy" Evans Symposium Series provided a collegial and friendly forum for presenting and discussing some of the ideas that made their way into *Meanings of Maple*. And on the home-home front, I extend my constant gratitude to my family, especially Carmen Lange for her unwavering support. I always know that at least one person will read my books. Special thanks also go to my brother, Douglas Lange, for the many chats we had as he tapped his first trees, but more importantly for his always watching out for me. He cares quietly, but I know he cares. He allowed me to tell his story to set up the discussion contained in this book, and that framing gave shape to the introduction.

Many sugaring people helped me with *Meanings of Maple* by sharing their time and minds with me. Whatever intelligence can be found in this book can be credited to them. Any idiocies are mine alone.

INTRODUCTION

Backyard Sugaring

My brother tried making maple syrup for the first time in the spring of 2015. Well, winter really, as the maple sap typically runs when the temperature is below freezing overnight and above 40° F during the day. Those conditions generally occur at the end of winter, but before spring has really sprung. We have both always loved to cook, and for several years now my brother has been increasingly interested in food sourcing, local produce, and a general sense of awareness of where the items he's cooking come from. Knowing an ingredient's origin and all the steps that go into its making are meaningful bits of knowledge for him. It matters to him to understand where the items in his kitchen come from. Making maple syrup—sugaring—offered him a good chance to know intimately an ingredient in the kitchen from its very beginning. He is a software engineer by day, which means that he thinks in digitized systems and is also a bit of a gadget head. Making maple syrup affords many opportunities for acquiring gadgets, as well as for organizing and optimizing numerical systems, so it seemed like a perfect outlet for his hobby impulses as well. Again, making maple syrup would be a meaningful activity for him because playing with the gadgets and balancing all the numbers is something that resonates with him. He enjoys it; it's meaningful. I was excited for him in his first year of sugaring, but also a bit jealous, as I have been doing research on maple sugaring in Vermont, where I live, for seven or so years now. I have helped Vermonters sugar, and I've taken part in pretty much all steps in the process, but I don't have any trees of my own. I have never made *my own* syrup on *my own* trees, and he was getting a chance to do so. By definition, he is a backyard sugarmaker, as the first tree he tapped was a maple in his own backyard in Ohio, but by the standards of Vermont, he is a backyarder because he is making syrup in very small quantities and for his own amusement and consumption.

Eventually, my brother added to that first tree and tapped a couple more trees in his yard and one on a neighbor's property, and he ended up with a decent yield of sap to work with his first winter. I would get periodic updates via text message about how much sap he'd gotten that day, and we would swap more messages about techniques and tools he could use on his first attempt at making syrup. In these conversations typed out with our thumbs, he also asked me questions about timing, temperatures, the vagaries and variations of sap flow, and many other topics, and he would report proudly his results. I was taking part in these conversations with two lines of thought. First and most important, I simply wanted to help my brother do something he was excited about trying to do. Second, I was listening in with my cultural analyst ears (as I always am . . . the curse of being an academic with no off switch), to hear what he was thinking about as he tried sugaring. He talked about the intensity of the flavors he was getting in his first couple batches, or where the best equipment came from, and I felt myself quietly filing those conversations away under "culinary meanings" or "geographic meanings." It is profoundly annoying to be related to an anthropologist, so I didn't tell him about the parallel course of analysis that was running through my head while we chatted, but he's been my brother long enough that he doubtless figured it was happening anyway. I was particularly struck during one chat when he said that he wanted to do right by the trees he was tapping. I knew what he meant without having to ask him to explain, as I've been his brother just about as long as he's been mine. He knew he was engaging in a process that was new to him, but by no means new, and he wanted to make sure he was doing it well. He wanted to sugar in a way that was respectful of the trees as biological organisms and mindful of the many others who have made maple syrup before him. "Ecological meanings," yes; "heritage meanings," check. All of these things mattered to my brother. He wasn't just playing around at cutting holes in his trees; he was doing something important and he wanted to do it well. Even from his first attempt, making maple syrup was an intensely and multiply *meaningful* process for him.

That sense of meaning is why I wrote this book. Maple syrup is poorly understood by most of the people who consume it. It's even less well understood by those who don't, who prefer artificially flavored corn syrup derivatives on their waffles in the morning, or for those who don't consume syrup at all. For the last group, my book probably won't mean much. For the first two groups, though—people who eat real maple syrup and people who eat artificial things pretending to be maple—this book will give greater understandings of what real maple is, how it is made, and most importantly, what roles it plays culturally for the people who make it. For anyone who has stood in a grocery aisle and wondered why a pint of real maple syrup costs five or six times as much as Aunt Jemima and Log Cabin, *Meanings of Maple* explores the process of getting maple from the tree and onto that store shelf. At every step of the way, and in many different forms, maple syrup is laden with meaning. By exploring those meanings, this book attempts to create a better understanding of a very misunderstood product.

This book is not just an extended commercial for Vermont maple syrup, though. On a larger scale, I want to explore meaning, or more properly, meanings. Using maple in Vermont as an example, I want to delve into the many and varied ways that humans make meaning with the objects and processes in their lives. The sheer variety of meanings that can be made with something as simple as a jar of syrup is obvious, but only if one looks. This book looks.

Meanings of Maple is situated in Vermont. I have been living there and talking with sugarmakers for several years, learning from them about all aspects of sugaring. The mechanics of it, the economics of it, its importance to who they are—all the different meanings that maple has for Vermont. Maple syrup is only made in a small corner of the world, and Vermont has claimed a spot right at the center of the maple-making world. When trying to understand the meanings of maple, it's the place to be. Some of the analysis in here is specific to Vermont, but most of it is applicable to any place where maple syrup is made. Indeed, much of the discussion can be used to inform analyses of any food item anywhere, but that's the nature of cultural analysis. We try to find the generalizable in the particular. In the case of *Meanings of Maple*, the particulars are Vermont and maple syrup, the general are meanings and the making thereof.

Setting the Scene

It's not hard to find maple in Vermont, to be immersed in it, to *feel* maple all around you. A drive out from Burlington north to one of my many interviews takes me from urban to rural in less than fifteen minutes. The trip up to Fairfield will take about forty-five minutes, but I'm out of the city and into the hills in no time. As I cover the miles along the road north, sugaring becomes more and more immediate, more present. It's all around us in Vermont, but it makes itself more obvious on the drive. I leave the city's hidden maples, the planted, landscaped maple trees that appear in yards and parks, and enter the hills where maples form stands and, with birch, beech, and ash, make up whole stretches of forest. Vermont is not a big place. We've got only two interstates, and there are still plenty of unpaved roads that get you from here to there. I'm not talking about the little unmarked tracks that lead from a road to someone's house—even being a genuine, named-on-the-map road in Vermont is no guarantee of paving. One of the effects of having more small roads is that, even when driving, it is very common to feel more of the presence of the landscape beside the road. Whatever is off the shoulder of the road here is generally closer to you when you're in a car, and that closeness is more than just spatial. You see the fields and woods, you feel them; they are part of your present situation, not just background that is whizzing by, merely a setting for the reality of driving that is taking place in the foreground. The fields and woods are part of the foreground here. You don't drive past the fields and woods here. You drive through them.

Fields and woods are the hallmarks of Vermont. Yes, the postcards show covered bridges, rustic barns, and pointy little churches, but those are images Vermont shows to outsiders. They are real enough, and we live here among them, but they are put on the postcards and shown to others because a visitor expects to see bridges and barns. The structures are always tucked into the fields and woods. As I'm driving through them on my way to Fairfield, maple gets closer. Even from the highway, I can see stands of maples, clustering together and asserting their presence among other species. I don't know that I could have done that ten years ago, but several years of studying sugaring and talking with sugarmakers has given me a greater familiarity with the woods and trees. Here and there, the tell-tale blue or green networks of plastic weave among the trees, ready to gather sap from all the maples hooked into a sophisticated web of tubing that now gathers the vast majority of maple sap and funnels it to a sugarhouse, where it is made into syrup.

Some people and some tourist brochures will tell you that driving out into the hills of Vermont is like driving back in time. That is, at best, overly simplistic, and at worst, patently false. The webs of plastic tubing are very obviously modern, and knowing all the technological systems those webs of tubing connect to just confirms that I am not driving into the past out here. Such a statement assumes there is only one way to be human in the present day, but the people who live and work in the small towns and hills of Vermont are members of today, just as much as anyone else. Driving to my interview in Fairfield is not a trip to the past, but it is a trip to a farm, which is a different way of life from mine. I live and work in the city now. I grew up among farms, but not on a farm, so there is a wonderful familiarity about the sights and smells for me as I pull into the driveway of Jon Branon's century-old farmhouse for my interview. Dairy is the main occupation on this farm, as it is for the majority of farms in Vermont. Jon greets me warmly when I arrive, and even before I am in the door, the conversation quickly turns to the most recent sugaring season—how well the area did, what prices are like, and so on. We sit down at the kitchen table, a familiar setting for my interviews with sugarmakers, especially in summer. A talk during sugaring season is going to take place in the sugarhouse or walking among the trees. I have been in Jon's woods with him during winter as well, but summer is as close to down time as sugaring has, so today we sit around the kitchen table, and I start asking questions. More importantly, I listen to Jon's answers:

ML: Tell me about your family's history in sugaring.

JB: I don't know exactly when we started making maple syrup, I would assume it was very early on. I know we had dairy very early on, and so I'm not sure of the actual date on our first maple process, but I think it's been a hundred years easily enough. And we've acquired a little bit of land over time, not a lot. The homestead is pretty much what it was then, I think. We're a fairly small producer overall, we tap about 3,200, some of that is over the fence on the neighbor's, kind of hedgerow-type tapping of significant woods. And as time has gone on in the maple world, 3,200 is a very small number. I've got some uncles that are doing tens of thousands, almost a hundred thousand actually. And so, economically, it's fairly insignificant probably, compared to some others local, but it certainly is a heritage. It's a way of life that we've fostered for years, passed on from one generation to the next, and we're hopefully instilling that in our children. I've got three children on the farm, and my brother, who's a big player in our maple, he has two children also, and so we're trying to encourage it to them.

As we begin talking about his sugaring operation, it is evident that at least two sets of meanings are interweaving from the outset—the economic importance of maple in the area, and its importance to his family in particular. How these two layers of meaning intersect catches my ear, as Jon juxtaposes the small number of taps he has, which is "fairly insignificant" in comparison with some of the larger operations near him, and the importance of his sugaring to his family's heritage. I want to know more about that heritage. . . .

ML: You used the phrase "heritage and way of life"; what do you mean by that?

JB: For us, maple means more than just producing a crop. On the dairy farm, we produce three cuttings of hay, so those would be three crops, sometimes corn would be a fourth crop, maple would be a fifth crop, actually our first crop of the crop season. And for us, it represents much more than that. For me personally, it's evidence that winter is tail-ending, we do the sugaring in the spring of the year. Typically winter for a lot of Vermonters gets to be long, drawn out, and so when we start moving toward sugaring, that means we're moving toward spring, new beginnings, new crop season, and so that plays a pretty big role in my personal feelings toward the spring of the year. I also am a science major in college, and I really enjoy being outside and in the spring of the year, that's the new beginning of all kinds of plant life and animal activity, and so by being out sugaring you see that. Whether you want to be or not, you're out there during the snowstorms, or rainstorms, or windy days, and so you see all the awakening, the new season. It puts you right there. And as far as the cultural heritage, as I said, we've been doing it in the family for generations. In fact, some of the equipment that we use was probably used by my great-grandfather and maybe even beyond. Some of the buckets, for example, got many, many miles on them. The manufacturing of maple syrup has certainly progressed. We used to be all buckets with horse-drawn tubs, that's how we collected the sap, and I was very active in that when I was younger. And the technology and the economics have kind of pushed us toward modern maple, which is much more pipeline and pumps. In fact, we have a team of horses, but we use them very little. We do have a few buckets still of that 3,200 total taps, probably 200 are buckets. And now we kind of look at gathering the buckets as almost a Sunday picnic. My father, who'll be sixty-seven this summer, he oftentimes will drive the tractor, and myself and my kids or some friends from town and their kids will come down, oftentimes on a Sunday, and we will do our little bucket run, which is on a nice, graveled road. The trees are pretty friendly, no side hills. When we used to gather buckets, when we had to gather buckets, you literally took a small army to get the sap collected. We were in some of the worst terrain, going over hillsides to gather trees on ledge, or ice-covered and that kind of thing, and asking the horses to take heavy loads down into swaley areas that were breaking up in the spring of the year the frost was going out, and the icepack and stuff. And so, now gathering buckets is kind of a fun chore, and years ago it was, if you had a big run of sap and then all the sudden the weather turned negatively cold, down around zero where it was going to freeze and split the buckets, there was a big hurry-scurry to get the buckets empty, to get that sap boiled before everything froze up. And so now the bucket component is handled much differently. And the pipeline isn't nearly as susceptible to freezing and damage as the buckets would have been.

A question about heritage evokes a response about agriculture, the farming calendar, and crops. I try to listen to the immediate conversation while, at the same time, analyzing the various lines of thought that are unfolding. Understanding a heritage meaning necessitates a discussion of the place of maple in the agricultural cycle, and understanding that agricultural meaning of maple necessitates a description of the local geography and ecology of Jon's sugarbush. That leads into a discussion of some changes in the technology of sugaring. While trying to keep up with these threads, I am trying to figure out how to organize them in my head, as well as in my analysis. Following up on the technological changes, I want to know a little more about how that meaning affects the heritage idea. . . .

ML: Given all these changes, you talk about the transition from buckets to pipeline, there've been other changes, too; when I was here last time we took a look at your RO setup, and there've been other changes that have been introduced into maple sugaring, how has that changed your personal connection to maple, or has it?

JB: It really hasn't changed my feeling to maple. We find it to be, maple's always very labor-intensive, but with the pipeline you can actually start the maple maintenance much earlier in the year. In fact, some will do it in the fall, go out and fix lines, and then they'll maintain them all winter. For us, it's usually more around mid-December, January, and so it takes a lot of pressure off. With buckets, you never wanted to get them out in the woods until it was close to time to hang them, for fear of them being blown away or buried in snow, and so you kind of watched the calendar, watch mother nature, it looked like spring was approaching, and you would try to break trails with the horses through the woods, through three-foot snowdrifts that were well-established pack from the winter snow, and next thing you know, you get a run of sap and you're not ready, so you lost it. And so now, with the pipeline, you can start much earlier and hopefully have things ready for when that change happens for sap flow. Some folks, and this wouldn't be myself, complain that the flavor of the syrup has changed with all of the technology, and I don't know if that's accurate or not. For us, we use reverse osmosis, but we only bring it up a few percentage points of sugar. Our sap typically tests between 2.5 and 3%, and our comfort level to boil it is about 7 to 8%. Some operations will process the sap to 18 and 20%, and so obviously that may have a flavor change in the final product. It's not in the evaporator as long because it's going in at 20%, the final product is 66%, so it's not there long. Hopefully that doesn't hurt our market or the consumer perception, too much technology. So, for myself, the pipeline and even the RO, on a big run of sap, my brother, who's a very big player in our maple, he does the boiling with some other help. He's a full-time schoolteacher, so typically, he doesn't get here until the evening to boil, and without the reverse osmosis, we'd have to evaporate every drop of that liquid to make the syrup. And now, with reverse osmosis, we've saved hours every night of boiling time. And there's something kind of romantic about boiling till two in the morning once in a while, but not every night during the sugaring season. And so typically now, we're done, cleaned up, back home, thinking about a shower and bed by ten or midnight, which is much better. And so it's taken a lot of pressure off there too. It's more efficient and it's cost effective. My grandfather used to have a saying, and I don't know that I ever heard him say it directly, but I certainly heard it passed on, modern-day sugarhouses of course have electricity, running water, some of them have heated rooms even. Ours isn't quite that way, we do have electricity and running water, the heat comes from the evaporator, the wood fire, but in the days of my grandfather, he passed away in '84, the sugarhouses were typically located in the actual sugarbush, at the lowest point because they didn't have pumps, everything had to be run to the sugarhouse on gravity. Holding tanks would run downhill. And also at these low points in the woods, would be your rivers, your brooks, so they had a source of water. And he used to have a saying that, with good sap, good wood, because if you burn poor wood, you lose efficiency, you don't have the BTUs, good sap, good wood, and good luck, from sunup till sundown, they would make about a barrel of syrup, which I'm guessing might have been 40 gallons. And now, with good luck and good equipment, our operation, we're doing probably 40 gallons an hour, hour and a half, and so that's kind of the difference. And we're not pushing, we've got some uncles that are doing almost a hundred gallons an hour, 70–100 because of the reverse osmosis. But that gives you a perception of how much time they must have spent, the old generation, in the sugarhouse because they would make a hundred drums of syrup some years. I think the winters were much different, they must've been. The trees were obviously younger, more vibrant, but they used to make a lot of syrup, and it was inefficiently made syrup. With today's closed system, with the vacuum and the sanitary adapters, we're making upwards of a half a gallon of syrup per tap, and the rule of thumb used to be about a quart of syrup was considered a good year, a crop of syrup, and so we've about doubled that. And so, to hear stories from the senior generation, they used to make a hundred barrels of syrup a year some years, and that was done with basically the same acreage, probably a lot more trees on those acres and their seasons were much longer, lot more flow apparently.

The dizzying balance of so many numbers comes back into the conversation again. A discussion of heritage meanings cannot happen without taking into account technological changes and the economic impacts of those changes. . . .

ML: There's going to be a different experience of the whole process for your kids, you said you're getting your kids involved and getting them into the process. How old are your kids? What age do they start getting into the sugarhouse and helping out?

JB: As I started to say earlier, for us, it's definitely a family affair, and that's where the culture would come in too and some of the heritage. Typically, when sugaring season gets here in full swing, there'll be lots of people in and out. My brother is here a lot of the time with his children and wife, and oftentimes, my mother will make a big meal at the end of the day, and we'll get together as a family and have some time there. And so I would say at a very young age, they're exposed to, this is a different way of life than the rest of the calendar year because all the cousins are around, especially on a Sunday, big meal, it's sugaring season. As far as actual productive help, that would come at a later date, although my daughter . . . , she's a terrific help with the buckets, she can put the covers on when we scatter them, install them at the beginning of the season, and she certainly can help gather them and stuff like that. The older kids, my son and his cousin, who's twelve, they are a very good help with the wood because we have to handle upwards of thirty cords of wood to produce the syrup, and so we can expect a lot of help from them in the woodshed to get the wood out for the evaporator and that kind of thing. So at the beginning of the season, we start to see a lot more family activity because of sugaring, spring of the year. And oftentimes, when we're in the woods, my brother and I, and sometimes my father, we can talk about different areas.

Every section of our woods has a different name. We've got places like the Snake Run or the Brown Bucket Run, and that all represents something that was passed down. The Brown Bucket Run, for example, was a very prime maple area, and they chose to hang the biggest buckets there because they were always high-producing trees. So at some particular point in our hundred-plus-year history, we had buckets that were oversize, and so that was the designated area for the Brown Bucket Run. And the Snake Run, I think, its name probably derived from the little gathering trail, it's very twisted, it follows a brook, very snaky-like I think. It's also kind of a southeast exposure with a lot of ledge, and in the spring of the year, besides the peepers and some other things coming to life, the snakes get active, and they use these crevices through there. And in the Branon family, snakes are not very attractive, and so that name probably has some significance too. It's an area that, at the end of the season, when the wild onions, the leeks, and whatnot are growing, and the little mayflowers are coming up through the leaves, you can expect to see more snakes than usual. Those are two names that come to mind. We've got the Cove, which is an old oxbow bend in the river, kind of made a small lake, and that's a very north-facing, cold area, late-running sap because it takes longer in the season to start flowing, and so that's all some heritage, passed on from one to the next. And then, the other thing with the maple, and we talked a little bit about crops, this is a crop that, I don't know that we've ever had a year where we lost money. Some years, we've made a lot less than others, probably, and as I said, we're fairly small potatoes anyway with the maple with only 3,200, but typically going into the sugaring season, we know that we can make a small investment and get the return on our investment at the end of the season. And in some years, it has greatly contributed to the farm income, paying taxes and past due bills, and so that certainly is another factor that we weigh in on as far as that particular crop.

Sugaring involves a very direct, very intimate interaction with the land. So, when I ask a question about family, it makes perfect sense that the response includes a discussion of the landscape, especially as a lived, worked landscape. The people Jon is talking about—his family, his children—are not living off the land. They are living with it and within it. He knows that I can't really make sense of his family's history in sugaring without understanding that land a little bit too. I'm starting to understand, so I seek more information about their land. . . .

ML: The names for the different parts, the Brown Bucket Run, the Snake Run, the Cove, because you said you've got some buckets but you run tubing, so when you don't have to go out into the sugarbush anymore to gather the buckets, does the knowledge of that name go away?

JB: It doesn't because, with pipeline, it's laid out much differently than gathering buckets on roads. Typically when you're gathering, it's just common sense, like putting the sugarhouse at the low point, you start your load empty on the worst uphill, then you get heavier, load your tub and come downhill back to the tank. And so, a lot of these gathering runs we would call them, were kind of built for that reason, it's just, you'd look at the lay of the land and figure out the best way for man and beast to gather it. We have a High Horseshoe Run, we refer to up on the Fanton woods, it's probably the highest point on our property, and it's a big U shape, and so you could start on the south end and end up back on, say maybe the south-east end and come back on the south-west end or something like that. Or you could do it reverse if you walk the lay of the land, and you knew you were going to be a team of horses trying to pull up a ledge, you would choose to go one way or the other. With pipeline, the way it's laid out, you kind of find a central point in your woods, a lot like placing your sugarhouse, where sap naturally wants to go, and you lay your lines accordingly. So now, for example, one mainline, which is the big conductor line that carries that sap, it might actually traverse part of the Big Maples, the High Horseshoe, and into the Berry Patch just because of the valley shape of the terrain. And so, this does pose a bit of a problem when I'm communicating with my brother especially, because he's older than I am, and he knows when we used to gather what the Berry Patch looked like, and so now we have to number our lines or put a name on the line, and these mainline tubing situations definitely change the old terminology to some extent. The bigger operators I've been in their sugar woods, my uncles, and they've got a pretty extravagant identification process because when they're talking to the hired help and they have to send them to a certain quadrant in the woods, they need to be able to identify that. And so these lines have some kind of a numerical identification, and a lot of times, the mainline has subsidiary lines that branch off from it which also have to be identified. For us, we're not quite that big. Our 3,000 taps are actually in three different woods, and so we would start the conversation something like, "we've got some line issues in the Hislop" so automatically, we'd know that's one of the three woods we'd go to. And then it might be the Snake Run line or the Fourth Knoll line, that kind of identification. And we know because we've walked these lines and built these lines that that actually encompasses the Third Knoll, the Fourth Knoll, the Snake Run, and ends up you know, up on the Brown Bucket Run or something like that. One line covers all those areas. And then also another line might, because of the topography, also connect some of the Third and Fourth Knoll too. When you're building a pipeline system, you try to use gravity in your favor, they ideally tell you to grade your lines at 2 to 5% slope, and so that dictates where you put your pipe basically, and it's all about terrain and topography as to how you build it.

We talk for an hour or so, and then it is time for Jon to get back to the never-ending work of a farmer. He has already been more than generous with his time, so I pack up my gear and a quart of his excellent syrup, and with my thanks, I head out the door.

The smell of hay lingers in my nose as I pull out of the driveway, just as the ideas from our conversation linger in my mind. Our discussion touched on so many aspects of sugaring, so many layers of meaning. The intense knowledge of the terrain and ecology of the sugar woods is always impressive to me, but I have come to understand that knowing the woods being tapped is second nature to sugarmakers. Hearing him describe how sugaring is part of his family's heritage and identity reminds me of how inextricable, how intertwined sugaring is in Vermont. I literally cannot imagine the place without maple. And as always, layered in with the abstract and sometimes nostalgic discussions of heritage, there is a constant practicality, the discussion of numbers of taps and yearly production. I am slotting the various bits of conversation into my categories, "ecological meanings," "agricultural meanings," but the reality is that these categories are made up. All of the many meanings are woven together, all parts of a hugely complex yet decidedly simple thing called maple. I may use my categories to arrange and begin to analyze, but all of these supposedly separate meanings of maple are really just aspects of one big web of meaning.

The drive back into town doesn't lessen the feeling of being surrounded by maple. A quick slip through the city of St. Albans on my way home reminds me that all the street signs there have a small maple leaf decal, right in front of the street name. I pass half a dozen roadside signs declaring, "Real Vermont Maple Sold Here." Business names like Maple Acres and Maple Tree Associates adorn the sides of buildings far from the nearest sugarhouse (which, to be fair, isn't that far in a state this small). As summer is in full swing, it seems that every side window of a business has become an opportunity to buy a maple creamee, the local term for maple-syrup-flavored soft-serve ice cream. Nearer home, I drive past the brand-new Stonewood Apartments complex with its maple leaf logo on the sign out front, and I pull into my own driveway and see the enormous maple trees that have been landscaped in as part of my suburban neighborhood. No one is tapping these trees, but that doesn't change the fact that maple is very much in all the parts of the landscape of Vermont, urban or rural, tapped or untapped.

The Story

This book is about maple, and it is about meanings. It is about both in pretty much equal measure, although that might not be apparent on first reading. In one sense, *Meanings of Maple* is an effort at writing a fairly straightforward ethnography of sugaring—the making of maple syrup and derivative products from maple sap. The research I conducted to write this book included talking with sugarmakers, the people who tap the trees and make the syrup, as well as others connected to the maple industry, such as bulk packers, government officials, academic consultants, equipment manufacturers and dealers, and so on. And the analysis and contextualization I do is more or less standard operating procedure in writing ethnography. I wanted to write a straightforward ethnography of maple because, surprisingly, no one has before, which is part of why maple is so misunderstood. There has been a wealth of academic attention paid to maple in the past, but it has looked at aspects such as the chemistry of the syrup, or the economics of maple sales, or the effects of sugaring on forest health. Very little attention has been given to the cultural meanings and impacts of maple, and that is a gap I want to fill. I could have told a detailed story of one sugarmaker, but to do so would have missed so much. Every sugaring operation is incredibly individual, and there are so many potential variables that one sugarmaker's story can only give the broadest strokes of meaning that can be applied to others. So, the narrative arc of this book is not to delve into one sugarmaker, or even to move from one to another. Instead, *Meanings of Maple* moves from one realm of meaning to another. Just as in the interview above, the meanings all interlace, and the real picture only comes together when you follow several strands and see how they crisscross one another. So the book looks at several threads in turn, before seeing how they come together to make one image. As I put the text together, I tried to balance the discussion. Drawing insights from the many sugarmakers in Vermont and beyond who shared their time with me, as well as the open perspective of my brother, who was brand new to sugaring, I have tried to craft a narrative that is of interest and use to a wide range of readers.

Structure

Meanings of Maple is divided into eight chapters. The introduction here sets the scene and provides some texture to the text. As with any cultural activity, trying to write about it can only convey a fraction of the fullness of the topic, so I want to give a taste, if you will, of how and how deeply maple is used to make meanings before turning to the arbitrary categories of meaning I have used to organize my thoughts. The following six chapters each approach one of those categories of meaning that maple has. First is "Economic Meanings," which looks at various economic aspects of the maple industry. Maple syrup and its derivatives are bought and sold, and the economy of maple provides an important stream of revenue for many sugarmakers, from the small producer paying their property taxes to the larger 70,000-tap operations, for whom sugaring is their sole income source. Additionally, a broader sense of economics is explored by looking at the commodification that exists in many parts of sugaring. Next is "Culinary Meanings," which looks at maple as food, and the manifold ways it is meaningful in that capacity. I examine the fluid and evolving role that maple plays in the culinary landscape, in the context of the historical role maple has played for the people who make it. The next chapter, "Geographic Meanings," looks at the effects of maple's limited geographic range on making identities for, and with, sugaring. Because making maple syrup on any scale is done in a limited portion of the globe, the process and product are strongly tied to place, even while being exported around the world. "Ecological Meanings" looks at maple as occurring at a boundary between the human and the nonhuman world, paying special attention to the interaction maple has with other processes that are understood as natural, while "Agricultural Meanings" explores sugaring as it relates to more obviously human processes. Maple syrup is in part a gathered resource, but in part produce of a farm, and this chapter explores that liminality. Last, "Heritage Meanings" analyzes maple's part in the making of Vermont identity through a sense of historical connection and ownership. The strong rootedness in place of maple, combined with the idea that it stretches far back in time in the hands of specific people, makes the notion of heritage a particularly powerful set of meanings in sugaring. The last chapter briefly summarizes and connects the six body chapters, bringing the analysis together and providing a sense of epilogue.

Sugaring

Before diving into the many and varied meanings that maple can have, most readers will benefit from some information on maple and sugaring itself. Tapping trees is not practiced everywhere, so the processes involved in creating syrup may well be unfamiliar to many of you, as it was to me when I moved to Vermont. Sugaring is a vernacular term for the making of maple syrup and other products by collecting and boiling the sap from maple trees. Sugaring on maple trees has been practiced in what is now the northeastern United States and southeastern Canada for many centuries—long before those names were attached to that geographic area. There is strong archaeological (Thomas, Jackson, and Guthrie 1999) and narrative (Wittstock 1993) evidence that sugaring was a well-developed process in this region among native groups stretching far back before European contact. The process was taught by local inhabitants to Europeans when they came into the area.

The process starts when sap is collected from trees, which is done by drilling a small hole in the side of the tree. The hole then receives a tap or spile, a small device that is designed to funnel the sap that weeps from the hole and point it somewhere—in previous years, most often into a bucket hanging below the tap, or more and more commonly now, into a system of plastic tubing that directs the sap flow from the tree.

If the sap drips into a bucket, the bucket must be emptied by hand, usually into some sort of larger vat that will receive the sap from many buckets in one go. If the sap drains into a tubing system, the tubing directs the sap from numerous trees into a centralized pipe that drains into some kind of holding tank, similar to the vat into which the buckets are dumped. Either way, the sap from individual trees is gathered and combined in larger containers.

Sap collections systems: maple bucket and tubing. *Author photos.*

The contents of those larger containers is taken to the sugarhouse, which is the building where the sap is boiled down into syrup. I would attempt to describe a typical sugarhouse, but there is no such thing as a typical sugarhouse. I have seen boiling taking place in everything from an open-sided lean-to that fought the wind to remain standing to an enormous heated, plumbed, and insulated building that met the highest standards of both government cleanliness and man-cave comfort. I've been in sugarhouses that barely had roofs, and I've been in sugarhouses with flat-screen televisions and wifi. The one thing that all these sugarhouses have in common is an evaporator—the device used to boil the sap into syrup. The evaporator is, in essence, a big pan over a heat source.

The simplest evaporators do not amount to much more than that, but the most elaborate and expensive have separate chambers through which the sap passes on its journey toward syruphood, as well as many different plumbing and electronic systems to increase the efficiency of the boil, thus reducing time and costs to the sugarmaker.

The sap comes out of the tree at anywhere from 0.5 percent to 7.5 percent sugar content, but it averages about 2 percent to 3 percent. The sugar content must be concentrated down to somewhere between 66 percent and 68 percent (depending on where you are) in order to be called maple syrup, which really just means that a whole lot of water needs to be removed. The sugar content of both sap and syrup is calculated on the Brix scale, which measures the number of grams of sugar as a percentage of the mass of a liquid solution. Brix is a useful measure of both the sap and the syrup, as the percentages of sugar in both are very important in understanding sugaring. The more sugar in the sap to begin with, the less time and effort needed to concentrate to the necessary 66–68 percent, so a tree giving 2 percent sap is going to take half the sap to make syrup as a tree giving out 1 percent sap. Two numbers are often quoted as shorthand to describe the amount of concentration that needs to take place: 40/1 and the Rule of 86. Neither of these numbers is mathematically accurate, but they are both used as rules of thumb, and anyone visiting a sugarhouse is likely to hear at least one of them mentioned. The Rule of 86 states that, for each one percent of sugar in solution in the sap, eight-six gallons are needed to make one gallon of finished syrup. So, a quick calculation of sap that comes in at 2 percent says that (86/2 = 43), 43 gallons of sap will boil down to one gallon of syrup. The Rule of 86 is a handy guideline, but unfortunately it is not completely precise, as the rule was calculated at a time when finished syrup was understood to be 65.5 percent sugar. Now, the legal minimum everywhere is at

Evaporator. *Author photo.*

least 66 percent, and in a few places higher (such as Vermont, where it is almost 67 percent), so the math no longer works quite the same. However, the Rule of 86 is fairly easy math and provides a useful estimation tool, so it maintains its currency.

Even less precise is the ratio of 40/1, which you will often see in tourist brochures or popular discussions of sugaring. This number just claims that you need forty gallons of sap to make a single gallon of syrup. Obviously, this number is less accurate and does not take into account sap with varying sugar content, but 40/1 is used primarily for an unknowing audience, and is less about mathematical precision and more about conveying the amount of labor and effort involved in sugaring: 40/1 dispels the notion that syrup flows out of the tree when you tap it. Forty is a number with a history of imprecision, and a tree giving a little over 2 percent sap would necessitate about 40 gallons of sap to make a gallon of syrup, so for an audience that does not need mathematical accuracy—the crowd that may assume syrup flows straight from the tree—40/1 is indeed a useful shorthand to communicate how much effort goes into making real maple syrup.

The sap is concentrated by removing its water content. Many commercial sugarmakers do some of the concentration with a reverse osmosis machine, which removes water by pressurized filtration, but all sugarmakers regardless of size use boiling to remove the majority of the water. For most of the boil, the sap will remain at roughly the boiling point of water. Since the sap is mostly water, this stands to reason. Only when enough of the water has become steam and floated away to coat the walls and rafters of the sugarhouse does the temperature start to rise above 212° F. As the sap is boiled down to approach the required sugar percentage, changes in color, viscosity, and flavor can all flag that the magical moment has arrived. Every sugarmaker I know uses some form of measuring device to do at least a final check of the syrup's Brix, but many, especially the old-timers, play by eye or ear. Different signals are sought: the look and sound of the bubbles that ride the boiling liquid (they should no longer pop as individual bubbles, but slide away and subside into the foam, like the head on a properly drawn pint of Guinness), the viscosity of the liquid as it falls back from a spatula (it should sheet off, instead of dripping in separate rivulets), or the color (translucent amber, rather than clear yellowish).

Some combination of these traits is watched, and then the syrup is worth testing with a hydrometer for accuracy.

When the syrup hits the required percentage, it is drawn off, which means it is removed from the evaporator and from exposure to the heat source. The syrup is then filtered to remove any unwanted inclusions, such as concentrated minerals, called nitre or sugar sand. Nitre always builds up in syrup because as the sap is boiled, everything suspended in the water gets concentrated, including both the sugar molecules and the other minerals present in the sap. While harmless, these concentrations of minerals can cloud the syrup, so many sugarmakers who sell their syrup work to remove any visible particles. Filtering can be done with small, gravity-operated mechanisms that simply drain the syrup through a physical membrane, much like making coffee with a drip filter, or through larger filter presses that use diatomaceous earth. Either way, the filtered syrup is then ready for packaging.

Syrup Grades

Maple syrup is usually graded before it is put into a container. All syrup sold in Vermont requires a grade (although if you're buying it from your neighbor up the road, the grade is sometimes skipped), but regulations elsewhere can vary a bit. Where my brother lives in Ohio, for example, grading syrup is entirely optional, as long as it meets the legal requirements to be real maple syrup. The grading systems vary from place to place as well, although they are all coming into closer alignment for marketing reasons. Because *Meanings of Maple* focuses on sugaring in Vermont, I will describe here the grading system used in that state, touching on other systems for context, especially of very recent changes in the grading system. For decades, Vermont syrup was assigned one of five grades based solely on the color of the finished syrup. The color had a rough correlation to the flavor, but color was the only criterion on which the grade was based.

The five categories that were used were, from lightest to darkest: Fancy, Medium Amber, Dark Amber, B, and C. All of the grades of syrup undergo the same amount and type of processing, with the variations in color being due to inclusions in the sap, particularities of

A window display demonstrates the wide range of possible colors in finished syrup. *Author photo.*

the collection system, time of year, boiling efficiency, or other factors. Fancy, the lightest in color and usually in flavor, has long been prized by Vermonters as the most delicate and highest quality. Medium and Dark Amber are darker and generally more intensely flavored, but have long been accepted onto Vermont dinner tables and waffles. Grade B had a reputation in the state for being more suited to cooking, where its strong flavor punch is useful for shaping the taste of beans, breads, cakes, and the like. Grade C in this grading system, with an intense, almost acrid maple flavor, was illegal to sell to individual consumers in Vermont, instead being shunted into secondary production like candy making or use as real maple flavoring in processed foods.

These five grades were the norm in Vermont for many years. An initiative out of the University of Vermont and the state Agency of Agriculture, however, changed the grading system used in the state to align more closely with systems used in other states and provinces in attempt to create a standardized, international grade scale. The thought was that too many variations from system to system caused confusion in the market, hurting overall sales of maple in established markets and hurting maple's ability to penetrate new markets. In 2014, Vermont sugarmakers had the option to use the old grading system described above, or to switch to the new system that came out of UVM and the Agency of Ag, but the new grades became mandatory as of the 2015 sugaring season. The new grading system, which is based on the amount of light that is transmitted through the syrup, uses vocabulary that touches on both color and intensity of flavor. The new grades do not overlap neatly with the old system used in Vermont, and there are now four grades covering what used to be five. In order from lightest to darkest, the new grades are: Golden with Delicate Taste, Amber with Rich Taste, Dark with Robust Taste, and Very Dark with Strong Taste.

The People

I have been doing fieldwork with people connected to sugaring since 2008, and every conversation I've had informs what is between these covers. Some of the conversations were formal interviews with the audio recorder running, but most of them were expedient conversations that happened when I visited their sugarhouse, or when we met at MapleRama, or across the counter of their storefront. The vast majority of people who shared their time and thoughts with me for this project are sugarmakers—the people who actually make the syrup—but other people connected with sugaring have been kind enough to talk with me as well. People in governmental or educational positions, makers or sellers of other maple goods, dealers and producers of the complex and varied equipment used in sugaring, all have shared a bit of their time with me to inform my analysis. For simplicity of presentation, and to maintain the anonymity of my interviewees, I refer to nearly everyone as simply "a sugarmaker," unless they have given me specific permission to name them. The sugarmakers with whom I have spoken have ranged from a young guy tapping a dozen trees in his backyard to a giant operation with almost 100,000 taps, but the focus of the sugaring in this book is on a range from just above the smallest to the largest.

I wanted to narrow my discussion to those sugarmakers who are involved in more than a backyard-and-neighbors-sized operation.

That choice was made for a couple reasons. First, there is a significant difference in the identity of the set of sugarmakers who work on such a small scale, compared to those who sugar larger. The backyard sugarmakers include many old, traditional Vermonters with generation after generation in the local cemetery, but they also include many newcomers to the state and to sugaring, who do it as a hobby or as some form of homesteading. In both cases, the connection between sugaring and the identity (of both themselves and the state) is different. *Meanings of Maple* is focused on the roles and meanings of sugaring to some sense of Vermont identity, as negotiated by individuals, but as communicated within and across a larger scale. Maple's place in that process is shaped very largely by sugarmakers who sell their syrup on some commercial level, so those are the ones on whom I have focused here. That is not to say that the smaller sugarmakers are unimportant or uninteresting. Far from it. They are different though, and their role in making and using maple identity is different. My focus on larger operations is not out of a desire to ignore the little fish, but only an effort to maintain a coherence in my analysis.

When I say "larger operations," I don't want to give the impression that there is such a thing as a maple syrup factory out there somewhere. In no case is there a concrete monolith on the bad side of a large city that boils down truckload after truckload of anonymous sap from anywhere and everywhere. At most, the largest common operations in Vermont can be described as successful, medium-sized businesses, nearly always owned and operated by an individual, single family, or in a few cases, a set of business partners. The majority of operations consist of a family-owned farm that sugars as some part of their income. That part could be very large, but it is still in the context of a family farming operation. That's where the vast majority of the real Vermont maple syrup comes from. As I will discuss in the chapters that follow, some forms of industrialization have been incorporated into the sugaring industry, but the family operation still dominates. When standing in the aisle of the supermarket, weighing the real maple syrup against the corn-based stuff, this idea is the first thing to remember. The corn-based stuff is made in an industrial factory somewhere that takes in truckload after truckload of corn or corn syrup. But real maple is very likely made by individuals who are tapping their own trees and boiling their own sap. It happens on a personal scale, which is why I think it is important to tell maple's story. It is a personal story.

Some of my friends laugh at my inability to pass by a bottle of syrup on a store shelf without checking the label to find out whose it is, or the fact that I'm drawn like a moth to flame by a sign declaring "Vermont Maple for Sale Here." Even when going to a farm to buy a Christmas tree with some friends last year, I noticed the farmer also sugared, and a conversation about maple ensued. He even let me peek at his evaporator rig, even though it was dormant in December, waiting for the sap to run again the following February or March. Most of my interviews take place in the summer, which reflects when sugarmakers have more time to sit down and talk to someone with a tape recorder and a notebook. It may seem counterintuitive to say that farmers are less busy in the summer, but many of the farmers in Vermont are dairy farmers who are not planting and reaping vast fields of grain. There are no off days in dairying, but summer brings a lull in some tasks of dairying that are not available for crop farmers. So, summer has always been a fruitful time for me to have conversation with those who sugar.

Vermont

Meanings of Maple is very Vermont-centric. I have spoken to sugarmakers in New York, New Hampshire, Maine, Quebec, Nova Scotia, New Brunswick, and Newfoundland, as well as sugarmakers from many more states and provinces, but most of my conversations have been with Vermont sugarmakers and people connected to Vermont sugaring. I have visited sugarmakers in every county in Vermont during the course of my research, and I have tried to mention statewide variations where they are valuable and mitigate them where they are not. Because this book focuses on the relationship between sugaring and Vermont identity, the extra attention paid to the state makes some sense. However, the analyses I do are not exclusive to Vermont. A Maine sugarmaker or a Quebec sugarmaker is in many important ways going to be different from a Vermont sugarmaker. In Maine, for example, sugaring is much more a part of the logging world than the agricultural world. Syrup is a forestry product in Maine more than a farm product. However, the process of making meanings that maple has in those places is often going to be similar. The things that are meaningful will be largely the same, even if the way they are meaningful, or the degree to which they are meaningful, will likely vary. So, I hope my book, which is unapologetically Vermont-centric (not unlike many Vermonters themselves), will be useful to an audience outside the state, in other sugaring regions and beyond.

Some Notes on Terminology

Throughout this book, I use the word *maple* in many different ways. It is in the title, so maybe that will come as no surprise, but some discussion of the various uses of the word is in order. The word maple can refer to different things: the tree, the wood, the syrup, the industry, the flavor. Sometimes, maple means the product, sometimes it means the process, sometimes, maddeningly, it means both. Often, I use the word maple in an almost generic sense, to refer not just to one of those possibilities, but to the concept of maple. Sometimes, this broad usage is designed to be encompassing of different aspects in one go, such as, "the value of maple to Franklin County's identity can't be overstated." In an instance like this, I am not talking about the trees, or the syrup, or the industry, but some idea or identity that wraps around all of them—trees, syrup, flavor, and more. The varying uses of the word maple can sometimes be confusing, but if you keep in mind that maple is often not *just* one of those things, not just a tree or just a syrup, then maple as a concept makes a little more sense.

There are some cases in this book, though, where I use the word maple, when what I am actually talking about is just the syrup. These uses are the most confusing of all. I have edited out many such instances, but some remain as a reflection of Vermont vernacular word usage. Many people in the maple industry will use the words "syrup" and "maple" interchangeably, and the context of the conversation is the only guide as to when maple means syrup, and when maple means something else or something more. I have decided to include some such usage partially as local color, but partially to attune the reader's ear (eye?) to the ubiquity and importance of maple syrup to

Vermont. Getting the terminology in something like the manner it is delivered within the state, at least among sugarmakers, connotes just how powerful a trope maple is there.

As you will read in the book, sugaring is still very personal, and syrup is sometimes very personalized, but the commercialization process has a slight but appreciable effect on the person in the personalization. One of the effects is that some of the person's identities become less important, while others become foregrounded. The sugarmaker whose name is on the bottle of syrup is made slightly generic—still an individual, but with a predominant identity (sugarmaker) that subsumes others. This book is about the answers sugarmakers gave me, about the meanings they make with maple in all its forms. Maple is poorly understood by many, many people. What follows is an attempt to convey some of the meanings—the understandings—that maple has for those who live deep within it. I want to communicate some portion of the depth and importance that sugaring has in Vermont, in the hopes that you as the reader will come to understand maple a little better. During interviews, people often say to me in an apologetic tone, "I'm not sure if I'm answering your question." My response is always the same—you're doing great. I'm more interested in your answers than in my questions.

CHAPTER 1

The Economic Meaning of Maple

You sugar because you have to, it's in your blood, you just love it that much. But then you have to sugar because you've got that cash outlay in the sugarhouse and the evaporator and the tubing and the marketing to get the customers to a place like this. —Sugarmaker, 27 May 2010

Maple is a commodity. By this, I mean that maple has undergone a process of commodification in the popular understanding, with economic meaning and a sense of "product" attached to it. None of that should come as any kind of surprise, of course, but the role that commodification—that economic transformation—plays in the use of maple as a meaning maker cannot be underestimated. Funnily enough, though, it often is. As with many forms of expressive culture, there is a tendency to focus on maple's traditional aspects and cultural history (as dealt with elsewhere in this book), and to see economics as somehow base, or perhaps a violation of the authenticity of maple or sugaring. Examples abound of similar romanticized notions of folk culture as somehow "pure" and therefore not subject to normal economic processes (for examples, see Hobsbawn and Ranger 1983; Handler and Linnekin 1984).

Nearly every sugarmaker who spoke with me was very comfortable with the economics and commodification of maple, however. While romanticizing was not absent from sugarmakers' discussions with me about maple (both process and product), the idea of maple as moneymaker is more or less ubiquitous. Sugarmakers with smaller-scale operations would often describe a mentality that sugaring pays the property taxes on a small property or farm, freeing up the rest of the year's work for economic sustainability and (it was hoped) profit. So, even if sugaring is not a huge economic driver, it earns its keep for many of the people who tap trees in Vermont. Every sugarmaker also knows the going price for a gallon, whether their syrup is sold to nearby friends and neighbors or at specialty shops in London and Tokyo.

The scale of distribution does not seem to matter in sugarmakers' understandings of the economic meaning their syrup (or anyone else's syrup, for that matter) has. Whether they are providing syrup for themselves, selling to neighbors up the road, sending it along to bulk packers, or distributing around the globe, the end location of the maple system has little effect on the meanings they make of maple to themselves, their families, and their communities. Regardless of the scale of distribution and consumption, the scale of *production* is always the same—local. Maple syrup in Vermont is not made in factories. There is no equivalent to a giant processing plant where maple is made anonymously. In Vermont, it is always situated in the sugarhouse of an individual, rooted in a spot. What held sway in 1974's *A Taste of Spring*, a teaching guide for Canadian educators, is still largely true: "The usual unit of syrup production is a family, or a family plus one or two persons hired for sugaring."[1]

The localness is important to the economic meaning of maple, both internally and externally. For sugarmakers, the knowledge that they are doing something that is theirs, that belongs to no one else (at least outside of the sugaring sphere), makes the sale of a quart of maple a sale of a bit of themselves. The syrup is a commodity, but the syrup is representational of Vermont and individual identity, so Vermont and the sugarmakers become a bit commodified themselves. I am not putting forth this analysis with a Marxist sneer, bemoaning the downfall of the oppressed proletarian sugarmaker by being commodified in the bottle. Instead, I want to recognize that there is a link between what it means to sugar and what the stuff in the bottle means.

These two meanings are linked, to the point of becoming very nearly the same, by the narrative that sells maple. The imagery of the land and people, the horses and buckets, roots sugaring in the place, and that narrative makes maple appealing as a product. People, both within the state and far afield, want to buy a bit of the clean, green, and serene chunk of Earth that is Vermont. Maple syrup does not remain local in its identity *in spite of* commodification . . . that very localness is part and parcel of the commodification and commodity that results. Because production remains local, locality is part of the commodity.

Vermont sells its maple syrup and other products based partly on the fact that they come from there, but the locality is more important than just being a place from which the syrup comes. Coming from a "there" is a potential selling point of any item. The "there" that is there in the case of maple, though, plays a powerful role in its commodification. Coming from Vermont is meaningful because of the reputation of the state—old, traditional, rural, a more "authentic" way of life. All of these tropes attach easily and well to maple, and they all help distill the place into the bottle, commoditizing both together. Localness is an important trait with which economic meanings are made by sugarmakers. As one sugarmaker expressed in an interview, "I love to see the branding of Vermont and the movement toward buying local and consuming more food close to home, and that's true, that would have benefits all over the world. But my rationale for maple is that since it is only made in seventeen states and provinces, except for those, we're local to the world."[2]

Even though maple is made in a particular place, in this case, Vermont, that place has become a commodity itself. Because the place becomes commoditized, the traits of the place (cleanliness, greenness, rurality, traditionality) can be made part of the economic meaning that maple carries to other parts of the world. The phrase "local to the world" may seem odd, even contradictory, at first glance. However, this person is expressing in their own words the concept of the "glocal," the intersection of local and global identity. Ritzer and Galli explain that the term "'glocal' is meant to imply that in the global age it is difficult to find much, if anything, that is not influenced in some way by the global (as well as the local). Culinary traditions that were once uniquely local now incorporate global products."[3]

The global product in the case of maple syrup is not an ingredient or additive (indeed, pure maple has no additives), but an awareness of the global market. Changes such as a new grading system that aligns more closely with international standards, or marketing that tells a broader story of a genericized localness to the customer, make the very localized product of maple syrup "local to the world." Maple is economically viable as a commodity outside of the locale of its production because it carries a bit of that locale with it. The localness gets commodified, so anywhere syrup goes, some sense of localness goes with it, making it local to the world wherever it hits the shelves. One sugarmaker explained it to me, "That is a big part, I think, of the marketing plan, is a lot of syrup that's sold over there [Asia, Europe] goes along with a little information packet on the bottle or can, whatever it seems to be marketed in. And it's a little explanation of how and where it's produced, and I think it really helps the marketing end of it."[4]

When Vermont exports syrup, it also exports the localness, and it does so purposefully, with a planned marketing strategy. Both syrup and place get commodified with a narrative explanation of where and what—where the bottle comes from, what is inside it, and how those two things are intimately tied together. The tying of Vermont and syrup together in this way is not always a comfortable process for sugarmakers, such as this one: "Vermont does have an identity, they call it a Vermont brand. I hate that word 'brand' because 'brand,' I think of Aunt Jemima's a brand, Philip Morris is a brand."[5]

This man is troubled by the branding that occurs when syrup is taken to other places with that constructed narrative, thereby taking Vermont to other places. It is interesting that the first two examples he comes up with for what he sees as the distasteful concept of brand are Aunt Jemima and Philip Morris. Aunt Jemima is, of course, a brand of corn-based pancake syrup, which is presented as representative of branding in a negative sense. I have yet to hear a sugarmaker mention Aunt Jemima in a tone of voice other than derision or pity because of the artificiality of that syrup. The implication made by this sugarmaker is that a brand itself is artificial, more corporate, more commoditized, and therefore less worthy of respect. To equate Vermont maple with Aunt Jemima is something close to heresy for sugarmakers, so when this man sees the branding of Vermont as approaching the Aunt Jemima end of a spectrum, his discomfort is made explicit. The fact that his next example is a cigarette company makes even more obvious the distasteful nature of branding for him. He paints a picture of branding as something done on behalf of the artificial, and even the dangerous. Aunt Jemima and Philip Morris are both huge corporate machines that make something unhealthy in this understanding. To subject Vermont maple to the same branding treatment appropriate for those products is problematic for him because real maple represents the opposite of all these values.

The commodification of maple and the scaling up that commodification allows (and often, demands) could not alter the notion that maple is produced by individuals, walking their sugarbush and tending the boil, responsive to the vagaries of local weather and other conditions. Part of the reality of maple syrup is that it is not large scale, not corporate. There are a few larger operations with a significant complement of hired labor, making the sugaring process more of an industrialized thing, but those operations are few, and more importantly, they don't change the narrative of maple as a small-scale, often individualized pursuit, even though "[p]eople almost never work in isolation from each other."[6] Such a narrative creates appeal for a growing portion of the specialty-food audience, where "foodie discourse valorizes simplicity in examples like labor-intensive (non-industrial) techniques for harvesting potatoes, 'simple' presentation styles in upscale restaurants, non-manufactured foods like hand-made tortillas or home-made ricotta, and the 'simple' pleasure of a vine-ripened, organic tomato harvested on a family farm."[7]

If that discourse of simplicity is one that sells, then maple can sell simplicity and syrup by the truckload. The family farm is the paradigm of Vermont sugaring, and the paradigm has, in this case, the added benefit of being largely true. The individual sugarmaker using labor-intensive techniques is the story of sugaring, and it is one that resonates and becomes economic meaning very readily. It is a story sugarmakers tell to customers, as they "struggle to instill in consumers a greater appreciation of commodities . . . that embody an ancient tradition."[8] Jim Weil, economic anthropologist, is here talking about Costa Rican ceramic artists, but both potter and sugarmaker are practicing a tradition that has long historical roots. A key difference is that sugarmakers don't really struggle to instill appreciation in the consumer, at least not in recent history. The Vermont Agency of Agriculture, the Vermont Maple Sugar Makers Association (VMSMA), and several other entities make part of their mission the instilling of that narrative in the mind of the consumer. That story is also one sugarmakers tell to themselves. Even for those who sell to bulk packers with enormous distribution networks, the knowledge that the sap they are boiling will become syrup perhaps on the other end of the world does not make the production of maple feel any less local or individual. Further, the story of locality is still part of the commodity, part of what sells the syrup because it becomes part of the syrup that is sold.

This is not to say that changes in scale are not felt at all. A story from the 8 May 2013 issue of *Seven Days*, a Vermont free weekly newspaper, quoted one sugarmaker as saying, "It's kind of scary around here. . . . We're not making hundreds anymore; there's people making millions, . . . as soon as someone starts making a million dollars, the game is changed."[9] An awareness of changes in the sense of scale is creating at least a small sense of unease in some sugarmakers, who perceive a potential threat to the localness, or perhaps to what being local means, as the economic meanings of sugaring change. Maple has been a moneymaker for a long, long time, but when the amount of money crosses a certain threshold (in the case of this man being quoted, a million-dollar threshold), something different is going on. The discomfort seems similar to the previous sugarmaker above, who was concerned about branding. Both see a threshold being crossed from local to corporate. One's threshold is marked with a number, while the other's is marked by product branding.

Not all increases in economic scale are understood as problematic, though. One sugarmaker recalled what it used to be like trying to get a bank loan to expand his sugaring operation: "When I went to try to borrow some money for a sugarbush [thirty years ago], it was just, 'what are you talking about?,' but now there are loans being made for sugar operations, half million dollars, and they don't bat an eye about it because it is acceptable now that it can be viable."[10] In this case, the change in economic meaning is viability—sugaring is now seen as being economically feasible as a larger-scale enterprise, and therefore more worthy of being supported by larger loans. In the past, to assign a meaning of viability beyond the local was unthinkable, but in today's economic climate, it is not only thinkable but increasingly common. While holding onto the sense of locality, sugaring's progression into a global economic process has made its economic meanings more intense. It is not more economized, but sugaring has become more monetized, with dollar amounts in the millions now being bandied about alongside the smaller-scale versions of exchange that took place between neighbors, sometimes involving trade, not cash.

The role of bulk packers in making economic meanings for maple is an interesting case. There are several bulk packers in Vermont who buy syrup from sugarmakers all across the state (in some cases, from outside the state as well) and package and/or further process it for sale under any number of brand and label identities. Some of the larger and better known bulk packers include Butternut Mountain Farm, Bascom Maple Farms, and Highland Sugarworks. The economic advantages to the sugarmaker are clear, as they get a more reliable sales outlet for their syrup, while foregoing the need to package, process, market, or distribute their syrup themselves. Bulk packers in Vermont serve some of the same purposes of price stabilization and using economies of scale that are provided to Canadian maple by the Federation of Quebec Maple Syrup Producers. The Federation functions as an enormous, governmentally structured economic cooperative, allowing sugarmakers in Quebec to act as a unit. Bulk packers in Vermont are not governmentally organized, and they work on a much smaller and less ubiquitous scale than the Federation, which produces over 70 percent of the syrup in the world.[11] However, a bulk packer is able to guarantee a price more reliably to producers than they can trust getting themselves, so the benefits to sugarmakers are clear.

The economic advantages of the process for the bulk packers are easily seen as well. They get to focus their business practice on marketing, processing, and distribution, allowing them to dedicate their time and resources to that side of the industry. "We're more of a service company than a maple company," as one bulk packer told me. Such a statement is not to be taken lightly, or dismissed as obvious.[12] The same man told me later that his primary identity was as a sugarmaker rather than a businessperson: "I clearly think of myself as a sugarmaker and a land manager and steward of the lands we have," so to make the statement that his company is more of a service company than a maple company is meaningful indeed.[13] Even while he runs a business that is not about tapping and boiling, he maintains his primary identity for himself as sugarmaker. He does still tap trees and make syrup himself, so his claim to that identity cannot be disputed, but it would not matter whether he tapped trees or not, honestly. The identity of sugarmaker is so powerful that it transcends how one gets their paycheck. As many people told me, sugaring is who you are, not what you do.

So, what are we to make of the statement that the bulk packing business is more a service company than a maple company? In describing it that way, this man is recognizing the separation of processes that has allowed his company to provide services to sugarmakers and the maple industry writ large without wanting to cede the centrality of sugaring, either to the industry or to his personal sense of self. By concentrating on the set of services that he does, he is able to be economically sustainable and to create more economic sustainability for sugarmakers and others in the industry by allowing them to focus their time, attention, and resources as well. His handling of the packing and selling provides space and resources for others to remain proper sugarmakers, to sugar well and to maintain their stewardship ethos, as well as making good economic sense for all involved. As this same man described to me later, sugarmakers, for example, "don't have the machinery to do these little bottles . . . we've got other competitors who, or customers who, pack a lot of their own syrup but they don't want to do the little leaf bottles."[14] The bulk packer takes on the task of packing syrup into specialized containers, leaving the sugarmaker to pack in more standard bottles or jars or simply to concentrate on making syrup. The work gets spread among the different parts of the system.

In straightforward anthropological economics, bulk packers are engaging in a form of craft specialization, "the ability to produce more efficiently by dividing labor among individuals or groups," wherein some entity takes a very specific role in a larger economic system and trades their expertise on that role for the increased results of combining their expertise with others' expertise in other roles.[15] In anthropology, economics has nothing necessarily to do with money. Economics at its most basic is about exchange: "Of course human beings have reproduced themselves in their environments and exchanged goods with other groups since the origins of our species, so in this sense we can say that the human economy is as old as humanity itself."[16]

Systems of exchange can involve money, of course, but that aspect is secondary and fairly unimportant to really understanding an economic process. Craft specialization is one result—perhaps a necessary result, perhaps a side effect—of economic exchange, and it forms the basis for many of the traits of contemporary economics that we take for granted, such as the assembly line and managerial hierarchy, even as basic as differences among professions. Sugaring can be seen as a process encompassing all parts of tapping, boiling, packaging, marketing, distribution, and sales, but bulk packers are involved in separating out certain parts of the process, allowing a more focused expertise on those parts and divesting the expertise of boiling on the sugarmakers from whom they buy their syrup. Sugarmakers who sell to bulk packers are just as much a part of this craft-specialization process, as they are complicit in allowing the bulk packers to focus on one part of the larger scheme, while themselves focusing on another.

In this manner, bulk packers intensify the commodification process of maple. Instead of a single pair of hands guiding the syrup from tree to evaporator to store shelf to consumer's kitchen, the bulk packer starts with the syrup, already the product of someone else's labor, and relatively undifferentiated as a product. Bulk packers do keep close track of which barrels come from whom, of course, both for quality control and to differentiate final use. Some syrups are more suitable for the bottle, while others are more suited to making maple sugar or candy, for example, but regardless of the final destination, the syrup a bulk packer buys enters into a set of processes that shape its final outcome entirely separate from the sugarmaker who boiled the sap down. It would be overly romantic to say that the identity of the syrup is *lost* in the process because that analysis would rely on an understanding of identity as a thing that can vary in quantity (rather like saying "we got a lot of weather last week," as if the calm conditions of this week do not qualify as a type of weather), as opposed to a thing that varies in quality, which understands identity in terms of its shape and the role it plays for the people or groups who have that identity.

A better way to understand the role of the bulk packer here is to say that syrup being bought by a bulk packer *changes* its identity by making the syrup a relatively undifferentiated commodity, rather than the evident result of a particular sugarmaker's efforts. Michael Pollan has gotten a lot of attention for writing about this re-identification effect of large-scale food economies in the United States, and there are some similarities between his example of commodity corn and bulk-packed maple. He describes commodity corn as, "as much an economic abstraction as it is a biological fact," but that description is too dismissive of economic meaning.[17] The commoditization he discusses is economic, but it is not an abstraction at all. The meanings being made are very real and very tangible. As Pollan explains about corn when it becomes a commodity: "My plan when I came to Iowa was to somehow follow George Naylor's corn on its circuitous path to our plates and into our bodies. I should have known that tracing a single bushel of commodity corn is as impossible as tracing a bucket of water after it's been poured into a river."[18]

For Pollan, the stark realization that there is a difference between corn-the-food and corn-the-commodity helped him understand what it means to take a single producer's yield and combine it with that from other producers.[19] The individuality of a single bushel of corn may be removed, but its identity does not disappear. It simply changes from a set of divisible, identifiably different *products* that share a label (ears of corn) to a mass of undifferentiated *product* that has a new, singular identity (corn). In linguistic terms, it transforms from a countable noun to a mass noun, which is marked by the grammatical forms of "ears of corn," with its pluralizing /s/, and "corn" without a singular or plural form marked.

Maple syrup that goes through bulk packers is subject to some version of this identity transformation, although the change is not as extreme or typically as irreversible. The corn Pollan is tracking from George Naylor's farm "joins the streams of corn coming off his neighbors' farms; later, that tributary flows mostly east and south from Iowa into the tremendous maw of the American food system," thereby becoming the mass-noun corn.[20] Some of the syrup sold to bulk packers gets blended with the syrup from other sugarmakers in a liquid flow that more closely resembles Pollan's metaphorical river of corn. Its identity is transformed from separate syrups from different sugarmakers to an undifferentiated, singular syrup. To be fair, though, this change is not that different from what an individual sugarmaker does if they are bottling and selling their own syrup straight to the consumer. Sugarmakers don't bottle the syrup from one tree separately from the syrup from another tree. They blend their sap and their boilings together all the time, as sap is collected from a wide area and processed together. So the blending and loss of differentiation that a bulk packer is doing is more a difference in degree, rather than kind. The ability to define a jar of syrup as coming from a particular sugarmaker or a particular sugarbush is lost, but the ability to determine an origin in the first place is not as precise as it may seem.

At whatever scale the blending of syrups into syrup takes place, it comes with an associated loss of differentiation in origin, either of tree or sugarmaker. The narrative of being from a particular place still remains, though. Locality then becomes negotiated on a different scale, although it is by no means lost from the commodifying equation. Even when a single bottle of syrup can't be tracked back to a particular sugarhouse or stand of maples, it is still localized, often with the words "pure Vermont maple" or some version thereof. Within Franklin County, it may be meaningful to say whose sugarhouse a bottle comes from. A visitor from southern Vermont may just find meaning in Franklin County, while a tourist up from New York City may be willing to pay a premium for anything called "Vermont maple." The scale of consumption alters the scale of location that is meaningful, up to a point. The name of Vermont carries meaning in New York, in California, and even in Australia, over and above other possible locators like New England or USA. Vermont maple carries an implicit trust that, no matter where it was produced within the state, the commodity in the bottle will include syrup and a story that is meaningful enough to elicit the price. Vermont has earned the ability in constantly expanding markets to trade on itself as a location by diligent oversight of the quality of the syrup it produces.

I came upon an interesting twist to this scaling of syrup identity in a tourist shop on the harbor of St. John's, Newfoundland. In many international markets, the words "Vermont" and "Canada" carry similar weight in terms of eliciting economic meaning. People think of those locations as the homes for maple, so will pay for those names. St. John's is a stop for cruise ships, so one shop owner experienced many tourists from abroad entering her store, looking for Canadian maple syrup as a recognizable souvenir. For the cruise ship tourists from Sweden or Poland, the difference between Quebec (which produces much maple) and Newfoundland (which produces almost none, and absolutely none for the maple market) was irrelevant. They had just stepped off a ship into Canada, and from their distant point of view, Canada meant maple. So, this enterprising shop owner, whose store specialized in Newfoundland souvenirs, bought Quebec maple syrup and had labels made that said, "This syrup is <u>NOT</u> from Newfoundland!" She was localizing the syrup in a joking manner by applying the word "Newfoundland," allowing her to sell maple to tourists who wanted to buy it while playing with the different senses of scale and localness that they had.

Bulk packing is not the only form of craft specialization, and therefore commodification, that has been introduced into sugaring. Green Mountain Mainlines in Fletcher, Vermont, has created an industrialized boiling operation that buys sap from many local tappers and boils it at a centralized facility. While the idea of buying sap from someone else and boiling it, or even leasing the trees on someone else's property, is nothing new, the scale and sense of specialized process that Green Mountain Mainlines brings to the system is at the very least a novelty in sugaring. Their boiling facility has two fairly large 4x14 evaporators, being fed by five reverse osmosis (RO) units.[21] The operation purchases sap from across a wide area and trucks it to their facility in Fletcher, where it is dumped into an in-ground piping system through grated ports in the ground, very similar to systems used to take grain off a truck at a grain elevator, evoking Pollan's experience of the corn mountain at an Iowa grain elevator. Again, the commodification process turns the different saps from particular stands of maples into a mixed, undifferentiated flow of sap that gets boiled at Green Mountain Mainlines.

Where Butternut Mountain Farm or Highland Sugarworks can track a barrel of syrup that they have bought back to a particular sugarmaker (who may be able to track that barrel back to a particular stand of trees on a particular day), Green Mountain Mainlines does not have as much ability to trace the origins of its product. This is partially due to timing. Highland Sugarworks can easily let some purchased syrup sit in its barrel for weeks, complete with a tag and tracking information because the syrup, once produced, is only minimally perishable.

Maple sap, on the other hand, is very perishable, with many sugar-makers telling me they would not boil sap more the twenty-four hours from the tree. Sap left out can easily begin to ferment because of the high sugar concentration in the liquid, so Green Mountain Mainlines works under a constant flow of pressure to boil sap as soon as possible, making the process of transforming the individual saps' particular identity into a genericized stream of sap a more immediate and pervasive process. Both bulk packing and bulk boiling commodify, but bulk boiling commodifies a bit earlier in its specialized step, and a bit more thoroughly through its process. Interestingly, Green Mountain Mainlines sells much of the syrup it produces from this bulk boiling system to one of the large bulk packers in the state, Butternut Mountain Farm. The forms of craft specialization line up with one another. Another large-scale operation, this time in the northeastern part of the state, is bringing a new level of industrialization to sugaring. Sweet Tree Holdings is a new company, starting production in 2016, that promises to make maple on something approaching an industrial scale, drawing on at least 200,000 taps—double the size of the largest traditional Vermont operations—and boiling in a factory-like setting.[22] The true impact of Sweet Tree will not be known for some time, but the mere fact that they are producing maple on such a scale is a step up in the commodification of maple, and a new economic meaning being made within the state.

How do these commodification processes of bulk packing of syrup and bulk boiling of sap shape the economic meanings of maple? Clearly, maple has become less of an individualized product of one producer and more of a commodity in these systems. There are still plenty of people who sell the syrup they make on the trees they tap, but the amount of syrup being distributed by bulk packers means that the sweet stuff in the bottle, for many end consumers, is just as often the result of some craft-specialized process as the more traditional understanding of sugaring. However, the narrative that the bulk packers attach to their syrup and other maple products is very much the same as the individual sugarmaker because the product is telling and selling the same story. That story involves not just the syrup, but the life and lifestyle that produced it. "Intimately connected to 'simple' food production methods are the 'simple' ways of life of those individuals who produce authentic food."[23] The man in the red-checked coat emptying buckets is just as prominent in the marketing and packaging materials of the bulk packers as it is in the neighborhood sugarmaker up the hill, both representing the simple way of life of the Vermont sugarmaker. The fact that the design and creation of packaging for maple products is most often the result of another craft-specialized process means that whoever is filling the bottles, the story the bottle is trying to tell is similar, and it is one of individuality and the simple, rustic charm of a red-checked coat and buckets.

There is another marker of the individual and the personal remaining in maple, even within the bulk packing and bulk boiling systems. Among sugarmakers, when I would hear someone talking about Butternut Mountain Farm, for example, I would not hear the name of the company used. Instead, the sugarmakers would refer to David Marvin, the owner. The expression was not, "I sell my syrup to Butternut Mountain," but rather, "I sell my syrup to Dave Marvin." In like manner, Marvin referred to several individual sugarmakers in a conversation with me. In both directions, even though the syrup was being commodified and its individual identity being transformed into a commodity identity, the people involved understood themselves and one another as individuals. Similarly, Green Mountain Mainlines was just as often referred to as the owner, JR Sloan ("my sap goes to JR up in Fletcher"), even though both operations employ a large number of people.

The similarities in Green Mountain Mainlines' operation to grain farming are clear, and those similarities make for an intriguing change in the meaning of maple. One of the stereotypical images of the Midwest United States is a wide-open swath of flatland, with the horizon interrupted only by a grain elevator. Having grown up in the Midwest myself, I can attest to more than a kernel of truth in this particular stereotype. Farmers in Vermont very often are quick to differentiate themselves from their midwestern counterparts, though, as their horizons are pierced by the next mountain ridge nearby, not a grain elevator far off. The gulf between the two in this narrative is clear—Vermont has small hill farms that are (or used to be) family owned, while midwestern farms are huge monocrop agribusinesses. The differentiation is similar to the ones made earlier with branding

and the million-dollar threshold. What is done in Vermont traditionally is small and local, by and for us. What is done in the Midwest is
impersonal, at Phillip Morris is corporate, and across the million-
dollar line is big business. None of those things accords easily with the
Vermont sense of localness and small scale that many people retain,
even despite economic changes.

Neither end of that Vermont/Midwest narrative is quite so simple
of course, but the narrative is used to make meaning for Vermont
farms. The use of a grain-feeder-type process by Green Mountain
Mainlines to get sap from trucks and into its processing facility is
the closest I have seen to a larger-scale, industrialized agricultural
process being introduced into sugaring. Such a process smacks of
agribusiness, which is not so much an aberration within sugaring,
but a violation of the Vermont version of agricultural identity. Grain
elevators are not a feature of the Vermont landscape because that form
of bulk consolidation and commodification of grain is much less part
of Vermont's agricultural identity. It is a part of dairy agriculture, and
Vermont's recent farming history is dairy, but maple is thought of as
a crop, rather than a year-round product like milk. To use a replica of
that grain elevator system in sugaring at the very least broadens the
meaning of maple to include an economic process that is, in its origin,
very foreign to the state. To be fair, no one I spoke with seemed to see
this as a threat to the authenticity of either sugaring or farming in
Vermont. I do not mean to suggest that it is such a threat or should
be. I merely want to point out that one trait of midwestern farming
has crept into Vermont sugaring, which provides an opportunity to
examine the economic meanings of farming and maple there.

Because sugaring is slotted into the realm of agriculture, the
identity of "sugarmaker" and the identity of "farmer" are still closely
aligned in Vermont, regardless of whether the person sugaring also
engages in any other agricultural activity or not. Farmers as a lot are
nothing if not economically practical. From the earliest days of agriculture, a person farming had to understand a wide range of inter-
connected processes with an eye toward generating some product at
the end. The sheer number of areas of knowledge that come into play
when one farms is staggering to the uninformed and still humbling to
those who know. Having to coordinate so many interrelated processes

tends to make farmers a fairly practical bunch, with a focus on the task and an eye on the bottom line. Because maple is understood as part of the agricultural world, many of the same ways of farmers' thinking can be associated with sugaring: "There's an awful lot of knowledge you need in order to make all that [sugaring] equipment work for you. It doesn't come with a lot of good instructions."[24] Sugaring equipment requires knowledge drawing on the realms of plumbing, electric, mechanics, fluid dynamics, basic physics and chemistry, and a host of other areas. None of that will come as a surprise to anyone who has done any farming, where such combinations of knowledge bases are the norm rather than the exception.

The practical, pragmatic mindset of the farmer very easily informs the general understanding of sugaring, so that even the most romantic notions of "the old ways" and "keeping heritage alive" that maple evokes are layered with a knowledge that what comes out of the tree eventually goes into a bottle and often onto a shelf with a price tag attached. As Anna Peterson puts it, "To speak of lived ethics points to the mutual shaping of ideas and real life and suggests that moral systems should not simply be applied to concrete situations but rather applicable to and livable in them."[25] Maximizing profit, even for the smaller scale of production, is often a priority over other considerations, as evidenced by a joke one sugarmaker told me: "You know the old joke about finding the mice. Sometimes you find [dead] mice in your buckets on the trees, and the old thing goes that over in New Hampshire, they just look the other way and take the mouse out and keep the sap. But here in Vermont, we like to wring the mouse out first."[26] The joke here is partially on the thriftiness of Vermonters, who have a reputation of being able to pinch a penny paper thin at times. However, also contained in this joke is a recognition of how important economic meanings are and have long been in maple. It is easy enough to romanticize the old ways and think of economics as a relatively new addition (intrusion?) into sugaring, but the joke above has been around a while. It's not a joke about mice in the vacuum receiver—it's about mice in the buckets. Economic meanings are not an intrusion into the heritage of maple; they are a part of that heritage.

When having conversations with sugarmakers about the balance of profit and heritage, their pragmatic approach sometimes reminded me of a man in Orkney, Scotland, who told me of his uncle, who would make a particular style of high-backed, hooded chair that was identified as traditionally Orcadian and sell them to the tourist market:

> It's such a pile of shit. My uncle . . . used to make Orkney chairs, now he didn't do it to keep heritage, he got money for it; he did it for money. He laughed at the people that bought them— these idiot tourists, he thought it was hilarious that they'd give him hundreds of pounds for this chair that he'd spin you know, *in his shed*; he did it for money, he didn't [think] "I'm keeping the old things alive. By god, you'll thank me for this one day." He did it for *cash*, same as did everybody else.[27]

This man's explanation of his uncle's work in a traditional craft could be described as not merely unromantic, but against the idea of the romantic, with its laughing dismissal of notions of heritage and identity being attached to material culture. While the sugarmakers I spoke with were rarely quite that dismissive, the unromantic idea of money and maple going hand-in-hand was one of the most common themes of our conversations. Far from being interpreted as a contradiction or a threat to authenticity, the economic view of maple is seen as a basic part of its identity. For much of its history among European descendants in Vermont, maple paid the bills, and even before that, it was understood as a thing with value of some sort.

The commodification and transformation into economic entity of maple happens well before the bottle hits the shelf, though. Sugarmakers are constantly balancing various sets of numbers: cords of wood or gallons of oil burned, number of taps set, gallons per tap, percentage of RO, acres of woods and yards of tubing, inches of pressure in their vacuum system. Each of these numbers represents some portion of the complicated dance that coaxes the sap from the tree and into an evaporator. Before the sap ever comes to a boil, it has been commodified umpteen ways to maximize the output of syrup at the end. Many sugarmakers are constantly tweaking their system, upping the vacuum one season, lowering the RO percentage another, in order to find the sweetest of the sweet spots, wherein they are making the most, best syrup they can off the trees they are tapping.

The constant push and pull of the various numbers is reflected in technological changes as well. Reverse osmosis machines were

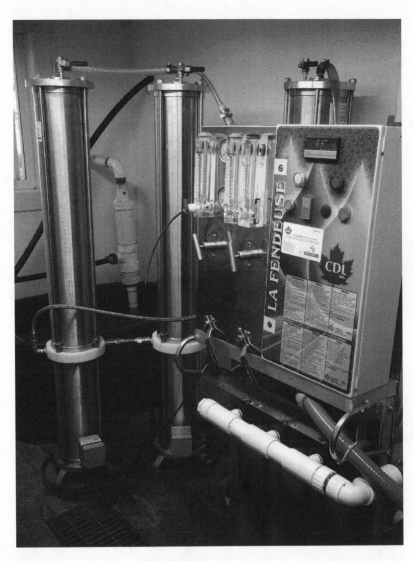

Reverse osmosis system. *Author photo.*

brought into sugaring to increase the percentage of sugar in the sap before setting it on the heat, allowing less fuel to be used to boil the sap down to the required percentage to be legally called syrup.

Interestingly, in sugaring, reverse osmosis machines are used in a manner opposite of what they generally are employed to do. The process of reverse osmosis separates water from particulate contaminants suspended in the water by running the water through some sort of filter under pressure. So, running liquid through a reverse osmosis machine generates two products: purified water (permeate) and a slurry containing the contaminants (concentrate). Usually, the goal of reverse osmosis is to remove the particulates (pollutants, salt, etc.) from the water. However, sugarmakers want to remove the *water*, leaving the particulate sugar in suspension. Purified water is the waste product of reverse osmosis in sugaring, although many sugarmakers put that purified water to some use. Because the process of reverse osmosis puts a lot of heat into the water, several sugaring operations use the hot, purified water to wash their equipment. In so doing, they are tweaking one more number in the complex of commodified systems by not having to use water from the taps or the well, or cleanser from the store. For those who wash with permeate, the trees provide not only the maple that comes out of the evaporator but the means to scrub the evaporator down. It is just another of the many ways that sugarmakers seek efficiencies and attempt to economize. The very process of economizing recognizes that economic meanings are very meaningful in sugaring.

Maple sells. It is a financially successful product because many different people in many different contexts are willing to pay a significant amount of money for it, enough to sustain its continued production and distribution. This is one way in which maple is economically *unlike* many other agricultural products—it is not subsidized in any appreciable measure. Governmental support is given for marketing and the like, but the product itself is not subsidized in Vermont in the way it is in other states, New York's "Maple Tap Act," for example, or the provincial and federal support of Quebec's Federation.[28] More than one sugarmaker chuckled at the false assumptions made by some newcomers to sugaring, who sought grants from the state government or academia to start up a sugar operation. Maple is profitable; such grants really don't exist because maple sells. The syrup and other maple products themselves are made into an economic commodity, but how? What is the value of maple syrup, and what are the values attached to maple syrup that allow it to be a commodity worth paying for?

A basic understanding of Adam Smithian economics says that profit ultimately comes from a difference between use value (the intrinsic value of an item based on the costs of its creation) and exchange value (the amount of value one can get for the item in an exchange process).[29] The use value of maple is pretty easily calculated, by taking into account the cost of the material input (the land and trees, the tubing, the releasers and tanks, the evaporator, the fuel, etc.) and then adding in the labor costs (the time and effort to check the lines, move the sap, run the boil, filter and bottle, etc.). The balance of all these numbers is the constant tweaking game that every sugar-maker plays, trying to maximize their output to achieve the lowest use value for a set amount of syrup. The use value of maple is not fixed, but it fluctuates within a fairly bounded range based on each sugarmaker's operation.

So, if that is the origin of syrup's use value, from where does maple derive its exchange value? What makes it a commodity in an eco-nomically sustainable sense, with profit potential? When looking at the retailing of maple, a particular set of tropes and motifs appears steadily and often.

Images of the sugarhouse and stands of maple trees are no surprise, but very often outside the sugarhouse is a man in a red-checked coat, and hanging from the trees are buckets.[30] Horse-drawn sledges are not an infrequent visitor to the eye, either, and wisps of smoke or steam from the sugarhouse suggest a wood fire as the obvious source of heat for the boil. These tropes evoke an old-timey narrative of sugaring, with what is perceived as a low level of technology involved, and with a process dripping (literally) with tradition.[31] The containers that carry these tropes are pretty stan-dardized, with the vast majority coming from a small number of companies. Sugarhill Containers, a division of Hillside Plastics out of Massachusetts, makes many of the plastic containers that receive Vermont syrup (as well as syrup made in other parts of the sugaring world), and their imagery very often includes the tropes of the red-checked coat, horse, and bucket.[32] The bottle itself, although made of injection-molded plastic, is shaped to resemble an old earthenware jug, again connecting to old-timey imagery. Sugarhill is by no means alone in evoking these tropes, but as one of the largest manufactur-ers and distributors of the maple containers, they have helped write a script that many others now follow.

Maple syrup container. *Author photo.*

The fact that few of the sugarmakers who package their syrup in those wholesale jars from Sugarhill actually collect on buckets and fewer still use a horse team to draw their syrup to the sugarhouse matters very little. It is not the process itself that is important to the commodification of maple. It is the *narrative* that spans the gap between the use value and the exchange value of syrup. People pay a premium for the story of maple. Don't get me wrong—real maple syrup is wonderful stuff, and I have tasted some amazing syrups in the course of doing the fieldwork on which this book is based. By pointing out the importance of the narrative, I am not diminishing the importance of what's in the jar. As more than one sugarmaker told me, if the syrup in the jar is not a top-quality product, all the fancy labeling in the world won't bring a customer back for more, and the same is true for fancy stories. However, the importance of the narrative in the commodification of maple is enormous. The story is what gets a price per gallon from the use value, which is just the cost of production, up to the exchange value, which is what the customer is willing to pay.

That exchange value can be influenced by any number of things, including not just the narrative of production that is distilled into the bottle, but also the narrative of acquiring the syrup. How a sugarmaker markets their syrup can be shaped by how they operate, but how they operate can also be shaped by how they market. One sugarmaker in southeastern Vermont summed up the impact of marketing on their operation by explaining the physical location of their sugarhouse:

> A sugarhouse like the one we're sitting in here now has no business belonging here from a production standpoint. It belongs at the lowest point of the sugarbush, especially back when they had horses, because you fill a tank up with sap, you want to go downhill and if you have pipeline, downhill, everything's downhill. The sugarhouse belongs down in the sugarbush at the lowest point. And [name] was one of the first guys, he actually hooked onto his sugarhouse with his tractor and pulled it up beside the road. And the reason he did that was because at that time, the roads were starting to improve and cars and tourists and roadside stands, that whole thing was starting up and [name] was looking to sell his syrup so, anyways, so that's all true. (9 June 2011)

The sugarmaker telling me this story is making the connection between production and marketing, between use value and exchange value. His operation sells primarily on the roadside, to a customer base that is driving through Vermont and wants to stop at the road for some maple syrup. In order to do so, he has located his sugarhouse in a spot that is illogical in strict terms of production. His sugarhouse, following the lead of the other sugarmaker discussed in his story, is placed at the side of the road, up the hill. There is use value to having the sugarhouse downhill, where gravity is working with the process (sap, being liquid, seeks a level, so it flows downhill), requiring less labor input to get the sap where it needs to go. But that bit of use value has been sacrificed for the sake of increased exchange value. This trade-off was made first by the older sugarmaker referenced in the story, several decades ago when automotive tourism was sharply increasing visitor traffic from Boston and New York up through Vermont's roads.

Having the sugarhouse easily accessible to the passing tourist doesn't make the *syrup* more easily accessible—jugs of syrup can be put by the side of the road without much trouble, regardless of where it is made or bottled. Having the sugarhouse there where the cars can see it, where the visitors can enter it, makes the *narrative* of maple more easily accessible. The experience of being inside the sugarhouse makes the story of acquiring syrup more special, more meaningful because the visitor is able to engage with more of the production process. Seeing a boil, even seeing an evaporator when it is not boiling, brings the visitors inside of something they normally cannot access. Being able to live that story, and then to tell that story as part of acquiring the syrup, makes the syrup worth more. The exchange value increases. For the sugarmaker telling this story, the majority of his sales are to the casual passer-by, making the sacrifice of use value for exchange value well worth the price.

Clearly, the intersecting stories of production and acquisition are worth something, as prices for maple have generally risen over time, and the customer base is constantly increasing. The meaningful visit to the sugarhouse translates directly into the economic meaning of dollars for syrup. One sugarmaker told me that he finds visitors so affected by seeing the evaporator at full boil that he goes to great lengths to provide that experience: "There was times I'd boil water out there to make steam, and be able to talk about it."[33] The experience of the sugarhouse, with the raging boil over the heat and steam dripping from the rafters and running down the walls, is so important that this sugarmaker admits to faking it, for the sake of giving tourists something closer to a real experience. The reality of such an experience is certainly open to question, though, as the steam created by running regular water through the evaporator will not have that evocative perfume of maple sap that invades your clothing and your nostrils for days. And the notion of boiling at a time of year outside of regular sugaring can undermine some of the realities of sugaring's seasonality, but the power of the experience trumps those considerations, at least for some sugarmakers such as this man. He boiled *something* to put on a show, because the show has such impact for visitors, and that impact helps create the narrative that he talks about. The show becomes part of the tourists' narrative of acquisition, while the story this sugarmaker tells is one of syrup production, even if the story is a little fudged by boiling water instead of sap. The show and the narrative help turn syrup into dollars, helping "tourists cultivate meaning attached to objects, service and experience at the level of exchange, not at the level of production."[34]

The visitor seeing the boil, regardless of *what* is being boiled, is more likely to translate the experience of the sugarhouse in action into the purchase of some syrup, thereby negotiating the meaning at the level of exchange. The line is admittedly blurry in this instance, as one aspect of the narrative of production is being faked by the man above (and he is not the only one who has boiled water for the sake of a tourist show). There is also fuzziness in that the level of production and the level of exchange are very close to each other. Indeed, that is one of the charms of maple—that the production of the product is easily accessible to the tourist because it takes place in and among people and their everyday lives, as opposed to having been created in a factory in some nameless industrial estate. This analysis ignores the fact that the people working in the factories on the industrial estates are, in fact, living everyday lives as well, but the physical proximity of production and product available for exchange in maple conveys a meaning of access and intimacy that very often translates into a visitor buying some syrup. An economic meaning is grafted onto the experience of visiting the sugarhouse the moment that happens.

Both narratives, of maple production and maple acquisition, have become commodities that play a role in the making of syrup's exchange value. The story of the red-checked coat, horse, and bucket has become commodified itself, as is made clear by how standardized that story has become on the containers. The story of the sugarhouse visit is made more available to the consumer and potential consumer by shaping the sugarhouse to meet the consumer where they are, in some cases literally, by placing the house on the roadside. Other sugarmakers shape their sugarhouse by crafting steps for children to be able to see into their pans or simply by opening their sugarhouse to the public, either on specific days or with a general open-door policy. The story sells because there is a mystique behind the syrup's production, even for those who might be expected to be in the know. Another sugarmaker who gets a lot of drive-by business discussed the lack of widespread knowledge: "Yeah, it's surprising how many people we get during maple season are Vermonters or from New Hampshire, Massachusetts, that really don't get it, don't understand the process, don't understand the different grades, you know, what makes the different grades."[35] Having the sugarhouse immediately available to the consumer allows them to explore sugaring and gain a little knowledge in addition to a little syrup. Even for locals, the process may be opaque. Because there is an unknown there, learning about the production process makes the narrative of acquisition more satisfying to the consumer. A sugarhouse at the bottom of the hill, far from the road, will not provide that part of the story, but one that has been dragged right up next to the road can, becoming a commodified version of "living history" that visitors can access.[36]

The commodification of all the different narratives moves the price from use value to exchange value, based on the desire of the customer to buy not just syrup, but *Vermont* syrup. The story above gained more meaning when the sugarmaker telling it explained that his customer base was largely tourists driving up into Vermont from south, Connecticut and Massachusetts, and stopping by his place to get some syrup on the way. The primary goal of his customers is to get a little Vermont, not to get syrup. Whether they are driving into the state for skiing or fall foliage, they are leaving their home to visit Vermont. Buying some maple on the way fits right into the plan because the syrup and the state are made synonymous by drawing on the same set of tropes. As one Vermonter who works closely with the marketing of maple discussed, Vermont trades itself on being a clean, green, and serene place, with a lifestyle that is rooted in tradition and authenticity, and the state is conscious of, and protective of, those meanings: "You look at the Vermont special food industry today, people just look at Vermont as being, right or wrong, something solid, something genuine. It's amazing how many companies from outside the state try to come in here, want to produce something one way or another, be able to utilize the name 'Vermont,' and it's a big discussion in the specialty food industry."[37]

The economic meaning of the state's name is protected by those who oversee the specialty food industry because they know that the name carries along other meanings, meanings of "something solid, something genuine," and that those meanings are important makers of exchange value. This person speaking, who is not a sugarmaker, knows how important the narrative of Vermont's solidity and genuineness is, demonstrating how important the connection is. It is not just sugarmakers who protect the value of the name. "Genuine" in this context might as well be "authentic," and authenticity is part of what makes Vermont and maple a commodity. Hearing about this kind of economic protectionism again put me in mind of one of my interviews from some previous fieldwork in the Orkney islands of Scotland. One of the locals recalled an incident when the name of Orkney was subject to the same kind of protection:

> Some years ago, there was a guy had requested financial assistance from the Islands Council [the local governmental authority] to help to start another jewelry industry, and he was going to call it, what was it . . . "something-something Orkney Jewelry," almost suggesting it was exclusively his prerogative, this "Orkney Jewelry." He would get the grant only if he changed its name because he had just settled here a few months, and he tried to get the exclusive name "Orkney Jewelry." [The Council] couldn't actually stop him doing the name, but they could give him no assistance, and clearly it was quite crucial for the start of his business, this assistance. So, he had the choice, either change the name or do without assistance.[38]

In both cases, Orkney and Vermont, there is a protectionist attitude on the part of authorities to the place's name. It is interesting to note also that, in both interviews, the speaker makes known that the entity claiming the name is in some measure an outsider. In the case of

Orkney, it is a man who had only lived in the islands for a few months, while in the quote from the Vermonter above, it is companies coming into the state from outside. There is something about using the state's name to sell a product that raises flags. The flags are not about the commodification of the name, but about the name being applied authentically—either by someone with a properly authentic claim to it or by what is understood as a proper, authentic version of the place, as explained by one sugarmaker: "The connection of Vermont to maple really works extremely well, and there's a heritage of Vermont supporting maple, and the purity and authenticity of the product, and the quality of the product."[39]

Here, the speaker is extolling Vermont's connection to maple, but the justifications being made are interesting. Why is the state's claim to maple valid? Because of the history and a heritage of supporting maple, which aligns nicely with the narrative of heritage meanings, but also with the purity and authenticity *of the product*, the quality *of the product*. The authenticity, heritage, and purity that are parts of Vermont's identity are here being given explicit economic meaning by being attached to the product of maple syrup. This speaker takes the discussion that connects the state's reputation to maple a step or two further. The purity is not a thing of Vermont that gets transferred to the syrup—it is a quality of the syrup itself. Vermont and maple become almost interchangeable in this construction, and the tropes of authenticity, heritage, and so forth are just as easily applied to the state as a place as they are to the syrup as a product, a salable commodity.

However, Vermont cannot claim to be the sole owner of all of these tropes that are attached to maple. Some of the authentic state identity that is commodified and placed in the bottle along with the syrup includes meanings of cleanness, greenness, and healthfulness. These are traits that are quite easily connected to Vermont, but not exclusively, especially in the marketing of a specialty food item like maple syrup: "Vermont stands for something that's clean, that's green, that's healthy, that's natural, and these are all words that connect really well with maple. They also however connect really well with Canada. I mean, if you ask an American consumer to describe how they feel about a food from Vermont or a food from Canada, they'd probably use the same language."[40] So the authenticity being brought to bear here is one that Vermont can legitimately claim (according to this speaker, anyway), but that others can as well. The ability for these meanings to be shared might not be that interesting or problematic, if not for the fact that they are shared with Canada, with whom Vermont theoretically competes economically on the maple market. Economic meanings can be made with cleanness and greenness, but they are not different economic meanings from those that can be made by Canada for its maple. The truth of the matter is, though, that the competition between Vermont and Canadian syrup is a relatively small economic factor, and it takes place mostly within Vermont, with Vermont consumers. Very little US maple is available in Canada, while a significant amount of Canadian maple can be found on Vermont store shelves. That has long been the case, but the growth in the maple market is in neither Vermont nor Canada, so this competition is meaningful on a fairly small scale. I am not dismissing the importance of that competition, mind. For a small sugarmaker in the state who is trying to convince neighbors to buy her or his syrup, rather than get some Canadian syrup at the grocery store, the competition is real and impactful. But on a larger scale, both Vermont and Canada are promoting maple in new markets in Australia, Japan, China, and elsewhere. In those places, the equal access to tropes of cleanliness and greenness matter less, as both places become fairly generic stand-ins for "far away, authentic, and healthy."

Closer to home, a sense of authenticity adds value to the commodity of maple, as well. It raises the exchange value significantly because people want to buy into (and then literally buy) a more specific story, the story of the old-timer up the road or the next county over boiling sap that he collected from buckets and dumped into a barrel on his horse-drawn sledge before hauling it to the sugarhouse. Earlier, I discussed how sugarmakers commodified their own identity and put it into the bottle right along with the syrup. That process only works economically if someone is willing to buy their syrup mixed with a story. That's where authenticity comes into play. Australian customers want a generic authenticity attached to Canada or Vermont. But visitors to the state want something that is "authentically Vermonty," and maple has been positioned not just as authentically Vermonty, but as paradigmatically Vermont.

In this way, the narrative of maple becomes part of the commodification process of maple. Even beyond that, though, the narrative itself becomes commodified. For many years, the standardization of the tropes that make the narrative was stunning. If one lined up bottles from states and provinces across North America, a similar story recurred over and over. A man in a red-checked coat is drawing syrup to the sugarhouse nestled deep in a woods, boiling over a wood fire, and using buckets and a horse team. To be sure, the imagery on maple containers and elsewhere can depict other things, and therefore construct different narratives. Maple leaves, a solitary sugarhouse, a simple state outline, and other tropes occur, but far and away the most common was for many years the man in the red-checked coat. This marketing standardization is changing, though, as the market for Vermont maple extends ever farther geographically from the state. The cachet of the name of the state means less and less as one gets farther away, to the point that, for example, "Vermont" means almost nothing specific in Australia. It evokes, but it does not evoke the man in the red-checked coat or the traditional ways of doing things. What it evokes instead is that cleanliness and greenness and trends in the labeling and marketing of Vermont maple are reacting to those new, more distant markets. In small steps, the horse team and red-checked coat are being replaced by images of mountains and unspecified trees. One good example of this shift is April's Maple, in Canaan, Vermont. April worked with a designer to make a custom label for her products depicting only a stylized tree. Her label evokes nature and simplicity, rather than the standard narrative of horses and buckets. The narratives are in the process of changing, but the reasons remain the same—the commodification of Vermont's story (whatever story it tells) to prompt the consumer to buy a bottle of syrup.

There is another form of commodification, or at least of quantification, that goes on in sugaring. When two sugarmakers meet, the first thing they typically talk about is how the current season is going or went, depending on the time of year. Next is often some discussion of the size of their operation. This part of the conversation can take the form of numbers that vary year to year, such as taps set, gallons produced, or cords burned. The conversation can also entail numbers that remain more fixed, such as the size of their evaporators' pans, or the output of their RO, measured in gallons per hour. A quick perusal through the discussion threads on the Maple Trader website (mapletrader.com, an online community and listserv for sugarmakers, "brought to you by The Maple Guys") shows that many of those who post questions or answers include in their signature a list of their equipment, the size of their operation, and/or some mention of their production. They communicate their operation through a commoditizing process, and in so doing, they make an economic meaning of their identity as a sugarmaker.

The economic meanings of maple are not strictly confined to syrup, though. I have written thus far of maple syrup as if it were the only end result for the consumer. However, maple syrup can be further refined or processed to make a wide variety of other, nonsyrup maple products. In the old grading system used in Vermont, Grade C syrup, the darkest and usually strongest flavored, was not permitted to be sold retail. It was sold mostly to secondary producers to become other products such as candy or real maple flavoring in cakes, cookies, sauces, and so forth. Now, with the new grading system, those darker syrups are being sold retail in Vermont, but much of the darker syrup still gets shunted into secondary production processes. Beyond flavorings, maple can be turned into maple cream, maple butter, maple sugar, maple taffy, and much more.

Some of these products are just maple syrup that has been processed in some additional way, such as maple cream or maple sugar. Maple cream is simply syrup that is heated and cooled in a particular sequence while air is whipped into it, giving it a creamy, spreadable consistency. Maple sugar is syrup that is boiled down until almost all of the water is gone, leaving just the crystalized sugar from that sap. Other products involve mixing the syrup with other ingredients to make some other end product. In either event, maple is commodified further in these secondary production processes, either by becoming merely one ingredient in a mixture or by being transformed from its "normal" state into the form of cream or sugar. In both cases, the draw for sugarmakers and secondary producers is to add exchange value to the syrup by transforming it into, or combining it with, something else, thereby getting an increased return on their use value investment.

The term *value-added commodity* is used in the food industry, and that term should be understood very literally in this case. A value-added item is an item to which more (exchange) value is added through secondary processing, thereby commanding a higher price. Interestingly, maple is understood to have a normal state in this formulation, and that state is syrup. Maple sugar used to be much more common than syrup, and more often the desired goal of a sugarmaker, as its lighter weight and longer shelf life made it more desirable to transport, sell, and stock in a kitchen. The commodity of syrup is now so central to the identity of maple that it is understood as the default setting, the place from which all other maple products come. Such a formulation ignores that syrup is the result of a human process in the first place, but that disconnect is probably not entirely unexpected, given the number of people who expect syrup, and not sap, to shoot forth from a taphole in a maple tree. Syrup is the baseline commodity in the maple world.

The understanding of syrup as maple's natural state is being challenged, or at least changed, by other secondary economies of sugaring. Unlike other secondary products like maple candy that are made from the product subsequent to boiling (i.e., the syrup), a few products that are now gaining popularity are made from the sap *before* it ever hits an evaporator. Maple soda has been around for a while, but there is a company in Vermont that has for a few years been bottling a soda made from maple sap, rather than flavoring soda with maple (real or otherwise). The Vermont Sweetwater Bottling Company makes a wide range of carbonated beverages flavored with maple. More recently, they have been marketing what they call Maple Seltzer, which is not carbonated water with maple flavoring, but carbonated maple sap. Several sugarmakers spoke to me of plans (either theirs or someone around the hillside's) to bottle and market the sap straight as maple water, a sort of performance drink. A few companies are doing just that, with brands like Seva and Oviva touting the healthful and natural benefits of their products. With the popularity of beverages like coconut water being sold on the minerals and electrolytes they contain, it was only a matter of time before someone got the idea to bottle maple sap, which also contains significant amounts of minerals such as potassium, manganese, riboflavin, and zinc. Several magazines and health-related websites (e.g., Klara 2015; Taylor 2016) even make the beverage comparison explicit, asking questions such as, is maple water the new coconut water?

The commodification taking place in the case of maple seltzer and maple water is in some ways the same as any other secondary maple product—a way for sugarmakers to expand their market by making another value-added product. The difference is that value is being added not to the syrup, but to the sap. Sap is commodified in sugaring, especially as discussed earlier in the chapter with Green Mountain Mainlines' industrialization of boiling sap they buy from all over the region, and Sweet Tree Holdings' massive scaling up of the sugaring process. However, in the case of maple seltzer and maple water, the sap is being commodified in a different way. It is being given a value all its own, separate from the default state of syrup and separate from the syrup-making process. For Green Mountain Mainlines and Sweet Tree, the commodification of the sap is an attempt to alter the use value end of the equation. Maple seltzer and maple water give the sap an exchange value, attacking the economics of maple from the other end of the equation.

Maple has many different economic meanings. It is a commodity in the most basic sense of the word, and it gets commoditized in many different ways, along all parts of its process. The very fact that "maple" describes both a product (or, more accurately, a set of products) and a process indicates how many different economic meanings can be made with maple. Because sugaring has long been an activity with economic aspects, making economic meanings with it has been a norm for a very long time. By understanding economics as a perspective not on money, but on exchange, commodification becomes a useful tool to make sense of maple. By looking at the basic difference between use value and exchange value, we can explore the ways that various meanings, such as the experience of seeing sap boiling, can translate into dollars for syrup. We can also begin to understand that economics is not some separate part of the process, but another set of meanings that people make and apply to a bottle of syrup.

CHAPTER 2

The Culinary Meaning
of Maple

*One of the perceptions that some of the people that come in here
have is that the darker syrups are less processed or more organic
or more something, you know. And you'll see people time and
time again saying, "oh yeah, that's what I want because that's
going to be better for me," kind of like white bread versus whole
grain bread. —Sugarmaker, 9 June 2011*

Maple syrup is food, a substance made to be consumed for nutritional
and culinary reasons. Food itself is a culturally determined identity,
as demonstrated by Marvin Harris when he describes a range of items
eaten by humans: "everything from rancid mammary gland secretions
to fungi to rocks (or cheese, mushrooms, and salt if you prefer euphe-
misms)."[41] By euphemizing with the labels we give to food, we explicitly (if unconsciously) take part in a process of making and assigning
meaning that is indicative of how powerful a conveyer of meaning
food is. It shows us how cultural food is. As Rebecca Hawkins puts
it, in what may be the culinary understatement of the twenty-first
century, "scratch the surface and it becomes clear that food is far from
simple."[42]

Eating is both a process of fueling the body with nutriment and an
aesthetic experience. The nutritional aspect of food we often understand as strictly biological, although it isn't. One glance at the shifting
nutritional meanings of eggs (They're good for you! They'll kill you!
Cholesterol! Vitamin E!) should tell us how culturally negotiated even
the biological side of food can be. Cultural analysts like Richard Wilk
have delved into the power of meaning in food: "Because food is both
a physical substance and a vehicle for the imagination, something that

nourishes the body, but also fascinates and moves the mind, it plays a protean role in the world, connecting the economic and the symbolic in ever-shifting ways."[43]

The meanings we assign to food are constantly shifting and morphing in reaction to cultural trends and new information. Even the parts that we think of as static—the scientific, the nutritional—change over time because that's how knowledge works. We don't "know things." We *make* knowledge—of things, with things, because of other things. Since food is a vehicle for the imagination (and a particularly fast and powerful vehicle it is), we make a lot of different meanings with food, both culinary and otherwise. In this chapter, I want to explore the culinary side of the equation, which deals with the aesthetic and other aspects of maple that are more obviously negotiated on a cultural level. Scholars of culture and identity have examined the role food plays in making meaning many, many times, so maple's importance as a culinary meaning maker is to be expected. From the cultural materialism of Marvin Harris (1985) through the Marxist-influenced analyses of Sidney Mintz (1986, 1996) to the interdisciplinary approaches that currently mark the burgeoning field of Food Studies (e.g., Sloan 2013), scholars have sought to connect food with human life. As Mintz explains in 1996,

> What was written about food and eating by anthropologists more than a century ago dealt mostly with feast and sacrifice— people's food relationships with their gods; with food taboos and injunctions, usually religious in nature; with the role of foods in how people were ranked socially; with cannibalism, and why people engaged in it.[44]

In other words, food was studied culturally for quite a while only as an adjunct to some other cultural phenomenon. Mintz continues to say that "it would probably be accurate to say that food and eating got much less attention in their own right as anthropological subjects than they really deserved."[45] Two decades ago, he called for an approach to food that moved beyond connecting it to some other aspects of human life and shifted instead to food's connection with human *living*, what consuming anything would come to *mean*.[46] Social science has responded, moving to explore the spot where the category of "biologically edible substance" becomes the category of "food," which is

THE CULINARY MEANING OF MAPLE

simply a biologically edible substance given a particular meaning by a person or group of people. This is where the edible becomes the culinary. Maple is a supremely culinary thing, and as such, of interest and worth exploring.

Maple is a form of sugar and a form of sweetness; while a sugar molecule may be chemical, the concept of sweetness is decidedly cultural. The high concentration of sugar molecules in maple slates it solidly on the sweet end of whatever culturally specific culinary spectrum one wants to use to map the flavor world. There are many different systems of flavor and taste around the world, so the concept of "sweet" can be understood and negotiated in different ways, or have more or less meaning for any given group of people. However, anything with a chemical makeup that is two-thirds sugars (such as maple syrup) is very likely going to end up categorized with other things that fall under whatever local label sweet things are called. It is going to carry the vernacular version of "sweet" in all likelihood. Sweetness itself is often understood as somehow fundamental in a culinary sense, a taste rather than a flavor. This understanding makes sweetness almost a biological thing, as opposed to a matter of personal aesthetic. The often-quoted system of four flavors (sweet, salty, bitter, sour) that many Western schoolchildren learned has recently been brought into question in a few different ways. For example, the notion that certain parts of the tongue are more responsible for certain tastes is generally no longer held, while many people, especially those in the culinary realm, have added a fifth taste to the canon—umami.[47] Umami is sometimes called "savory" in the Anglophone world, and it represents the mouth-filling, meaty taste triggered by the action of glutamates and nucleotides on the tongue. The existence of umami is why MSG does what it does as a flavor enhancer. MSG (monosodium glutamate) triggers glutamate receptors on the tongue, making us experience a taste to which we assign meatiness, savor, richness, or some other similar meaning.

There are physiological structures on the tongue and in the mouth that react to different stimuli, so, to be sure, there is some physiological process taking place that can be understood through a lens of biology. It is because of a genetic anomaly among mammals that cats generally cannot taste what we think of as sweet, for example. But the fact that our understandings of, and labels for, those biological processes has changed over time demonstrate that what we mean by "sweet" is not a simple matter of biological structure or action. Sweetness may be a name we apply (a meaning we assign) to the action of sugar on the tongue, but because it includes a process of assigning meaning, it is not strictly biological. The changes that our four tastes have undergone highlight that, while there are certain chemical actions that happen when we put food in our mouths, the *meanings that we make* of those chemical actions result in a less absolute system of taste than many of us learned. In this sense, sweetness is not just a biological fact of maple, but a meaning that we make with maple. That meaning is negotiated culturally, in the realm of the aesthetic and the culinary.

Historically and prehistorically, the number of naturally occurring forms of pure sweetness available to people was limited, especially depending on where they lived. By "pure sweetness" I do not mean uncontaminated or unadulterated. I am referring here to a taste whose primary culinary function is to sweeten, rather than another flavor that happens to have some sweetness to it. Perhaps a good synonym to convey the concept would be "strong sweetness" or "sweetening." Very few animals that are consumed by humans contain high concentrations of chemical sugars, a notable exception being certain social insects such as ants and termites, which sometimes store sugar-rich liquids in their bodies. These sugar stores can be accessed by people, simply by eating the bug. The sensation of a biting down on a termite swollen with sugar water is similar to eating a ripe berry or a piece of candy with a liquid center, with a burst of pure sweetness in the mouth. But, beyond the ants and termites, which are a regional foodstuff at best, not many animals themselves are significant sources of sugar that is consumed by humans. Bees produce honey, but one does not consume the bees themselves to get the sugar, so the animal is not the direct source of the sweetness.

So, many of the sources of pure sweetness that are nutritionally available to humans are botanical, rather than zoological, in origin. In a tropical climate, for example, many forms of fruit are generally going to be available, and for a larger portion of the year, making sweetness derived from fruit easily accessible.[48] In more temperate or even colder climates, though, pure sweetness is derived from other, usually more limited sources, many of which require great effort or intensive process to obtain. Sugar beets and sugarcane, for example, need to be harvested and processed (and often cultivated in the first place) to extract the sugar for separate culinary use, and each needs specific growing conditions that are not ubiquitous. The use of corn as a source of sweetness is a relatively new phenomenon in human history, but it is subject to the same limitations as beets and sugarcane. Honey is available anywhere honeybees form colonies that people can get to, and its sweetness is immediately available with minimal processing (at least by humans . . . the vast majority of the rather intensive work is done by the bees in this case). But again, not all climates conduce to the reliable existence of honeybee colonies, and extracting the honey can be some effort when it is available, depending on where the bees have built their hive. Domesticated honeybees that build hives in boxes provided by humans are generally pretty easy to harvest. However, in many parts of the world, the honey that people use comes from wild bees, building hives and storing their honey on cliff faces, in caves, high in the boughs of trees, and other places where people must expend considerable effort and/or face danger to access it.

Maple certainly requires quite a bit of process as well, but it is a form of pure sweetness in a climatic area where other forms are naturally absent or much less frequent. There is simply not that much sugarcane being grown in New England or Quebec. Beets, being a decently hardy root vegetable, do better in those northern climates, but the growing season in Vermont is short, and the cultivated land is generally put to different uses. The 2012 USDA census listed a total of six acres of Vermont land dedicated to sugar beet production, demonstrating their relative unimportance as a local source of culinary sweetness.[49] For much of Vermont's history, the only locally available sweetness was maple syrup and its derivatives, a fact pointed out to me by one sugarmaker, when speaking of Vermont's history in sugaring: "They sugared back at the time where that was how you got your sweet. I mean, if you wanted sugar it was maple sugar that you used."[50] In the absence of sugarcane and sugar beets, maple plays an important role as a botanical source of sweetness, both culinarily and biologically, with an entirely different set of cultural meanings in tow. Unlike cane sugar, whose story involves colonialism and international slavery, maple is understood as home grown and not historically reliant on exploitation of human labor.

Pure sweetness is not only aesthetically pleasing on the tongues of many, but it provides a powerful injection of calories from sugar, making it attractive as fuel. The cultural materialist approach of anthropologists like Marvin Harris or Roy Rappaport would suggest that the caloric density of maple in a cold climate is particularly important in understanding maple's meaning. While I do not subscribe to a strict materialism, some Vermonters like the author and sugarmaker Burr Morse have a similar interpretation to Rappaport and Harris: "You see, for some elderly Vermonters, living till maple sugar season and drinking sweetness from the front pan strengthens their spirit and prepares them for another year."[51] The meaning being made here is not strictly biological, but it certainly has a biological component of survival from year to year in it. In addition to the calories that maple syrup provides to either body or spirit, it is very easy to make a strong culinary meaning of maple. In a geographic area where other forms of pure sweetness are difficult or impossible to obtain, maple fills a culinary niche as source of sugar *qua* sugar.

However, in addition to being a source of sugar and pure sweetness, maple does indeed have a particular and distinctive flavor profile, making it culinarily more than just sugar or even more than just sweetness. It is both nutritional and aesthetic. The chemistry of maple has been studied several times (Childs 2007; Heiligmann 2006; Willits and Hills 1976) in an attempt to isolate and identify all of the chemical components that make up the flavor we call maple. Few food items have been the subject of this much flavor scrutiny—vanilla comes to mind, perhaps chocolate and coffee as well—which seems to indicate that the flavor of maple is complex, powerful, and evocative for both the human tongue and the human mind. Such foods, that carry meanings of depth and complexity, have a culinary appeal all their own, as the analysts of food and culture Johnston and Baumann explain: "Related to the quest for ethnic and exotic flavors, as well as the desire for authentic and ecologically-friendly foods, is the growing American demand for gourmet and specialty food products such as artisan cheese, gourmet coffees and single-source dark chocolate."[52] Maple, with its richness and complexity of flavors, fits very easily into the same paradigm that seeks the niche, the artisanal, the complex, and the specialized corners of the food landscape. Within Vermont, one of the mantras of the maple faithful is that the complexity and uniqueness of real maple syrup makes the simple, crass sweetness of the corn-syrup-based likes of Log Cabin and Mrs. Butterworth an insult to the palate. While sugarmakers concede that these "pancake syrups" are indeed sweet, they are just that—sweet, and little else. The artificial maple flavor is the result of compounds such as sotolon (which is often derived from sources like fenugreek seeds), and these compounds impart an aroma superficially similar to maple, but unable to replicate the complex (and complicated) flavor of real maple.

Interestingly, the dismissive attitude toward artificial table syrups is justified by an appeal to dual meanings—both the sweetness of maple *and* the particularities of its flavor profile. To be sweet is not enough, and to be maple is to be more than just sweet. Food is understood as "authentic if it can be categorized in certain ways *in relation to* other foods, particularly inauthentic foods."[53] Sugarmakers and maple fans alike simultaneously make culinary meanings of flavor complexity and biological meanings of sweetness when comparing maple syrup to the inauthentic pancake syrups. So, while maple is a source of pure sweetness, it is also by definition more than just pure sweetness—it is a sweetness with a unique and irreplaceable flavor. That flavor is best understood, and perhaps for some, only understandable, in relation to the imminently forgettable flavor of the imitations, whose blunt sweetness provides a counterpoint to the complexity and variety of real maple's more "authentic" sweetness.

The uniqueness of maple's flavor has made it a niche, specialty food in the foodie movement. The identity labeled "foodie" has been around since the early 1980s, when the word was coined as a satirical and derisive term. The term has grown out of its satirical meaning to be embraced by a whole set of people with an approach toward food and eating that emphasizes some form of consciousness or purpose, and foodie identity has received academic attention elsewhere (notably Johnston and Baumann 2010; Peterson and Kern 1996; and Arnott 2003). The foodie culture makes meaning with food in a very particular set of ways, but it is perhaps most marked by the sheer amount of meaning it makes with food, to the point that food knowledge can be central in making an identity: "When the term 'foodie' is taken as a marker of identity, it is thought to describe a category of people that love good food, and want to learn about good food. . . . Foodie-ism, whether the term is accepted or rejected, is also strongly associated with food knowledge."[54] Concerted intellectual attention to the varied traits of food is fundamental to being a foodie (it is right there in the name, after all), so any food item that has a set of unique traits about which one can learn is going to have a lot of potential as the focus of foodie attention. Food knowledge is fundamental to claiming the identity, but the maple knowledge a foodie gets from a bottle of syrup is, in some ways, second-hand, similar to the relationships between restaurant customer, chef, and the food they share: "Cooking creates known-ness for those who are involved in the practices, right? It doesn't create known-ness for those who are not involved in the practice, so . . . in a professional setting, it creates known-ness for the producers, not necessarily the people that come in and eat it."[55] To sit in a restaurant and eat the food of a chef is to gain understanding of the dish served, but not necessarily of the food items that went into that dish. In like manner, to gain knowledge by buying and consuming maple syrup is to gain knowledge of the syrup, but not necessarily of the production process. A sugarhouse tour can help in that regard, as discussed in the previous chapter, but the intimacy of the sugarmaker's knowledge of the land and trees is not accessible to the foodie, at least not by just stirring maple into their coffee or their crème brûlée. Nevertheless, foodies seek, and claim to find, knowledge of sugaring or some sense of a Vermont way of life by consuming real maple. In doing so, they make culinary meaning that includes geography, heritage, and history.

Many foodies are probably unaware that they are echoing Marvin Harris's discussion that food is both good to eat and good to think with.[56] Maple, with its unique flavor profile, ready-made culinary role as source of sweetness, and complex flavor and story, fits very easily into the foodie approach to the culinary world. Maple is both good to eat and good to think (which is to say, to make meaning) with. One of the most common thoughts made with maple is a sense of authenticity, which is hugely important to a foodie's choice of food.[57] They are drawn toward foods that exhibit traits including locality, creativity, and simplicity.[58] They tend to appreciate the new and the exotic as well, and maple, like any choice of commodity, can be used to mark status.[59] One of the meanings that foodies seek in food is rarity or novelty, that which they (and perhaps others[60]) have not yet experienced. Exoticism sometimes comes from an ingredient or technique that is from far away geographically (galangal or the tagine to a foodie in the States, for example), and maple's geographically limited production makes it distant from many places. The connection to a place far away communicates a worldliness and awareness that sometimes even transcends place, to convey culinary sophistication or even political consciousness. Paige West, writing about coffee and the various social meanings it can contain, explains that "consumers who buy a blend of Javanese, Sumatran, and Papua New Guinea coffees with a bit of East Timorese thrown in for a 'note of wildness' may be attempting to show how developed their tastes are. Today, people often attempt to derive and express identity and politics through the coffee and other commodities that they buy and serve."[61] The choice of a food item can communicate traits of awareness that the buyer wants made known—awareness of other places, other climates, or other politics. Identity is only useful if others make and apply it to you, and a person can help others make the identity they prefer by offering them, or displaying for them, certain commodities that connote exoticness, such as coffees from East Timor or real maple syrup from Vermont. Especially if one lives outside the state, having Vermont maple to hand guests conveys a sense of consciousness of the state, including perhaps its politics or social attitudes, but most certainly the culinary value of real maple and the culinary values of a rural, agricultural place.

Even if someone in California or Turkey is not attempting to make a political statement with what syrup they pour on their waffles or ice cream, they are communicating at least that they recognize and place significant meaning on maple by having a substance that is made in only one area of the globe. This understanding is very similar to the draw in tourism of places that are far from where one lives. Going to a particular place is sometimes less important than going to someplace that is very evidently not home. Maple syrup easily carries this cachet of meaning in California, for example, where tapping maples for syrup is barely known and not widely understood. Even in places like Boston and New York City, which are geographically close to where sugaring happens, maple carries an exoticism of distance because it takes places outside the city.[62] It is understood to be a rural phenomenon.

Not all foodie exoticism comes just from distance, then. Often the exoticism of a food item like maple can come from another source of separation. Miles can create separation in a geographic sense, but in a culinary sense, many other forms of separation can make an ingredient meaningful. Exoticism is about gaining access to something that one does not normally have access to or that others in the area do not have access to. That form of exoticism can be the result of traveling across oceans easily enough. However, one can just as easily gain access to something that is geographically near, but which is not a usual part of the local life. Eating food that is traditionally associated with another economic stratum, for example, can be just as exotic an experience for the foodie culinarily as dining on another continent. The culinary rise and fall and rise of various parts of animals is a good example of this process. Offal (organ meat) has drifted from the category of "trash" meat to the menus of royalty and back again several times in European culinary history, and even something as paradigmatically "rich people's food" as lobster has moved from the plate to the dustbin and back. An example from Belize, documented by the anthropologist Richard Wilk, demonstrates how "lobster was a common and low-value food. An elderly man told me that when he was a boy buying fish in the market, the vendor would throw in a couple lobsters for free. But when he got home his mother would not allow them in the house, since they were 'trash fish.'"[63] Wilk discusses the class ramifications of living in between the high-class plate and the dustbin, eating what he calls a "style sandwich," where shifting fashion and cultural trend give culinary meanings to the foods you eat, as well as those you don't. Where I live in Vermont, ox tail is currently haute cuisine, but by whatever date you are reading this book, it could be relegated back to the poor folks' plate again. Foie gras is an organ meat with a fancy name, but (if you'll pardon the anatomical metaphor mixing) at its heart, it's just chopped liver. So, geography is not the only maker of exoticness when it comes to food, and exotic food can come from right next door, if it is from another class or other identity category.

Funnily enough, one of those separations of identity can come by being right next door. Local food is often an important part of foodie identity, to the point that localness has its own separable label as a food-oriented identity: localvore or locavore. A food item's attraction can come from the fact that it is produced locally, making it separate from the mass market of agribusiness food production. This trend is, in a way, a reaction to the globalization of food systems, where a perception of detachment and distance is the norm. Industrialization of food production and the influence of corporations makes many consumers cautious, even uneasy about their food at times. The influence of these large, faceless corporations is to separate the consumer from the producer. The farm and the farmer are the exotic other in this construction because, in the mass-market agribusiness structure, they are typically separate from the ultimate consumer of the food items they produce. Seeking out and consuming local foods makes the foodie separate from the mass-market food system that creates such a large gap between producer and consumer, so that even readily available foods like offal are given a patina of rarity because they are rarely part of the average consumer's dietary options. Exoticness comes in this case not from distance, but from infrequency. If something is simply not the norm on a mass-market-driven plate, then it is going to have a certain cachet for the adventurous or self-styled conscious eater. The exoticness of eating locally derives from crossing a boundary that large-scale food systems create. The faceless corporation is subverted and supplanted with a farmer who presumably has a face. The separation from the normal system that creates the farmer as exotic actually removes a separation between the consumer and the farm/farmer.

So, even for someone living in New England or Quebec, where maple could be produced not far from their front door, it can still qualify as a foodie item because it is not mainstream, not a part of the large-scale food system that generates most of what is on market shelves. This, of course, feeds the sense of exclusivity as well. Anyone can get hold of a food item if it is mass marketed, but being one of the few who is in the know about maple makes it more appealing. Knowing a particular sugarmaker is an even more powerful draw. Its very localness makes it an exotic item. For the foodie who seeks the exotic in the local, the specialness of being from here, even if it is secretly from here, maple fills the bill. As one sugarmaker described it, "We're one of the very few ethnic American foods."[64] Maple is rooted in a place, and being in that same place provides an opportunity to access localness and locality at the same time. Consuming a food that was made nearby has an appeal, but knowing and expressing that food's local aspects carries an additional appeal. To call maple an American ethnic food is to emphasize its uniqueness of place and attachment to a particular group of people. By attaching to a sense of ethnicity, separation from the industrialized food system is again achieved, just as if someone mentions kimchi (a Korean pickled vegetable dish) or doro wat (an Ethiopian chicken stew), foods that are identified with particular ethnicities and regions.

It could also be argued that the sense of separation for maple comes from its rootedness in the rural, beyond just the city/country divide mentioned above. A food item that comes from outside a city can feel farther away geographically than it actually is on the map. However, the sense of separation can be less about the food item and more about the person eating it. Foodie identity is a distinctly urban phenomenon. It started in larger cities and stems at least in part from a desire for that which was beyond the mainstream, industrialized food system (the city being a paradigmatic example of the industrialization process, of course). Foodie identity, with its roots then in an overt modernity and overt urbanity, comes complete with layers of supposed sophistication and worldly cosmopolitanism. Even though it may have spread to less urban areas, foodie still smacks strongly of upscale neighborhoods in trendy cities, complete with the class distinctions that those tropes convey. Pointing out that foodies seek distinction makes it clear that having a sense of separateness, of specialness, is important to the foodie identity. It does not necessarily matter from where the distinction comes, as long as the food is distinct somehow. Separateness from the norms of industrialized food production is an appeal of its own, and maple, with its tropes of the rural farmer, boiling sap on a small scale, feels very separate from the mass market.

Johnston and Baumann delve deeper into what makes a food item appealing to a foodie in their 2010 book, *Foodies: Democracy and Distinction in the Gourmet Food Landscape,* finding traction in the concept of authenticity. There are several potential sources of authenticity in a foodstuff. Their list includes geographic specificity, simplicity, personal connection, history and tradition, or ethnic connection.[65] Maple hits four of their five dimensions without even trying, and an argument could be made for ethnic connection as well, as when the sugarmaker earlier described maple as one of the few ethnic American foods. Geographic specificity, personal connection, and history and tradition are all discussed elsewhere in this book, but simplicity is relevant to culinary meanings in the current discussion of separateness and exoticism. The sense of simplicity that lends authenticity is tied in maple's case to its rural origin. Even in a place where maple is made locally, it is far away culturally from the linen tablecloths and eight-burner stoves of the urban foodie world. The separation of city and country is emphasized from both ends, by maple's rural simplicity and foodie identity's urban sophistication. The gap between the two is part of maple's appeal for foodies.

How then does simple little maple fit into the cosmopolitan meanings made in the culinary world? In the foodie mindset, there is a certain pride of place given to flavors that are stronger and more difficult to access in a culinary sense. A location that is easily accessible to anyone is not a very exotic tourist destination, just as a flavor not everyone can obtain is appealing because of its difficulty to access. Additionally, a flavor that anyone can easily *like* is not as interesting to a foodie, while foods that are less easily palatable are sought after and prized. The entire appeal of Andrew Zimmern's *Bizarre Foods*, a television show running on the Travel Channel in the United States since 2007, is the supposed difficulty of the food items the host seeks out, consumes, and reviews. The unique flavor profile of maple has made it a more interesting ingredient to many people in the foodie world, giving it cachet already. Maple has a sweetness that brings other traits along for the ride, so liking it requires liking all of its traits. A similar rationale that combines the culinary and biological is employed here, where just anyone can like the corn-heavy pancake syrups that provide only sweetness, but it takes a knowledgeable tongue to like real maple and all its complexities. The appeal is to transcend the simplicity of pancake syrup's one-note sweetness, and to delve into a meaning understood as more complex with maple's intense and unique flavor profile. Interestingly, both the foodie and the farmer have the same set of motivations, drawing on both culinary and nutritional explanations, to explain the appeal of maple over Mrs. Butterworth's tepid offering.

However, there are some important differences in the approach the two categories (foodie and sugarmaker) take. The two groups both choose maple based on culinary and biological meanings, but their two choices have very different ramifications. The pursuit of the stronger, more difficult to access flavors that is a mark of the foodie's motivation has caused changes in the way food is produced, presented, and consumed across the board.[66] This trend has created an interesting effect in Vermont's maple industry specifically. For many old-timers in the Vermont sugaring game, the lightest colored syrup (until recently, called "Vermont Grade A Fancy," or simply "Fancy," now referred to as "Golden with Delicate Taste," when the grading system was changed in 2015) that was typically the lightest flavored, was by far the most desirable. Michael Farrell, director of the Uihlein Forest, a maple research center at Cornell University, explains that lighter syrup "has traditionally been considered the highest quality among the maple-syrup-producing community. This bias dates back to the times when it was more difficult to produce light syrup and only the best sugarmakers were capable of producing it. Back then darker syrups were much more prevalent and could contain serious off-flavors."[67]

Sugarmakers themselves are prone to the same appeal of the difficult and the rare, in this case equating sugaring skill with quality of syrup. In a culinary sense, Fancy's light, delicate flavor was most prized by old Vermonters as straight eating syrup, while the other, darker grades were more for cooking or selling to tourists. As such, Fancy syrup commanded a higher price in the bottle. However, as the foodie culture gains more influence on the marketing of food items, and more influence on the palates (and/or wallets) of consumers, the desire for stronger, harsher, more difficult to access flavors means that darker syrups are increasingly in demand. As Farrell continues, "Although sugarmakers may pride themselves on making light syrup and prefer the flavor of it, it is important to realize what consumers like and market our syrup accordingly."[68] To put it briefly, delicacy has fallen out of favor. The title of a 2008 article from an online magarine[69] is but one example of many that demonstrate the value placed on the more intense flavor of darker syrups: "Maple Syrup Grades: Sometimes B Stands for 'Better.'"[70] This shift has meant that now, all grades of syrup usually sell for the same price on the shelf. Some Vermont sugarmakers still prize the lighter grades for themselves, and a few bemoan the loss of the larger economic premium that their Fancy used to command, although generally the price of darker grades came up rather than the price of lighter syrup dropping much.

While Fancy does not bring the premium it once did, the prices of all grades in Vermont leveled off together, closer to the high end than the low, following the changing tastes of the consumer, as made clear by one sugarmaker: "We sell all of our syrup, same price across the board. Our best seller is A Medium, and second best is A Dark, and our third is Fancy, or the light. And then we sell some cooking, the B grade, which is cooking. So if they're just allowed to just, with no pressure from me, taste it, lots of them choose the medium, and then the dark is the second best."[71] Consumers, more and more of whom do not carry the traditional bias toward the lighter flavor of Fancy grade syrup, and perhaps influenced by foodie trends of seeking out and preferring stronger flavors, now buy more Medium and Dark syrup from this sugarmaker. As a result, he sells all his syrup for the same price regardless of grade.

As I asked this man to explain why tastes have drifted, he put some of the cause on the growth of maple's popularity outside its home region: "The lighter is more of a local, connoisseur type flavor, but for the general population, A Medium at least, or darker, is probably what suits their palate."[72] The lighter syrup still holds the place of respect it long has among locals, which in this case is probably code for sugarmakers, while those less "in the know" have palates that want stronger tastes. Even those people who live nearby but seek the exotic in the local tend toward darker syrup, so this man's use of "local" to describe a preference for Fancy has little to do with geography. Being local in this sense is not being close to where the syrup was made, but close to the knowledge of good sugaring. Close to the center of the identity of sugarmaker.

The center of sugaring's identity has recently changed, though, with the arrival of the new grading system to Vermont. The new system, optional in 2014 and mandatory for all Vermont sugarmakers as of 2015, aligns more closely with international grading norms, making Vermont less idiosyncratic. One sugarmaker I visited very shortly after the new system came into existence talked to me about the culinary changes that it was causing. After the usual chat about his boiling rig and his sugar woods, I indicated that I wanted to buy a quart of syrup. I tend to like the darker syrups because I have a fairly dead tongue, so I asked for "Dark Amber or B," using terminology from the old grading scale.

He had started using the new labeling system on his containers, so my request for Dark Amber or B had to be translated into the new terminology. He had syrup that under the old system would have been classified as Dark Amber, B, and C, but in the new system was all either "Dark with Robust Taste" or "Very Dark with Strong Taste." While I had known about the new grades for some time, this was my first encounter with the new system as a consumer, so I genuinely did not know which one I wanted. Unfortunately, the sugarmaker was not able to be of much help either, as the changed terminology was new to him as well. Neither of us knew how to make a coherent culinary meaning with the new grading system yet, which put us at a bit of an impasse in this situation.

The sugarmaker here was no great fan of the new system, which he thought was both unnecessarily confusing and promoted skewed values. In his reckoning, he was bottling syrup for the consumer that previously he would have discarded or sold only to secondary food producers (Grade C, which was for commercial use as a flavoring or ingredient only[73]), and this was a problem. He showed open disdain for the Very Dark and Strong syrup he had bottled, to the point that he pushed me toward buying a quart of the Dark and Robust. I did so, only to have him throw in another quart of the Very Dark and Strong for free. He had produced just a handful of bottles of it, and he did not expect a large market. Further, he did not want to make money from a syrup he did not feel represented well his sugaring operation (or his skills, in all likelihood). In essence, for this sugarmaker, the Very Dark and Robust syrup was a bad representation of his syrup and Vermont maple in general. I got the impression he was as happy to have it out of his house as anything else, and he only requested that I let him know

Maple Syrup

Pure Vermont Maple Syrup has been made for generations to the same exacting standards, creating the signature product of Vermont. It's no wonder it's the Official Flavor of Vermont!

Starting in 2014, Vermont will begin using a new system for grading syrup, meaning the same great product will now have easier to understand grades.

www.vermontmaple.org

Golden with Delicate Taste
Light, golden color with a mild, delicate taste. Excellent as a table syrup or over ice cream or yogurt.

Amber with Rich Taste
A light amber color and full-bodied flavor, this class of syrup is the product of choice for consumers who desire the classic maple syrup flavor.

Dark with Robust Taste
A dark amber color with a more pronounced maple flavor, this class will satisfy those consumers who desire the strong flavors of what has been known as Grade B.

Very Dark with Strong Taste
Nearly black, this syrup has a strong flavor that translates well to cooking, where the maple flavor will carry through to the finished dish.

Find Your Favorite Syrup
Have you always loved Grade A Medium Amber? Use the chart on the right to find the new grade that will best match up. Our new grades expand the range of maple syrup available but rest assured it's still the same great, high quality maple syrup you've come to expect. We hope that you'll explore all of the grades to discover new uses for the entire range of flavors that exist in Pure Vermont Maple Syrup!

Why the Change?
The maple syrup grades we had been using were based on a system created when maple syrup was a substitute for cane sugar, which was not widely available. Our new grades provide better descriptions, with each of the classifications having a color and flavor descriptor, helping our customers pinpoint the exact syrup they want to purchase.

International Alignment
For years, Vermont's four grades of maple syrup had differed from New York's, Maine's, Canada's and others. This created confusion within the marketplace and our new grades will be aligned with all other states and provinces, so that we all use the same grade names.

Vermont's New Maple Grades

VMSMA
Vermont Maple Syrup

the Official Flavor of Vermont!
VERMONT MAPLE SUGAR MAKERS' ASSOCIATION
491 EAST BARNARD ROAD, SOUTH ROYALTON, VT 05068
WWW.VERMONTMAPLE.ORG

A card from the VMSMA shows the old and new grading systems together. *Image courtesy the Vermont Maple Sugar Makers Association.*

what I thought about the flavor once I cracked it open at home. The tone of his request was less eager anticipation, and more sympathy for what I was going to taste.

Despite this sugarmaker's disdain for the new system and its placing of very dark syrup directly into the hands of the consumer, the new grades and the new sense of taste they reflect have had some economic benefits for Vermont maple. The desire for stronger, more particular flavors that foodie culture has engendered has allowed Vermont's maple industry to be more sustainable in the face of Quebec's dominance of the industry. In numerical terms, Quebec outstrips Vermont in gallons produced, market share, and more, and it is not a close race at all. According to the Federation of Quebec Maple Producers' statistics, "Quebec maple producers are far and away the main producers of maple syrup in Canada and the world, with 71% of world production (in 2004). . . . The Canadian provinces that produce maple syrup are Quebec (90.7% of domestic production), followed by Ontario (4.4%), New Brunswick (4.4%) and Nova Scotia (0.5%)."[74] Quebec makes 90 percent of the maple syrup made in Canada, and at least 70 percent of the maple syrup made in the whole world. Because Vermont can never compete with Quebec in terms of volume, the state's maple producers need to rely on their product having a cachet of uniqueness within the uniqueness maple already carries. Vermont maple must be a niche within the niche, in a process found in many places (see, for example, my earlier work on Orcadian identity, Lange 2007).

The state has carved out that niche in the form of specificity of flavors and uniqueness of place. Vermont maple is marketed not simply as special because it is maple, but as a particular flavor profile *within* the range of maple that is the result of a particular sugarmaker or a particular stand of maple trees. It is a specialty item that reflects the very local situation that produced it. This marketing approach is one of the forces that led to the changing of the grade labels. Instead of the old system, which relied entirely on the color of the syrup, the new system explicitly includes flavor references in the grades.[75] The new system is based on light penetration, so color (or more accurately, opacity) is still the determiner, but flavor is communicated on the label as well. To be sure, there is a general relationship between the color of maple syrup and its flavor. Lighter-colored syrups tend to be lighter in flavor, while the darkness and strength of flavor tend to increase proportionally. This relationship is only a strong tendency, though. I have tasted very intensely flavored syrup that would have graded out as Fancy, and delicately flavored stuff that was Dark Amber in color in the old system. In the new system, color is described along-side strength of flavor, so that the foodie's palate can anticipate the richness of the aesthetic experience with both tongue and eye. The new system places culinary meaning more at the forefront, even if the reason the syrup is there is still primarily the intensity of its color rather than its flavor. The foodie movement has made flavor more prominent in the labeling, as well as making stronger, more difficult flavors more desirable.

As the sugarmaker mentioned above indicates, not everyone is happy about changes being introduced to the way maple is understood in Vermont. However, some sugarmakers are embracing the changes and using the culinary traits of maple more fully and directly in their marketing. One sugaring operation was for a time marketing their syrup using tasting notes straight out of a wine catalogue:

> distinctly rich, creamy, buttery, and full of maple warmth. Notes of brown sugar and medjool dates back up the sweetness that lingers on the palate

and

> hints of vanilla, nutmeg, and sweet melon

and

> the Dopple Bock of maple syrups. German dark wheat bread, molasses, burnt sugar, raisins, dates, and smoke

and

> baked apple and golden sugar notes are backed by a subtle but clear maple flavor. (http://bit.ly/2coCtKj)

The appeal to standard tropes from the foodie and haute cuisine realms (medjool dates and nutmeg), as well as the explicit comparisons to other favorite categories of foodie attention (beer, with "the Doppel Bock of maple" comment) make this kind of marketing of maple more aligned with the increasingly common tropes familiar to the foodie.

Even for other sugarmakers who don't market directly with such language, there is a recognition of the effects of place on their syrup. One old-timer who tapped trees within a town gave me his understanding of place, saying that "trees in the city produce much sweeter sap than it does out in the country." [*Why so?*] "Well," (laughing), "I always said it was the dogs."[76] This man is both making a joke and making a point. He recognizes that the very particular parts of a tree's environment will shape the sap that comes out and eventually the syrup that results. He was not kidding about the higher sugar concentration of his urban trees, even if his explanation, that the city's dogs using those trees for a urinal sweetens the sap, is perhaps facetious.

Marketing is a process of creating and communicating an identity in order to manipulate someone into buying (or buying into) something. The identities being communicated are brands, and the sugarmakers using the tasting notes above are constructing a new brand for their maple. The selectivity and distinctiveness of Vermont's maple—which the state needs to evoke to compete with Quebec's greater production—is making a state maple brand separate from just any maple, playing what writer and cultural critic James McWilliams calls a brand game: "As the French reliance on *terroir* proves, a nation, a region, and a locality can play the brand game just as well as any corporation."[77] The sugarmakers quoted above are attempting to make their region and locality play the brand game to manipulate people to buy their syrup because of its distinctiveness. Manipulation can have a negative connotation, and for some sugarmakers it does, which makes branding feel distasteful or inappropriate for maple. But manipulation is at the heart of marketing, and the word does not necessarily need to carry a stigma. Many cultural processes that we take for granted are done in order to convince, cajole, persuade, and influence people to act or think in ways we would prefer. All of these processes are forms of manipulation.

Interestingly, the "Vermont terroir" website from which the maple descriptions and their tasting notes above were drawn, which was active in 2012, was a dead link as of the beginning of 2015. Perhaps this attempt at marketing, crafting a specialized brand using such a thorough employment of tasting notes, was not wholly successful. Regardless, maple's place in the culinary imagination has been on the move for better than a decade, and the shift is at least in part a reaction to the different meanings the general public makes with food, with taste, and with the particular and specific traits of products.

It is easy to get upset about branding, thinking of market economics as some sort of icky encroachment on the purity or natural order of Vermont life. Before we do, though, we should heed what Amy Trubek, author of *Taste of Place*, said to me in an interview about branding and Vermont identity: "At this point it's about selling Vermont, in a certain way, but I would say working with these people all the time, it's not a cynical thing, it's really a lived thing, like 'We're from here, this is our identity, this is our place, and we understand that people in other places are attracted to Vermont and the image that it now has related to food.'"[78] Vermonters, including sugarmakers, understand that what they are doing is selling maple by crafting very purposeful identities, but that crafting does not necessarily need to be thought of as a cynical act. Indeed, it's a very common act, one that most people engage in at some point during their day. Using tasting notes more familiar from the wine world as part of the crafting is not any more or less problematic than any other form of crafting, at least not by itself. Playing "the brand game" is nothing more than creating and communicating a particular meaning to someone. If the meaning is something actually lived by people, or at least rooted in something lived by people, then automatically viewing it too cynically seems shortsighted.

It is no accident that some maple has been marketed using language that sounds as if it comes from descriptions of wine. The tasting notes of wine come from a French culinary concept called *terroir*. In her book *Taste of Place* (2008), Amy Trubek has written very usefully about *terroir*, which she explains as "a connection between the symbolic and practical definitions of the earth and the tastes of food and beverage" (xv), and its spread through various food movements such as foodie and localvore. Vermont's maple industry draws on the ideas behind *terroir*, and as evidenced above, sometimes on *terroir* explicitly, to place its maple as not just a standardly excellent product, but as a product whose excellence comes from the unique circumstances of each bottle's production. Positioning the state's maple in this way helps the competition with Quebec, by fulfilling what Johnston and Baumann identify as a desire for authenticity: "For people who seek authenticity in their lives, the connection between an identifiable producer and a cultural artifact is an essential part of cultural experiences."[79] Or as Trubek quotes Tod Murphy (owner of the Farmers Diner in Vermont), "food is local as long as it is knowable."[80] Maple is most certainly a cultural artifact, laden with meaning and meanings by both the people who make it and the people who want it. Knowing the specific person who made the specific bottle of syrup enhances the amount and quality of culinary meaning that can be assigned to that bottle's contents because the "uniqueness, originality, and sincerity of an identifiable individual or group finds expression in their cultural production."[81] Maple conveys the sincerity of a sugarmaker, not just the state.

The need for sincerity on an intensely personal level is recognized by sugarmakers as well. Burr Morse, a well-known sugarmaker just outside Montpelier, Vermont, explained his understanding of sincerity to me: "I guess I just draw from my inner soul and try to be sincere. I say, 'Burr, do your best, understand these people are your friends and they came to learn about maple syrup making.' Oftentimes I ask them about what they do, where they come from, you know. Besides being sugarmaker and customer, I think you have to be friends. A drill sergeant and his trainee can't be friends, a college student and his teacher can't be friends. You gotta keep a little bit of separation, but with a sugarmaker and a potential customer I think you can be friends."[82] Burr makes it part of his job to form as much of a personal relationship to his customers as he can, stressing the sincerity and realness he tries to bring to the encounter. For the foodie who roots authenticity and sincerity in a personal connection to a known individual, it doesn't get much more known than making a new friend with your sugarmaker. That personal relationship enhances the culinary meanings a customer can make with the syrup.

Food does not always automatically stir the consumer just because it is attached to a specific person in a place, though, even if the place is very specific and localized. Drawing another example from the world of wine (with which maple shares so much culinary approach and economic meaning), scholar Damien Wilson describes how, in France, "[d]espite the central role of gastronomy in French culture, it seems to

THE CULINARY MEANING OF MAPLE

be relatively inconsequential in the minds of tourists. However, linked to the concept of *authenticity*, encompassing *history, tradition*, and *nature*, it takes on greater importance and meaning."[83] The sincerity of the individual sugarmaker that Vermont brings to bear conveys not just the maple, and not just a broad sense of "mapliness." In order to be useful in the branding game, that sincerity needs to carry along with it a sense of authenticity, including perhaps some versions of history, tradition, and/or nature. In Vermont, indeed it does, as the marketing of Vermont maple using tasting notes exclusively would be an enormous bust. The *terroir* approach needs to be situated in a place and with an identifiable person to really resonate as selling Vermont maple. The individuality of the syrup, communicated with the tasting notes, needs to be linked to an individuality of location and person in order to effectively play the brand game.

While Quebec can rightly boast of the reliable quality of all of its maple syrup, that quality is generally a trait of the syrup as a bulk commodity—Quebec maple is Quebec maple is Quebec maple. Vermont, on the other hand, is selling its quality as a trait of the individual sugarmaker and the individual batch of syrup. In this case, *terroir* and authenticity are conjoined by the ability to connect place to food item. For relatively local markets, not just any place, but only a very specific place, will do, as many people place a strong sense of authenticity in a specific place geographically. The more one can zoom the map in on a foodstuff's origin, the more appeal that foodstuff has. The bottle of Vermont syrup that a customer holds in her hand is supposed to speak of the specific place *within Vermont* whence it comes, as opposed to Quebec's maple speaking of a quality that applies equally across the province. The higher level of geographic specificity makes Vermont's syrup more special in the mind of the consumer, and the mind of the consumer is directly connected to the wallet of the consumer. As discussed in the chapter on economic meaning, Quebec is the biggest player in the maple world, and the Federation, the cooperative economic structure that oversees the vast majority of maple production in Quebec, allows them to speak a singular message about their maple with a unified voice. There are statewide organizations, such as the Vermont Maple Sugar Makers Association and the Vermont Maple Foundation, that help create unified narratives for the state's maple, but these groups must speak with many small voices of many specific locations scattered across the state to compete with the one, loud statement from Quebec.

When trying to understand the relationship between Quebec and Vermont syrups in a culinary sense, and why *terroir* has a logic to it as a marketing tool for Vermont, an easy parallel can be made between maple syrup and Scotch whisky. Blended scotches are the result of many different distillations being brought together and mixed (blended) to make for a uniform, reliable flavor. Single malt whisky, on the other hand, is the result of the distillation of one batch of malted barley (the "single malt" implied in the name), and is therefore much more variable from one label to the next, as well as from one year to the next within the same label. The very particularity and uniqueness of single malts is part of their consumer appeal. They are, by design, *not* reliably the same or evened out to meet the expectations of a palate, at least not on a larger scale. Single malts are made to be individual, and they are marketed on their individual characteristics. In much the same way that wine can be described with terms like "jammy" or "plummy," single malts can be described as "salty," "peaty," or, in one unforgettable instance from my own past, "like creosote." Such flavor notes are much less often used with blended whisky, instead being replaced with more generic terms such as "smooth" or "rich" (although the foodie norms have crept in here as well, and more distinctive vocabulary is now sometimes used to market blended whiskies). The mixing of distillations from different places makes the particularities that tasting notes draw on less evident in blended whisky, but a consistency of product more of an expectation. In like manner, most of the Quebec maple is drawn from the many, many sugarmakers who are part of the Federation and mixed together to produce a reliable product whose particularities have been evened out. Quebec maple from the Federation is mostly a blended whisky. Vermont maple markets itself as a single malt, where each producer presents their maple on its individual characteristics that result from the particularities of its production. And, just as with a whisky connoisseur, the foodie often seeks out the particular in the culinary world and is willing to pay a premium for it, translating the culinary meaning into an economic one.

There are culinary meanings made with sugaring that are not necessarily part of the syrup, funnily enough. A big vat of boiling sap affords sugarmakers the chance to do some cooking in the sugarhouse, and I was told many stories about eggs poached in the sap or hotdogs cooked in the front pan. A small café called Joey's Junction, in Highgate, Vermont, serves a breakfast consisting of half a dozen eggs poached in a cast-iron skillet filled with maple syrup (not sap), carrying on in a way the tradition of eggs poached in the front pan of the evaporator, where the sap is very nearly concentrated to the point of being syrup. The chef at the café is a sugarmaker himself, with a substantial operation. As a sugarmaker, he has doubtless heard stories of eggs poached in the evaporator, but whether those stories were a direct inspiration for the dish, I don't know.

These stories of sugarhouse cuisine were always set in the past, at least when they were told to me. The implication is that current health and hygiene rules make cooking up a hotdog in the sap impossible because it is against the rules today. Also implied by such stories is the all-hands-on-deck, twenty-four-hour-a-day nature of sugaring when the sap runs. Historically, with sap coming in and needing boiled as soon as possible, often there simply wasn't time to break for meals, so eating, and often cooking, was done right near the evaporator. With efficiencies introduced into sugaring by technologies such as reverse osmosis, the twenty-four-hour boil is becoming less common, which also places the stories of sugarhouse cuisine more into the past. Several sugarmakers told me of their memories of meat being hung over the boiling sap to cure, and wistful mention was often made of the perfumed quality of the meat that resulted. Hanging meat in this way served a dual purpose, apparently, as fat would drip from the meat into the boiling sap as it cured in the smoke and steam. The drops of liquid fat served as a defoaming agent, keeping the sap from bubbling over as it boiled in the front pan. I was told that meat hung over the sap was a technique still used in Quebec, but I was told this by Vermonters. The small economic and large identity rivalry between the sugaring in these two places makes one wonder whether this technique, considered unhygienic according to Vermont law, is applied to the Other in Quebec to make them foreign and their syrup less desirable. Whether it is entirely extinct in Vermont, among small producers who do not sell their syrup beyond friends and family, is also up for question.

Defoaming agents are a standard part of sugaring, albeit a part that would seem at first blush to violate the culinary purity of maple. Defoamers are not considered an ingredient (and therefore not allowed to be culinarily meaningful) in the syrup because a very small amount is used in a huge vat of sap, and because the defoaming agents "will evaporate without a noticeable trace in the syrup," according to Penn State's agricultural extension service.[84] Chemical defoamers such as propylene glycol are widely available and often used, but any syrup certified organic, and many that aren't, use simple vegetable oil. Because vegetable oils work less efficiently than chemical defoamers, more must be used per gallon, although the amounts are still very small. An oil with a neutral flavor, like canola or safflower, is preferred, as anything that alters the flavor of the syrup would be a violation of maple's culinary identity. Whatever form is being used, the defoamer, just like the dripping animal fat of yore (and lore), breaks the surface tension of the boiling sap, preventing it from bubbling up too much to the point of boiling over. According to Michael Farrell, too much foam on your boil also insulates the sap, reducing your boiling efficiency.[85] When understanding the role defoamers play, culinary meaning is forced to intersect with the numbers game of economic meanings that sugarmakers constantly engage.

There are many other sugaring memories that evoke culinary meanings having little to do with maple syrup. To be a sugarmaker is to be a sort of culinary insider, knowing the sugaring process more intimately. A foodie may be able to track down the finest, rarest syrup in the state, but it is much less likely that they will be able to know sugaring in the depth that would allow them memories such as this one, shared with me by a sugarmaker as we sat by his evaporator: "They made maple whiskey, which was just fermented, it's not distilled, but they made this stuff that they would roll out every year, and we kids would have a little tiny taste. Sometimes they cooked bear meat."[86] People who sugar get to have culinary experiences that consumers of maple products never do. As such, they get to make culinary meanings that consumers never do. This man recalled with some fondness a maple beer of sorts that was produced and distributed very locally, likely among neighbors and no further, which stresses the localness and insiderness of this culinary memory. Also rooting his memories very locally is the cooking of bear meat. Bears are not hunted in many places, and they are eaten in even fewer. Connecting this memory to the sugarhouse places both culinary meanings firmly in the rural, and firmly in the local, as well as fairly far from the maple syrup that is the most evident and widely known result of sugaring. This is a meaning only an insider can make.

Another beautiful example of insider culinary knowledge from the sugarhouse is given by Burr Morse in his book *Golden Times*, a collection of essays on life in rural Vermont, where he writes of an old man who visited him one day when he was boiling a batch of sap:

> Age had diminished his stride to a feeble shuffling. He came across the sugarhouse, seemingly led by a white, ceramic mug. He shuffled up to where I was boiling and, without words, offered the mug to me. Both being Vermonters with sugarhouse roots, neither of us needed words; he was asking me to fill his mug with sweet sap from the front pan. I took it, scooped into the steaming liquid with my dipper, and filled it to the top. I handed it back to him, offering no words of warning. He knew how hot it was.[87]

This memory, shared with the public in Burr's book, depicts something deeper shared by two Vermonters "with sugarhouse roots." The culinary moment that needs no words to unfold speaks to a common knowledge and a common meaning that the two men can make with drinking sap from the front pan. The front pan is one of the last stages in the transformation of sap to syrup. The boiling sap from the front pan will have been concentrated quite a bit already, perhaps almost to syrup, making this drink very sweet, and very tasty, indeed. The fact that I need to explain the implication of dipping from the front pan here sort of highlights one of the points of the story—both these men know what culinary beauty the front pan holds, while if we have never sugared, we may not. It is a culinary meaning only available to those who have shared the experience of the sugarhouse. It is a culinary meaning that carries with it meanings of identity, heritage, and so much more for those in the know. Tod Murphy said that food is made local by being known. It doesn't get much more local than shuffling into the sugarhouse and right up to the evaporator's front pan, and it doesn't get much more known than sharing a wordless set of meanings about what that front pan can provide.

The culinary meanings of maple are many and varied. The variations in the meanings come from several different sources—the identities of the people making meaning, such as foodies, consumers, and sugarmakers; the traits of maple being used to make meaning, such as its sweetness or its unique flavor profile; the ways culinary meanings intersect with other kinds of meaning, as in the cases of branding and *terroir*. The overlap of different realms of meaning is indicative of just how powerful a trope maple is culinarily. If it were just food, the meanings wouldn't ripple across to other fields beyond the culinary, but they do, to economic, ecological, and other meanings. Regardless of who is making the meaning, or what meaning they make, maple is very obviously a powerful and flexible conveyer of culinary meaning. As a food item, this is perhaps to be expected, but it is not to be assumed. Exploring the wide range of meanings that get made with maple allows us to understand it as more than just food, or even as more than just a foodway. Maple is a complex flavor and a complex set of meanings that intersect and overlap among many realms of human life. Culinarily, maple is a lived and living thing.

CHAPTER 3

The Geographic Meaning of Maple

That's something we were lucky enough to inherit. . . . Fifty years ago, very little if any syrup came in from Canada, so Vermont was the maple syrup producer in the United States.
—*Sugarmaker, 20 July 2010*

As much as anything, this book is about meanings of place. Vermont is a place, Quebec is a place, and these places are important and powerful causes and effects of people making meaning with sugaring. A lot of cultural process is involved in making a place meaningful because, as Tim Cresswell explains in his exploration of place, "places are the products of society and culture, [. . . but] place, in a general sense, adds up to a lot more than that."[88] A location, a place, a space— these terms get used in different ways, but they all involve some version of meaning being assigned to, or derived from, a spot. And it is very often the case that both occur simultaneously. Anthropologists Andrew Strathern and Pamela Stewart discuss the variety of avenues of meaning that the landscape provides:

> If there is one thing the study of landscape can do, then, it is to make clear that landscapes are culture, inscribed in fields, woods, crops, animal stock, buildings and roads, and in the sensory impressions and memories these evoke for those who live in them.[89]

The cultural inscription that is being described is the assigning of meaning to a place, thereby making it cultural. People doing the things that people do mark a place as theirs in some way, and sugaring is no different.

Maple is geographically identified with a specific portion of the globe because a density of the maple trees suitable for tapping is found only in a confined area. While there are well over a hundred species of maple (botanically defined as anything in the genus *Acer*), the number of species that predictably produce enough sap with a high enough sugar content to boil is much smaller, around ten or so (depending on the taxonomic system being used). Trees in other genera can be tapped, notably some birches (genus *Betula*) and several nut trees (especially those in genus *Juglans*, the walnuts), but no sap product has quite the same cachet as an edible item that maple does. Other tree sap items are certainly renowned and respected, but not necessarily as a food product. Amber, for example, is valued as a jewel, while frankincense and myrrh are prized for both aromatic and medicinal qualities. You can eat myrrh, but that is not its primary use. Only maple has the prominence of a tree-sap-derived product known primarily for its edible qualities. Such being the case, maple's value as a food product and importance as a flavor are geographically situated by the range of the trees, even when a particular maple product is not. A bottle of maple syrup on a store shelf in Dakar is still rooted in a different geography, and it still carries with it different geographic meanings from its place of origin, no matter where it is.

The area where maple sugaring occurs is located on the eastern side of the North American continent. In New England especially, questions of place and geographic meaning have long been at the center of discussions of identity. New England identity is often discussed in terms of ethnic/national (English, Scots, Irish) identities or religious identities (Catholic, Protestant). Those play a role, of course, but the particularities of place in New England help just as much, especially when discussing a place-based activity that is so important to regional identity, such as sugaring. The epicenter of sugaring is a border-crossing area of northern New England in the United States and southern Quebec in Canada. Vermont sugarmakers will tell you that you can zoom the lens in even further and place the epicenter of world sugaring in Franklin County, Vermont, despite the enormous volume produced by Quebec, which produces about 90 percent of the maple made in Canada, and over 70 percent of the maple made worldwide. One sugarmaker told me that the heart of sugaring was

Fairfield, Vermont, a small town in the hills a bit east of St. Albans, the county seat of Franklin County. This statement is not entirely braggadocio, as Franklin County is consistently the largest producer by county in Vermont, and Vermont out-produces every other state and most provinces where maple is tapped (the sole exception being, of course, Quebec). A recent report from the USDA tallied Vermont's production in gallons from 2012 to 2014 far above any other state in the United States, with the nearest competition from Maine and New York State hovering around half of Vermont's totals, and the most recent five-year USDA Censuses, conducted in 2007 and 2012, listed Franklin County's production as tops in the state.[90] In 2011–2012, Franklin County *by itself* out-produced every other state and province, save Quebec.[91] Clearly, Franklin County has some evidence to back its claim as *an* epicenter, if not *the* epicenter, of the sugaring world.

Several of the largest producers in Vermont are located in Franklin County. Two families, the Branons and the Howrigans, are well known as having long histories in the county, and each family has many branches that sugar to some extent. One sugarmaker, who, it must be said, was from southern Vermont and was not connected to either family, described the situation jokingly by telling me that in Franklin County, you couldn't swing a Howrigan without hitting a Branon, or a Branon without hitting a Howrigan. There was no disrespect in this man's variation on the "can't swing a cat" phrase, he was merely recognizing the number and importance of these two families to Franklin County's maple reputation. Each family name appears across several farms and sugarhouses in the county, and it is very common to see a cousin dropping in on a cousin during sugaring time, either to help with a big sap run or to compare in a manner half joking, half competitive, how many gallons each one made per tap. Unsurprisingly, both the helping and the joking often take place simultaneously. There is a strong sense of rootedness in Franklin County for these two families because "these farms were handed down for generations, and it means a lot to the families."[92] The "it" in that sentence is in fact several things—the land, the farms, the sugar woods, and the sugaring process. The last part of that statement, that it "means a lot" to the families, is true in every epistemological sense of the term "to mean." A lot of meaning, and a lot of meanings, get made for these two families and many others in Franklin County, and the intense interrelationship of person and place, process and product is more on display there than anywhere else I have been during my sugaring research. Franklin County is to many of its residents "an exemplary kind of place where people feel a sense of attachment and rootedness," as the geographer Timothy Cresswell might put it.[93]

John Gray tries to capture the ineffable quality of place when discussing shepherds in the Scottish borders, who take part in and construct a sense of belonging and home in a place very far from where most people live. Quoting one of the shepherds he interviewed, Gray tells us:

> One shepherd, Jim, expressed what I came to understand as the special, sensual, and intimate attachment people feel toward the hills in which they spend so much time—a feeling of being in their proper place, a feeling I try to capture with the phrase "being at home in the hills."[94]

Gray might as well be talking about Vermont's hills here, as the sense of being at home among them was often expressed to me by sugarmakers, old and new alike. Kent Ryden explores similar conceptual ground in New England, looking at how place is a conveyer of meaning in the region.[95] The meaning of properness of place is hugely important for many Vermont sugarmakers, as is the intimacy of their interactions with the landscape they sugar.

There are other sugarmakers in Franklin County who are not connected with either family, of course, and several of those producers have very large operations as well. The sheer intensity of sugaring in Franklin County is a bit staggering if one steps back from it, but the county has a very high concentration of sugar maple trees and a reputation for making lighter, and therefore historically more prized, syrups, so the number of sugarmakers and the sizes of the operations make sense. The reputation for lighter syrups is not just a comment on the county as a geography. It also notes the skill of the sugarmakers there, as the ability to make lighter syrup has long been a sign of expertise in sugaring. The reputation of the county's syrup is still geographized—it is made geographic, given geographic meanings— though, as the place, people, and syrup are all thought of as a unit, inseparable and fully meaningful only in the context of one another. To have the reputation as the epicenter of sugaring requires the geography, but also the people who are in some ways a fundamental part of the geography, so the trees and the skills of the people can come together. The result is not just the most maple syrup, but the best maple syrup, according to the narrative of geographic meaning that is widely applied to Franklin County.

The connections among place, process, and product are important in many realms, not least of which is the marketing of the syrup. As I was wandering through one of Vermont's large syrup bulk-packing facilities talking with a manager there, we chatted about the labeling and distribution processes in evidence. The importance of place of origin came clear as we were looking at one particular stack of barrels among the hundreds in front of us. The manager described one section of syrup as "New York fancy, . . . if we were packing pure Vermont maple syrup, we can't have a sniff of something that's not from Vermont, so like this [other barrel] is Vermont, from Franklin County."[96] New York's grading system does not use the terminology "fancy," but this man is translating New York light amber into Vermont's vernacular. However, even New York's equivalent of fancy, the lightest colored (and therefore regarded as highest quality) syrup that New York has to offer, is not allowed to come near the Vermont syrup, at least any Vermont syrup that will retain its geographic identity on the label.

The need to keep the syrups separate based on their geography has several reasons. There are legal requirements for the labeling, for example, that mean only syrup whose geographic origin is entirely within Vermont can use that name on the packaging. Amy Trubek's brief discussion of maple in *The Taste of Place* is a bit dismissive of the importance of place in labeling syrup, compared to French wines, but the power of place in maple is negotiated differently, and not as strictly legalistically.[97] The importance in maple is controlled by laws, but it goes well beyond the legal. The labeling laws are in place because so much geographic meaning is made with places like Vermont and Franklin County. One sugarmaker summed up the point that when "you put the Vermont name on a container of maple syrup, there's no other word you could add to it that's going to make it any more salable."[98] The word "Vermont" is a placename, but it carries so much other meaning along with the place. The word denotes the state, but it connotes the cleanliness and purity I have discussed elsewhere. To say a bottle of maple is from Vermont is, in this man's estimation, the highest praise and guarantee of attractiveness that could be given to the syrup. Maybe that's not surprising, given that the speaker is a Vermont sugarmaker. More importantly, applying the geographic meaning of "Vermont" to the bottle directly translates into the economic meaning of being salable. The name of the state is a very important and powerful meaning maker, so protecting that name is a high priority. Not only would it be taboo and illegal for the bulk packer above to package New York syrup and call it Vermont, but the New York syrup cannot even sniff the Vermont maple. The other barrel, which contained Franklin County syrup, had a different destiny still because it came from that county, which was understood to be the center of sugaring, at least in this situation.

Regardless of where one places the center, the outer edges of maple sugaring's area are pretty well defined as the area where tap-worthy maples grow in numbers. Sugaring of any scale is done in the provinces of Ontario, Quebec, New Brunswick, and Nova Scotia; and the states of Maine, New Hampshire, Vermont, Massachusetts, Connecticut, Rhode Island, New York, Pennsylvania, Ohio, Michigan, and Wisconsin. A quick scan of license plates at the most recent MapleRama, a trade show and conference of sugarmakers held each year in a rotating location within Vermont, showed vehicles from Virginia, Minnesota, and Nebraska too, suggesting something above a scattering of hobbyists in those states as well. Too far beyond that footprint of southeastern Canada and the northeastern United States, though, sugaring is not much more than a novelty activity. While working on this book, I took a sabbatical position at Memorial University in St. John's, Newfoundland, an area not known for maple sugaring. However, there was a growing handful of people tapping maples, mostly as a backyard hobby and a chance to eat local and/or produce local foods. These people seemed to be making a meaning of maple that was either culinary or local in identity, but explicitly not geographic. There was little sense of Newfoundland identity about their sugaring, and even a sense of maple being an aberration of the identity of the island. So, place and activity are separable conceptually, even if they occur together. As John Agnew puts it, "Confusing place and community is widespread in the social sciences. . . . community was conceived as both a physical setting for social relations (place) and a morally valued way of life."[99] The common desire to equate place and community would suggest that, because people are sugaring in Newfoundland, it must be part of the sugaring world just like Vermont. But even though people are sugaring in the place, sugaring is not a part of the community's identity in Newfoundland, so this sort of backyard sugarmaker does not make much geographic meaning, despite sugaring in that geographic place.

Part of the reason that sugarmakers in Newfoundland do not make much geographic meaning on the island is that maple is not a very important part of the culinary imagination there. According to Canadian folklorist Diane Tye, the sweetener of historic choice in Newfoundland is molasses, rooted in the town's past as a seaport in the trade between Europe and the Caribbean.[100] As such, molasses is much more culinarily meaningful for Newfoundlanders, and the geographies of molasses are much more meaningful as well. Sweetness in Newfoundland is already rooted in a triangular trade route connecting the Caribbean, Europe, and Africa, so the geographic meanings of sweetness in the island are taken. The predominance of molasses in various traditionally named "Boston" foods (Boston baked beans, Boston brown bread) is doubtless of similar origin in another port city on a western shore of the Atlantic. Not much geographic meaning is made with maple in Boston either, despite a fair amount of sugaring occurring in Massachusetts.

I should note that for the purposes of this discussion, I am focusing on areas where maple sugaring takes place with some breadth and intensity. Sugaring can technically be said to be done anywhere someone drills a hole in a maple and boils what comes out. Indeed, Michael Farrell, in his book *The Sugarmaker's Companion*, starts his fourth chapter by wagging a finger at some of the geographic meanings made with maple: "Given the vast resource of maple, birch, and walnut trees throughout the temperate forests of the world, there are two widespread myths that I would like to dispel in this chapter: 1. Maple syrup can only be produced in the northeastern United States and Canada. 2. Maples are the only trees that can be tapped to produce syrup."[101] He then goes on to provide an anecdote about a maple sugarmaker in Denmark, of all places. I don't want to be seen as perpetuating the same myths, but this book is about meanings, not just maple. The areas where only a handful of people are tapping trees and making syrup do not yet have maple as a part of their identity. A few people in those areas might identify with maple, and some day an area could if sugaring expands, but these places as a whole do not make meaning with maple. The trees may be there, and there may be a few people making syrup, but it is just not as *meaningful* there geographically. So, while I agree with Farrell's statements, my analysis is not just on the ability to produce syrup. Because the focus of this book is identity and meaning, these scattered small producers, while not unimportant, are negotiated on a different scale, and they don't geographize their syrup in the same way. Because of those differences, they fall outside the scope of my current research. That's not to say that they are unimportant or even uninteresting.

As an indicator of the geographic importance of maple in Vermont, and the geographic centrality of Vermont in the meaning of maple, one need look no further than MapleRama, the annual conference and trade show by and for maple sugarmakers. MapleRama is sponsored by the Vermont Maple Sugar Makers Association (vermontmaple.org), and it draws sugarmakers from the widest extent of the sugaring world. The event rotates every year to a different county in Vermont, with hosting duties being taken on by that county's local sugarmakers' association for the year. Many regions in the maple world have similar meetings for sugarmakers, and some are quite large, but MapleRama continually has the widest reach in drawing participants, recognizing that the whole maple world points toward this event yearly. While large conferences of sugarmakers are held in New Brunswick and Quebec, New York and Maine, these conferences draw largely from their home territories, and much less from outside. MapleRama brings in sugarmakers from Nova Scotia to Nebraska as a matter of course.

MapleRama itself, and its being rooted in Vermont, speaks to the geographizing of maple, as does the annual Maple Festival, another event in the Vermont yearly calendar. Maple Fest is very much like any other town fair or festival rooted in agriculture. Corn Fest, Strawberry

Fest, Summer Fest, Pumpkin Fest—such fairs can be found scattered all across North America, anywhere that has a history and identity with agriculture. Because sugaring is often slotted into an agricultural identity, the fair celebrating maple feels an awful lot like any other small-town agricultural festival, complete with carnival rides, variations on the fried-dough theme, and chances to win stuffed animals and mirrors screen printed with various popular music groups. It is not a generic festival, completely devoid of uniqueness, though. The presence of a mobile sugarhouse on wheels, and the availability of a warmer weather version of sugar-on-snow and maple cotton candy mark Maple Fest as much "maple" as "fest."[102] Maple Fest takes place in St. Albans, Vermont, every spring (usually late April), and, while it is not the only maple festival of its kind, it is the most prominent and widely known. A permanent sign at the edge of St. Albans declares, in medium-size type at the top, "Welcome to St. Albans," and in type significantly larger, "Vermont Maple Festival." The city is laying claim to geographic centrality for maple, or perhaps geographically centralizing the celebration of maple within the boundaries of the city. It is not just any maple festival, but a *Vermont* maple festival, which takes place there, and the festival is given more prominence as one enters town than the town name itself.[103] St. Albans, in Franklin County, points the maple world toward itself geographically when it comes to honoring maple. Maple Fest is, in real, practical terms, less dominant and less unique as an event than MapleRama. Similar agricultural festivals held elsewhere have the same draw and the same cachet. So, while MapleRama indicates the geographic meaning that Vermont has across the maple sphere, St. Albans's Maple Fest indicates a geographic meaning that Vermont *thinks* it has or *wants to claim* it has. Both events, in different ways, speak to how geographically meaningful the intersection of maple and Vermont is.

MapleRama achieves its geographic claim to fame in a different way, and for a different audience, from the various agricultural maple festivals. While St. Albans's Maple Fest is for the general public, both Vermonter and outsider, sugarmaker and sugar consumer, MapleRama is for and by sugarmakers almost exclusively. It is one of the few places where sugarmakers from all over the sugaring world meet face to face to talk only with one another and those intimately involved in sugaring. In this instance, Goffman's discussions of face (1973) and Urry's tourist gaze (2002) can help us understand how and why a different conversation about sugaring will happen at MapleRama, which has no pretense of the public narratives generally connected with maple marketing. Sugarmakers tell stories of horses and wood fires when selling their maple to the public, but MapleRama is not for the public. It is a private, insider affair, so the public faces are not in place. They are often topics of conversation, as sugarmakers discuss the latest in marketing or maple economics around the globe, but no one wears those masks, only possibly discusses them at the meta-level of analysis.

The geographic meaning made with MapleRama is not situated in one location, like Maple Fest. MapleRama takes place annually in summer (typically late July) in a rotating location around Vermont. Because each county's maple sugarmakers' association takes turns hosting, the geographic centralizing takes place, but with a moving target. Vermont has fourteen counties, and all have a county sugarmakers' association, save Essex County in the far northeast of the state and Grand Isle County in the far northwest. Essex County is the most rural of Vermont's counties, and it has a very low population in comparison. Grand Isle County consists of the islands in Lake Champlain, and as such, has always had a slightly different identity from the other counties in the state. Sugaring in Essex and Grand Isle counties generally is attached to neighboring counties (Caledonia and Orleans for Essex, Franklin for Grand Isle) for any business conducted at the county level.

It is important to note here that the geographic target that MapleRama creates moves, but only within the bounds of Vermont, within the outline map of the state. MapleRama draws sugarmakers from all across the United States and Canada, as mentioned above, but all those sugarmakers converge on Vermont. It is at a rotating location within Vermont that sugarmakers gather to talk among themselves, share what is new, hear from industry leaders, and learn from and with one another. I have been attending MapleRama for half a dozen years now, and I have met sugarmakers with operations of all sizes, from the largest 70,000+ tap setups down to a couple from Indiana tapping half a dozen trees in their backyard. Vermont serves as the geographic home for this occasion, claiming a sort of spiritual central-ity for sugaring that transcends the tourist encounter of a maple fes-tival. These are not outsiders to sugaring coming into the sugarhouse to gaze on the syrup making and makers. MapleRama is by and for sugarmakers. Indeed, I am routinely one of the very few participants in MapleRama (we can always be counted on one hand, usually on one finger) who is not a sugarmaker or actively involved in sugar-ing in some way (maple retail, equipment sales, bulk packing, etc.). So MapleRama is giving geographic meaning to sugaring not for the consumer, but for sugarmakers themselves.

Vermont's claim to centrality seems to fly in the face of economic and geographic realities. The state has not always been the leader, even within the United States. There are many more maples being tapped in Canada, and there is a whole lot more syrup being made there. In the past, perhaps Vermont had more of a claim to maple centrality, for example in the interwar period, when the state made "probably more than Canada at that time. Up until World War II, the Canadians only produced about a third of the world's crop, and since then, between World War II and 1970, they went from whatever that was up to about two thirds. And today they're producing probably 85% of the world's crop."[104] In that crucial moment just after the second world war, when regional and national identities were being forged and made global at a rate greater than any time previous, thanks to the invention and penetration of electronic media and transportation advances, Vermont was the biggest wheel. It became the maple state when internationally known identities were being solidified. Even when Canada, specifically Quebec, surpassed Vermont, the identity didn't change. The situation is analogous to Wisconsin laying claim to the title of "The Dairy State." California produces more milk than Wisconsin, and has for quite a while, according the USDA's agricul-tural statistics.[105] To be fair, Wisconsin still produces more cheese, but the time when the state could claim leadership in all dairying is past. The identity remains, though, and Wisconsin is the spiritual center of dairying just as Vermont is the spiritual center of maple. Because the maple making in Vermont took place historically at such a small but widespread scale, with nearly everyone having a small hand in it, maple is more pervasively a part of the state's identity. Even as production concentrated and fewer people were involved, the pervasiveness remained and maintained the identity. The maintenance is not all show, however. The state has taken real steps to maintain its geographic understanding of the place. One Vermonter told me about the state's history of protecting its natural environment from development, that "Vermont in particular has a kind of reputation. We've got 500,000 acres now conserved permanently, so this is a place that people really care about our sense of place in Vermont."[106] So, Vermont's claim to centrality in the maple world is not entirely fictional. It is a bit fictive—that is, created by narrative—but all identities are fictive when it comes right down to it. Regardless, the state draws strong and clear connections between maple and the place where it is made, and it centers that image squarely on Vermont.

This centralizing is only possible because maple is understood as occurring in a limited geographic footprint, Michael Farrell's caution notwithstanding. Maple has a "where" to it that not all agricultural products do. Oranges are from Florida and California (a statement which is true for many fruits and vegetables), peaches are from Georgia, dates are from Turkey, and rambutan are from Malaysia, but these associations are mild in comparison to maple's geographized identity. Some agricultural products have almost no geographic meaning attached to them at all, as recognized by one Vermonter who produces both maple and milk. He explained, "I feel pretty fortunate to be involved in making something that is unique to a certain part of the world. We also produce milk. You could go pretty much any place in the world, and they would know that milk is from dairy cows. That's not the case with maple."[107] Of course, there are places where milk is not a part of the diet or the culinary imagination, and there are places where people use milk that does not come from cows, but this sugarmaker's point is that milk is not geographized in the way maple is. There is a universality to milk that makes it harder to pin down, while much of maple's identity is based on the fact that just the opposite is true. It is very pinned down on the map, and that is one of the things that makes it special.

Because maple has such a strong sense of *where* it takes place, those places can easily use maple to make some sense of geographic meaning for themselves. Canada does this overtly, with a maple leaf being the most dominant design feature of its national flag and an NHL team named the Toronto Maple Leafs. Granted, the discussion over the adoption of the maple leaf design on the flag (what Peter Marshall refers to as "the interminable and emotional disputes involved in the devising and adoption of a Canadian flag") was controversial and, in some quarters, rancorous.[108] Internally, the maple leaf is not as much a unifying symbol of Canadianness as it is perceived now from without. But that maple-leaf-wearing flag is now seen from without as paradigmatically Canadian. The hockey team, the Toronto Maple Leafs, is vernacularly called "the Leafs," which could easily be dismissed as a simple shorthand, a nicknaming process that is very common in professional sports ("the Pack" for the NFL's Green Bay Packers; "Hibs and Hearts" for two Scottish soccer teams, Hibernian and Heart of Midlothian; "the Sixers" for the NBA's Philadelphia 76ers; even "the A's," with their misplaced punctuation, for baseball's Oakland Athletics). However, it is also easy to entertain the notion that the Toronto Maple Leafs becoming just "the Leafs" suggests that the species of tree from which the leaf comes is so widely understood to be maple that it need not be stated. Non-Canadian companies will sometimes pass as Canadian or brand their Canadian divisions by slapping a maple leaf onto their logo, including such corporate giants as Sears and McDonalds, so clearly there is a ready equation being made between Canada (or Canadianness) and maple. In a way, Canada claims maple centrality with its flag and its hockey team, much the same as Vermont claims sugaring centrality with its Maple Fest and MapleRama.

The Canadian national flag is indeed a claim of maple centrality, but that claim is not very old. The design of the flag was adopted only in 1965, to create a symbol for all of Canada and distinctly Canada, which until then had used flags incorporating symbols of British Empire. The maple leaf was symbolically powerful in both Ontario and Quebec and had long been used informally as a pan-Canadian symbol, in military regiments of the British Empire, for example. In World War I, plants were often used to mark regiments from different parts of the empire in their regalia, such that Scotland became the thistle, Wales the leek, England the oak, and so forth; so too, Canada became the maple. Therefore, it was one obvious option to create a legally recognized national symbol when the Canadian flag was being formulated in the 1960s. The fact that it was an obvious option (even in the face of internal arguments and dissent), as well as the fact that it was the option that won, is attributable to the connections between maple and Canada that were already in place in the cultural imagination.

Maple is not symbolically used on the same national scale in the States, but it is certainly used on a regional level. Several states have a species of maple as their officially recognized state tree, with the sugar maple in New York, West Virginia, Wisconsin, and Vermont. Rhode Island, always one to be a little different, goes with the red maple as its state tree. Within Vermont, the symbolic use of the word *maple* and/or the maple leaf is enormously popular in brands and corporate identities. At the University of Wisconsin–Madison, I used to teach a course on the cultural history of the Vikings. As part of each day's discussion, the class would explore some instance of the Viking as a trope in popular culture—Viking brand sewing machines, Viking brand yachts, the Viking NASA missions to Mars, the Minnesota Vikings . . . the list goes on. It would be just as easy, perhaps easier, to do a similar set of class discussions of the trope of maple within Vermont. Placenames abound, such as Maple Tree Place, Maple Ridge, or Maple Corners. Companies as wide ranging as Sugarbush Investment Properties and the Maple Leaf Inn surround Vermonters with maple imagery far outside of the woods or the sugarhouse. Even some companies and organizations that have nothing to do with sugaring and don't have the word maple in their name will use a maple leaf as part of the graphic design of their brand identity. The landscape, as shaped by people, narrates, communicates, and maintains the "mapleness" of Vermont.[109]

Narratives and landscapes as forms of communication, as makers and transmitters of meaning and culture, have been explored elsewhere, and many of those discussions enlighten the case of sugaring in Vermont. As Keith Basso tells us in his brilliant and beautiful book, *Wisdom Sits in Places*, "In short, historical tales have the power to change people's ideas about themselves. . . . After stories and storytellers have served this beneficial purpose, features of the physical landscape take over and perpetuate it. Mountains and arroyos step in symbolically for grandmothers and uncles."[110] People and places narrate the connection between Vermont and sugaring constantly, and because of the multigenerational aspects of sugaring, these stories are passed down as if a prized possession, a container of identity. The stories of sugaring that pervade the area change and shape Vermonters' ideas about themselves, making sugaring a part of the state's identity, not just that of sugarmakers. The constant reinforcement of maple words and images in the places that inhabit the state then take over, stepping in for the grandmothers and uncles of Vermont to reinforce the narrative. That narrative is then communicated to all people living in or visiting the state, not just sugarmakers, and not even just those who visit a sugarhouse, as Burr Morse notes, "Maple season, indeed, brings magic. Its magic travels a road called nostalgia and may knock at doors all over the world or simply stay t'home in a steamy sugarhouse."[111] Burr Morse recognizes that even the romanticized notions of maple, while they may travel the world geographically, have a home in the sugarhouses of Vermont.

The connections between the geography of Vermont and sugaring are brought into stark relief in the design of the syrup container shown here.

The outline of the state of Vermont is depicted with a tap coming out of it, with sap literally pouring from the state itself into a bucket. Interestingly, the sugaring process being depicted here involves the old tradition of buckets catching the runoff from metal spiles (taps). The use of the state image really drives home how strongly and how completely maple is equated with Vermont, and the evoking of an older technology roots maple in the past of the place as well. That outline map beyond which MapleRama does not roam gives more geographic meaning to sugaring here. The sap bucket is poised under the state, and the tap is drilled directly into Vermont (right near the state's largest city, Burlington, funnily enough). The state is literally in the place of the maple tree, but the ubiquity of sugaring imagery means that the depiction and the meanings the viewer is supposed to make are clear. Vermont is maple. Further, and more importantly, maple is Vermont—it is the place. To tap into a maple is to tap into something fundamental, something definitional about the identity of the state, and maple sap runs through the place like blood through

Maple syrup container, showing the state of Vermont with a tap and bucket hanging on it. *Author photo.*

the veins of an animal. One of my informants from another research project once told me, "If you scratch the surface of Orkney, it bleeds history."[112] Well, apparently if you tap Vermont, it bleeds maple sap. The meaning being made is clear. The place, geographically defined and geographically represented with an outline map, is synonymous with maple—the tree, the sap, the process and the product of sugaring. It is, as Burr Morse puts it, "a mystique that's part of our Vermont being."[113]

The use of the outline map of Vermont here brings geographic narration into the discussion. People make stories, and elicit certain kinds of stories made with certain kinds of narrative epistemologies, through the use of maps and geography. On the one hand, a map is sort of by definition geographic, although it is probably more accurate to say that a map *geographizes*. It makes a place geographic, using a particular set of assumptions and knowledge to apply meanings to a place and make it orderly. So, while a map is in a sense geographic, it can also be understood as having a more active role, in making a place geographic, by using a certain epistemology (system of making knowledge and/or meaning) to tell a certain story about a place. Again, Basso is useful in explaining how places can be used by people to contain, explain, and maintain culture. The preface of *Wisdom Sits in Places* makes very clear the power of place in narrative and narrative in place when it states, "And so, unavoidably, senses of place also partake of cultures, of shared bodies of 'local knowledge' (the phrase is Clifford Geertz's) with which persons and whole communities render their places meaningful and endow them with social importance."[114] To use a certain epistemology to create an understanding of a place, to have a sense of the place, is to endow it with social importance. To endow a place with social importance is to render a place *meaningful*, to give it a meaning that people can share, negotiate, communicate, and (making me the millionth customer to reuse Lévi-Strauss's phrase) to think with. Once a place has a shareable meaning, it is left only to have two people who share in that meaning to use the place and the narrative culturally. In the case of a place or a map, the meaning is at least partly, and usually largely, geographic.

The map of Vermont on the side of the maple container renders the state meaningful by assigning a particular idea—maple syrup making—to the place. Interestingly, the meaning being assigned combines both the product and the process of maple. The depiction of the state with a spile coming out and sap dripping represents the process, with the obviously human-made spile and bucket interacting with the stand-in maple tree of Vermont showing part of the activity cycle that results in the product of maple. The end product is part of the narrative through the reality of the container and its contents. That paradigmatic shape of the maple jar does not contain sap, and it is not used as part of the sugaring process. It only comes into the picture when the process is finished. It contains syrup, and within areas where sugaring is common, that shape contains nothing but syrup. So the product, process, and geography all come together in this instance, creating and communicating an incontrovertible link of meaning and social importance.

Showing maple sap dripping from a tap bored into the map of Vermont endows the state with social importance, but not just any social importance . . . it is a hugely important importance. As the discussions above make clear (and it is hoped, as this entire book makes clear), maple is not just important to Vermont's identity; it is of utmost, paradigmatic importance for many people within and outside of the state. Other symbols are sharable with other places, but maple, even though it occurs elsewhere, is exclusively Vermont's symbol, according to many within the state. The maple sap dripping into the bucket demonstrates the depth and vital nature of maple and tapping to Vermont. It makes the state not just a source of maple; it makes the place into the home and ur-source of maple. One sugarmaker put it very succinctly, by telling me that "if you want real syrup, you get it from Vermont trees."[115] Other things that pretend to be syrup can come from other places, but *real* syrup comes from the source, from Vermont.

The image on the front cover of this book is another nexus point of meanings and social importance.

Another outline map of Vermont, this time carved from maple wood, makes for an obvious connection between the state and the tree, at least for anyone who can recognize the grain and texture of maple by sight. On this level, the process of sugaring is hinted at, as the trees themselves are the first step in making syrup. However, with a little more knowledge about the carved image, more layers of connection and meaning unfold. The small holes visible in the wood, as well as the dark vertical streaks stretching above and below those holes, are not natural parts of the wood or tree. A close inspection would show that each hole is precisely the same diameter because the

Carving of Vermont made from taphole maple, Chuck Mitchell, artist. *Photo by Judd Lamphere.*

holes were drilled by human hands. Given the nature of this book, it will come as no surprise at this point to discover that the holes were drilled to accept spiles. They're tapholes. In sugaring season, the sap flows up the tree vertically, as the tree draws nutrition from its base up to the new growth about to occur in the branches and tips at springtime. Drilling a hole in the side of the tree interrupts that vertical flow of sap. The dark streaks above and below each taphole are the direct result of these drillings, which kill some of the tissue above and below the hole by depriving that wood of the nutrient-rich sap. There are other forms of discoloration in maple wood that are also seen as desirable aesthetic elements. Spalting, for example, is a streaking caused by fungal action on a tree. The dark vertical streaks of taphole maple, though, are the direct result of human action, drilling a taphole to sugar on that maple tree. As such, the taphole maple used in decorative or functional woodworking speaks of that human interaction and the process of sugaring.

This wood, explicitly called "taphole maple" when used in woodworking, is representative not only of the tree, but of the process of sugaring itself, as it presents evidence of the human interaction with the tree in the form of the holes and the dark vertical streaks. Further, that evidence is used as a design element, an aesthetically pleasing aspect of the wood that is incorporated into its artistry. Jennifer Anderson discusses how the natural aesthetics of wood can be used as an artistic element by a woodworker in her book, *Mahogany*, and the same holds true for the wood of the maple tree. Indeed, "in the hands of a skilled woodworker," this taphole maple had been "manipulated to achieve a remarkable array of visual and tactile effects."[116] When this nexus of symbolism takes the form of another outline of the state, as on the front cover of this book, geographic meaning is created yet again. All the pieces of the puzzle fall together in this image, with the place, the process, and the tree being graphically (and beautifully) communicated to the viewer of the image, as well as to whomever owns the taphole maple artifact itself.

In this case, that owner would be me. I bought this piece of artwork at a stop during MapleRama in 2011. The artist, Chuck Mitchell out of Brandon, Vermont, was displaying his work in front of Sugar Brook Maple Company, one of the stops on the annual sugarhouse tour. At that point in time, the genesis of this book was already cooking in my head, and my immediate thought at seeing this piece of woodwork was, "That's the book cover right there." After admiring the other art pieces and items of furniture that Chuck, now retired from woodworking, had made, I bought the carving shown on the cover with joy, but also with a very slightly heavy heart. I knew that the artist communicated in this carving the complex set of ideas I wanted to write about more straightforwardly and more eloquently than I ever could with my words. I wish I had that instinct.

The outline carving of Vermont then stands as a symbol of the relationship between the state, the people, and the trees. The geographic representation of place is communicating a complex set of relationships, an identity expressed through a system of making artistic meaning. The carving makes its own set of meanings, and in doing so communicates not only those meanings, but the system of meaning making itself. The ideational system, the epistemology, that makes use of geography here in the form of an outline map not only uses the system to transmit what it is trying to say about the map, but it creates and perpetuates the system as well. To see a map of Vermont laid out in maple wood, especially taphole maple with its evidence of sugaring activity, is to be shown a meaning and a way to make meaning. Just as the image on the bottle, of Vermont with a tap coming out its side, tells the viewer not only a meaning to make but that they *can and should make that specific meaning*, the taphole carving demands a certain kind of reaction from the viewer too. Any artifact is made up of various elements. In the case of the maple container, the container itself (and by association, its contents), the outline of Vermont that geographizes, the depictions of the tap and bucket that speak to sugaring as process, and lastly the placement of tap into state all make up the language the container image is communicating. For the carving, the elements are the species of wood itself, the tapholes and their associated dark streaks, and again the outline of the state. Bringing together the various elements of either image does more than just suggest a connection. These sets of elements disallow a viewer from seeing maple and the state as separate, perhaps even from seeing the two as *separable*. These images tell someone how they should understand Vermont, maple, and the relationship between the two. The system of meaning making and its resultant artwork are culturally instructive, and therefore culturally constitutive.

Vermont often makes use of its limited geographic footprint to symbolically represent and communicate itself. The outline map of Vermont is the most common symbol used in this way within sugaring, but it is not the only one.[117] I want to explore for a moment another example of this kind of geographic meaning making within the state, but one that does not function in the same way in terms of sugaring. Another prominent symbol that is used to represent the state is the number 802. Those three digits are seen and used all over the place to convey an understanding of Vermont in shorthand form. On the surface, there is nothing particularly geographic about the number 802, unless one knows that 802 is the telephone area code for the whole of the state. Vermont is one of the few states left that is still covered in its entirety by one area code. The other states for which this is still true fall into one of two categories: small states geographically (such as Delaware) or large states with a very small, scattered population (like Alaska). In states with only one area code, the number becomes a geography, as the boundaries of that number's use are coterminous with a geographically bounded zone. The term itself, *area* code, indicates how spatial these numbers are, at least in their original conception. Area codes are distributed based not on geography, of course, but on population. When first conceived and applied, population and geography overlapped to a great degree. Now though, more people necessitate more available phone numbers in a given space, especially as the telephone becomes identified with a person, rather than a place. In the past (a distant past for the generation getting their first phones today), calling a telephone meant calling a specific geographic location—the house or business where the phone was located—with some sense but no certainty of who might be there. Now, as telephones are not rooted in a place, but mobile, calling a telephone very often means attempting to reach a specific person, perhaps with a sense but certainly no certainty of *where* that person might be (if they pick up at all). Area codes have become de-geographized by the phone becoming the cell phone.

With the advent of the cell phone, and more importantly with the wide spread of universal in-country long-distance charges included in a cell phone rate plan, the solidity of the connection between an area code and a geographic place is weakening all the time. People carry their phone number with them through moves, sometimes across the country. Despite this shift, 802 is a symbol that communicates "Vermont" more often and more consistently among younger people

in the state, the very people for whom, because of their greater identification with cell phones, an area code does not as strongly communicate a particular geographic location, a particular area. According
to Matt Dodds, founder of a Vermont marketing firm, the number not
only doesn't communicate geography, it barely communicates *anything* concrete to its young target audience, for whom Dodds worry-
ingly states, "the more reductive you can get, the better."[118] Instead,
the number communicates a sense of values associated with Vermont,
including in this case, coolness. Advertisements and branding use 802
as shorthand for the state in products and services aimed directly
at a younger set of consumers, such as ski companies or neo-hippie
organic products. By using 802 in much the same manner as the outline map, marketing employs 802 as a geography. It maps the identity
of the state as surely as Rand or McNally ever did, and in so doing
re-geographizes a de-geographized thing. But funnily enough, even
though the number 802 and the state outline are employed in many
similar ways, 802 is not really a symbol used that often in sugaring.

The easiest explanation for the predominance of the outline map
and the absence of 802 in sugaring's geographizing of maple is that
802 is recognized on a much smaller scale. Not many outside of
Vermont and the states that border it know what its area code is or
care that the state has only the one. Pretty much every schoolchild
in the United States learns the shapes of the states, though, so it is
a symbol that can communicate across a much wider range culturally (even if many people mix up Vermont and New Hampshire,
reversing which one is wide at the top and narrow at the bottom,
and which is the other way around). That explanation seems to run
counter to the intense regionalization of sugaring, though. Especially
earlier in its history and prehistory, maple products didn't often go
that far from the places where they were made. So why is the more
regionally understood symbol (802) of maple's location not more
connected with sugaring? Especially considering that regionality is
a hugely important part of sugaring's narrative, a regional symbol
seems particularly well suited to the marketing of maple. Well, part
of the answer is that sugaring goes back much further than the telephone, so 802 is a johnny-come-lately in terms of symbolism. Just
as the formation of spiritual centers discussed above happened in

the past and therefore transcends later cultural changes, 802 is a late arrival at the maple party, so it is less useful as part of the symbol system that communicates maple.

Also, 802 is overtly technological, being derived originally from the telephone.[119] Even though the amount of recently made technology used in sugaring is impressive, the publicly communicated image of sugaring is decidedly un-recent, especially when talking about technology. The red-checked coat, horse-drawn sledge, and wood-fired evaporator are the images that build sugaring's public narrative. Marketing is simply an applied form of public communication, so to use an overtly technological symbol to communicate Vermontiness just does not fly in marketing maple, which often communicates itself with older symbols. It works to use 802 when one wants to communicate a ski destination to younger hipsters, riders, skiers, and other similar markets, but maple has a different set of demographic targets in its sights. Using the state outline to communicate the geographic identity of maple makes much more sense in that case. An older symbol for an older audience communicates an older-fashioned way of doing things. The current boundaries of the state were determined longer ago than the current area code coverage, so the outline map speaks more to a longer history, a longer memory that sugaring often tries hard to evoke. That longer memory is one shared by sugarmakers, sugaring, the state, and (it is hoped in this situation) the customer who buys the syrup.

It certainly helps making those connections that Vermont as a state has a very strong and separate identity, disregarding sugaring or anything else. The state was the first to join the United States after the original thirteen colonies, and it was, for a short time before that, governed as an independent republic. This history has given the state a strong libertarian bent and a strong sense of a separate geography and special identity. Vermont is only as special as every other state is, but that doesn't stop a very small portion of the population from agitating for secession and the establishment of a "second Vermont republic." These agitations are much louder than they are politically or culturally important, but the fact that they exist at all helps us understand at least a little how Vermont's geographic identity can be so readily used in the creation and marketing of a maple identity. Vermont has long had a strong separate identity, so employing that identity to give maple a story is relatively easy.

Because maple production is very strongly associated with a geographic region, many geographic meanings are made with and for sugaring. Species of maple are available in many parts of the world, but the concentration of tappable maples in the area of eastern Canada and New England has helped make that region sugaring's geographic and conceptual home. A culture of maple has grown up there, and sugaring is culturally meaningful in that region in ways that it simply isn't elsewhere. Even in other places where people tap maples and make syrup, sugaring is not as much a part of the region's identity. The regionality of sugaring has become part of the story, part of the narrative communication of what maple products are and represent. When maple syrup moves from Vermont, very often it takes some set of meanings of the state with it, and those meanings are often geographic. Even meanings that are not overtly geographic become geographized, to heighten the sense of place that is so important to maple. The process, the product, and the people are all understood through a geographic lens, and all are given geographic meanings in the process.

CHAPTER 4

The Ecological Meaning of Maple

I really enjoy being outside, and in the spring of the year, that's the new beginning of all kinds of plant life and animal activity, and so by being out sugaring you see that. Whether you want to or not, you're out there during the snowstorms or rainstorms or windy days, and you see all the awakening, the new season. It puts you right there. —Sugarmaker, 11 June 2010

In this chapter, I explore maple as an arena for the intersection of the human and the nonhuman worlds. By "ecology" here, I don't mean simply looking at maple trees as a part of nature. I am exploring more the thinking frameworks that people use when they think ecologically, primarily dualisms such as nature and culture. This chapter isn't about the nature of maple trees; it's about how people think with the naturalness of the trees. The social sciences have for quite some time questioned a simplistic dichotomy between "the natural" and "the cultural" (Agryrou 2005; Hastrup 2014; Gingrich 2014; Palsson 2014), exploring various epistemologies, other theory systems that make different kinds of sense of the ultimately Cartesian separation between human and nonhuman. René Descartes's response to what is known in philosophy as "the mind/body problem" was to formulate and codify a dualistic understanding of the self—that a human is made of a corporeal, mechanical body and a nonmaterial mind. This dualism bled through much of European-derived philosophy for centuries, shaping approaches to many other issues about which philosophers think (which is to say, most everything). The dualistic understanding of nature and culture has other roots, but the intellectual taproot is planted firmly in a Cartesian dualism, while anthropology currently spends a great deal of energy exploring the natural and the cultural not as separate poles, but as entwined aspects of human life. The newest, best thinking about ecological meanings is taking place in the murky border area, what Anna Tsing calls the frontier where human and nonhuman interact and share identity.[120] Many disciplines are now exploring ecology through something other than a dualistic, Cartesian lens of separate categories of nature and culture. I have no desire to elide these ongoing conversations by simplistically using here the very complicated and very un-universal categories of nature and culture. Rather, I want partially to use maple sugaring as a case study, to see the various theories of "a unified view of world(s) as the combined product of natural and social life," as Hastrup might say, to see the views in action, as it were.[121] Additionally, I want to explore sugarmakers' understandings of the place maple holds in their worlds, a place that often straddles a boundary between their constructs of natural and cultural, of human and nonhuman. Because I am exploring the meanings that sugarmakers and Vermonters in general make with maple, delving into the structuring mechanisms they use is not only useful, but necessary. Even while anthropology questions, complicates, and in some cases outright rejects the dualistic categories of the natural and the cultural, that critique does not negate that nature and culture are categories used by sugarmakers.

Sugaring is increasingly understood as a human process in terms of its impacts on the natural environment, and this chapter delves into the meanings, positive and negative, that maple can have in terms of environmental impact. Again, this is not a discussion of whether tapping a maple is good for the environment or not. Rather, I delve into how people make ecological meanings with maple. Vermont is well known for being an "eco-friendly" place. As ecological awareness becomes more a part of people's identities, the ecological meanings of maple become more prominent not only in the sugaring world, but in the public discourse around Vermont identity. At first glance, it may seem hard to guess the degree to which sugarmakers would be environmentally conscious or eco-friendly. Sugaring in European-derived Vermont has its historical roots in small farming, and farmers certainly pay a particular form of attention to the natural environment and ecology. And Vermont has a mostly deserved reputation for environmental awareness—it is not called "the *Green* Mountain State" for nothing. Granted, the nickname derives from the connection between the name of the state and the French words for "green" and "mountain," *verts* and *monts*, although the Green Mountains seemed to be a placename used in the region before the name "Vermont" was in common currency.[122]

Regardless of the name's origin, Vermont has long had a reputation for its natural resources and an attitude of stewardship and appreciation toward them. Evidence of this part of Vermont's identity can be found in many a tourist shop up and down Church Street, the downtown shopping district of Burlington, the state's largest city. Bumper stickers and t-shirts can be widely found bearing the slogan, "Vermont: We Were Green before it was Cool." It is worth keeping in mind that the omnipresent slogan is evidence of Vermont having eco-friendliness as part of its identity, but not necessarily for Vermont being eco-friendly, by whatever measure one wants to use. Self-reported understandings should always be approached with at least a modicum of caution, so with that in mind, what the t-shirts tell us is that greenness is a part of the self-proclaimed identity of the state that is on display in Burlington.

On the other hand, most of Vermont's sugarmakers are in rural parts of the state (a state made up of mostly rural parts), far conceptually if not geographically from Burlington and Church Street. As can be found in many places, there are standard jokes that recognize the separation (another Cartesian dualistic split, if we want to analyze it) between the city of Burlington and the state of Vermont. Typically, these jokes go something along the lines of, "Burlington is a great place, and the best part about it is that it's right next to Vermont!" or "Burlington is ten square miles surrounded by Vermont," or even more pointedly, "Burlington is ten square miles surrounded by reality." Folklorists can tell you that the same jokes are told about Austin, Texas; Madison, Wisconsin; Portland, Oregon; and many other places (to the point that a website covering the history of Madison has the URL "surroundedbyreality.com"), making the joke less a description of a reality inherent to Burlington, and more a trope-cum-stereotype, a sort of Jungian archetyping of the city and state. The reality that surrounds Burlington in this case is a supposedly more pragmatic approach to life and social issues, as perceived from the rest of the state. Such phrases create an understanding of Vermont that is made up of two parts—the urban and the rural. The separation is pointed out, and indeed embraced, by people living on both sides of this supposed divide. The notion of being joined by something that separates is another common trope in vernacular speech. I've been told by many British friends that, "The US and UK are two cultures separated by a common language," for example. In the "surrounded by reality" construction, Burlington is a place where ideals and idealism can run free, while the rest of the state is thought to have a more practical, realistic view of the way things work. The two are understood to exist in balance.

In the more rural parts of the state, both social conservatism and social liberalism are generally flavored with a strong libertarian bent, not necessarily conducive to the widespread acceptance of traditional definitions of ecological awareness. Sugaring is also rooted conceptually in "old Vermont" (the realities of who all actually sugars aside), and there is a strong current of old-timers-vs-newcomers in the state, similar to the situation in many rural and peripheral areas. Many residents of Vermont, both urban and rural, old and new, attach the popularized form of ecological awareness/eco-friendliness to a post-1960s back-to-the-land mentality, a trait associated with incomers and that unbridled idealism that marks the supposed nonreality of Burlington by one sugarmaker: "Most of it . . . is definitely related to the back to the land movement, so we're talking about the 1960s and 1970s."[123] This connection can be traced back to Helen and Scott Nearing's book, *The Good Life* (1954), which was all about moving to Vermont for a better (understood as "more natural") way of life. The back-to-the-land movement that stems from this form of eco-friendliness prioritizes a "first, do no harm" edict that seems to see human interaction as, at its base, damaging to the natural world, or at least as potentially damaging. This mentality draws directly on the Cartesian human/nonhuman dichotomy, with all its potential to over-romanticize nature (often in this construct, stylized as Nature). The sugar woods are viewable as spaces where people move, live, and interact, with one another and with nature. And they can also be seen as places where improper or thoughtless action can result in dramatic and unpleasant consequences.

The Nearings had published another book four years earlier, *The Maple Sugar Book* (1950), which would seem to be more directly relevant to the topic at hand, the meanings of maple. However, their 1954 book, *The Good Life*, was the book that, if it didn't start a movement, at least can be credited with naming that movement within the United States. "Good Lifers" is a vernacular term for people who come to Vermont from elsewhere seeking what they believe is a more simple, honest, peaceful, and/or authentic way of life. The sense of authenticity comes from a combination of embracing that which is understood as natural and rejecting that which is understood as "too cultural," although that line gets drawn in different places by different people, and even in different places by the same people in different circumstances. Donna Haraway discusses the residual effect of a dualistic nature/culture system when she analyzes how humans think about other species in her book, *When Species Meet*. Wherever the line is drawn in sugaring between the natural and the cultural, the presence of the line is important in a Good Life mentality, because if "one loves organic nature, to express a love of technology makes one suspect."[124] The good life is livable on only one side of a perceived divide between the human and the natural, and humans must leave their side to enter that realm.

For people like the Nearings and their followers, crossing the line to enter that realm is as easy as driving across the Vermont state border. Once there, according to this version of an ecological meaning, a person can live a better, more natural life of simplicity, honesty, peace, and authenticity. Every scholar of social science and many longtime Vermonters will rightly raise an eyebrow at those adjectives—simple, honest, peaceful, and authentic. The term *good life* is not unique to Vermont. A British television series from the 1970s called *The Good Life* centered around a couple in England who attempt to live off the land in their suburban townhouse. Much of the comedy in the series comes from the clash between romanticized ideals of simple living, the realities of the hard work of farming, and the cultural differences between the couple and their neighbors, who live a more typical suburban lifestyle. The same dynamics of ideal surrounded by reality are in play in both Good Lives of the sitcom and the Nearings.

Incomers who move to Vermont often bring a romanticized ecological notion of the place with them, what one sugarmaker jokingly described to me as "a certain yearning to get back up there, a pull . . . call of the wild."[125] He was recognizing and mocking the over-romanticizing of Vermont's wildness and separation from the urban world that infuses many people's image of Vermont, insiders and outsiders alike. Interestingly, an urban part of Vermont—Burlington—is where the idealizing runs free, but the rural parts of the state are very evidently the object of, and made subject to, that idealization as well. In the hills and fields of Vermont, the ideal and the real are in constant negotiation with each other.

The over-romanticizing of a nature that relies on a strong separation between the natural and the cultural is a direct precursor to the concept of the Noble Savage—a person or group who supposedly lives closer to nature and closer to some understanding of the natural state of humans.[126] The hugely problematic notion of the Noble Savage is, at its core, an ecological idea. The key component of the Noble Savage's nobility is in a more natural existence in two senses—living more attuned with and more intimately among nature, and therefore being in a more natural, less culturally corrupted, state of human existence. An ecological meaning is being made when one uses the trope of the Noble Savage, and it is a trope that is used to describe Vermont and Vermonters, albeit without the name. Vermont's appeal to people seeking a Nearing-esque good life is the more natural way of life that can supposedly be found there. The 1960s version of eco-friendliness, rooted in a strong dualism, wants to meet and live among the Noble Savages of rural Vermont, while maintaining its dualistic concepts of nature/culture, insider/outsider, and old/new.

Sugaring, though, is understood as something of old Vermont. Old Vermont is rural but not simplistically natural, as it is a place whose post-contact history is farming. The attention paid to ecology in the agricultural mindset is structured through an interactive lens. People interact and intervene in nature as a matter of course. This different epistemology gives eco-friendliness a different feel from the standardized Nearing version from the 1960s or its descendants of the present day. Farming ecology focuses on stewardship of the land and a sense of intimate interaction between people and nature. Sometimes the relationship is dominant, sometimes it is symbiotic, but in either event people and the nonhuman world are understood to be intimately intertwined, rather than supposed to be potential threats to each other. The dualism is often there, but the gulf between the two sides of nature and culture is not that difficult or dangerous to cross in an agricultural understanding of ecology. Human action is not seen as threat or even potential threat, but as basic to the identity of human and nonhuman both. As Anna Tsing explains in "More-than-Human Sociality," while the "social lives of plants and fungi may or may not include humans . . . it is hard to find a place where humans are not relevant."[127] Sugaring is a place where humans are extremely relevant because they coexist in a nearly symbiotic way with the stands of maples. In this mentality it is the right and proper role of a person to tend the land, take from it what they can, and possibly to leave it in a condition to provide again.

Several sugarmakers expressed this exact sentiment to me when describing their understanding of their role and responsibility to the woods. One sugarmaker made a comparison to gardening, explaining that the forest "is like this patch of carrots, it's so thick that they're mostly still alive, but they're too thick. They'll stay little tiny carrots, but if you thin them out, you're going to have some nice carrots. And it's the same thing with the wood that we cut in here, we don't just go in and mow down a bunch of trees and throw them in the wood shed. . . . We have a written forest management plan. . . . What we're doing is good stewardship."[128] Human interaction, even action that can be seen as destructive, such as thinning the forest by cutting some trees, is understood as proper maintenance and care. Thinning is given eco-logical meaning as purposeful, rather than haphazard, and it is done in a larger context, with a larger eye toward the benefit of the forest as a whole. Having that control is the proper role of the sugarmaker, as the human in this human/nonhuman interaction, and exerting that control does not limit either the human or the nonhuman. In proper interactions, both sides benefit. What this and other sugar-makers expressed to me is a form of design-level thinking, what is popularly called "seeing the big picture." Anthropologist Tim Ingold has long been arguing for the application of design-level thinking in understanding people, nature, and the intertwined roles of the two in forming and participating in an ecosystem. He argues that, "rather than setting the parameters for our habitation of the earth, design is part and parcel of the very process of dwelling."[129] What Ingold discusses as design is the same set of meanings that the sugarmaker above describes as good stewardship. The purposeful interaction with nature that has as its aim the continued ability to interact in such ways, or at least in reasonably acceptable versions of those ways, is Ingold's design thinking. Sugarmakers who take a long-term view and manage the forest not just for themselves, but for some sense of posterity, and not just for the trees that are cut but the forest as a whole, are thinking with design, and thereby dwelling in and with the forest in a more sustainable manner. Ingold's dwelling implies a sense of awareness, purpose, and higher-level point of view, and that is exactly what many sugarmakers see as their role in controlling and stewarding the forest.

The most obvious root of this approach, at least in a Vermont context that is predominantly Protestant Christian, is Genesis from the Old Testament, where Adam is given dominion over the land and the creatures within it. The dualistic approach discussed at the beginning of the chapter, which plants maple and person on strongly separated ends of a spectrum, is undergirded by an understanding that the separation suggests, and perhaps demands, one end of the spectrum (our human end) to exert rule, control, and usage over the other. Dominion can sound an awful lot like a hierarchical separation, and certainly it can be understood that way, especially in a New England context that is not that far removed historically or conceptually from a legacy of European colonialism, as Vassos Argyrou discusses in his exploration of colonialism's influence on environmentalism. "It is difficult today to understand the nonchalance with which European 'man' proclaimed his power over the physical world. It appears as sheer arrogance—indeed, for many environmentalists, nothing less than hubris. It is even more difficult to understand the uninhibited manner in which he denigrated all those 'men' who were different from him."[130] The separateness of human and nonhuman that a dualistic model requires, and the dominion/domination that follows, seem almost quaintly absurd today, but this epistemology held sway for a long time and still does for some. But the form of control I encountered among sugarmakers that is rooted in (and justified by) such a biblical reading necessitates direct involvement and interaction of the controller and the controlled. It is a fairly parental relationship, where the control is interpreted to be in the best interest of the things over which dominion is held.

Post-1960s understandings of ecology can take several different forms, starting with the approach of the Nearings and their followers that is strongly dualistic. This preservationist mentality holds a firm sense of humans and nonhumans as fundamentally different entities, seeing each other on an alien shore until they are made to share space. The sense of separation here between the natural and the cultural worlds causes any human involvement to be seen as a potential threat to nature's harmony. The next form of ecological understanding is an eco-friendliness that shifts to a conservation mentality that acknowledges humans as an integral part of the ecosystem. The root of both "ecology" and "ecosystem" is the Greek word *oikos*, which literally means "house" or "household," the implication being "a place and everything in that place." The "everything" is very important here, as it implies that all the parts of the system relate to one another in some way. In this approach, people are not separate from nature (or at least not *as* separate), and they have a valid role to play in interacting with the environment.

The most recent form of ecological understanding to emerge is the current focus on sustainability, which brings a diachronic dimension to the mix, viewing human/nonhuman interaction as a thing that unfolds over time. The focus on process, on actions unfolding, in this approach is explained by Tim Ingold when he says that sustainability "is not about projections and targets, or about the achievement of a steady state. It is about keeping life going."[131] Sustainability is not about the static, or maintaining a status quo. Instead, it looks along a path of change and process, recognizes that parts of an ecosystem are moving along that path, and tries to keep them going, as Ingold puts it. These latter two forms of eco-awareness share many similarities to the stewardship model from agriculture discussed above. The threat-to-harmony school of thought relies on an understanding of ecosystem as balanced, sometimes precariously so, among many different, interrelated forces. The image of a fine china dish in a vaudeville plate spinner's show, teetering, spinning quietly and gently on the end of a pool cue, comes to mind. To this approach, drilling a hole in a tree to collect sap has the potential to knock the plate off its delicate perch, just as a stiff breeze could. The conservation and sustainability models view tapping a tree with less trepidation because of the greater involvement of human and nonhuman in those versions of the system.

Conservation and sustainability have become more prominent in ecological discussions as time has rolled on from the 1960s to the present. Of course, ecological discussions did not start in the 1960s, but the particular form of eco-friendliness that is found in Vermont is rooted firmly in (among other places) the sixties good life approach that sees people as threat to nature, while viewing a more natural way of living a form of nobility. Environmental science tells us that the fine china trope of the delicate, fragile, sustained balance may not be the best metaphor, though. Ecosystems exist not in states of stasis, but as a form of "dynamic equilibrium" that is capable of adjusting and correcting itself.[132] Instead of an ecosystem that is finely tuned, with every part in its place until humans come along and muck it up, many ecosystems are the result of long series of sharp disruptions, over-corrections, and adjustments, including human actions. The plate is not balancing gently by itself—it is wobbling violently and constantly because of internal forces (including us), and then being brought back into alignment, if only for a moment. If this understanding is brought to bear on sugaring, then the goal of human interaction in the system is to understand them as parts of the system, and to time and balance the effects of the wobbles, so that the plate doesn't get knocked off the cue.

Sugaring then sits in a liminal space between old Vermont agricultural understandings of stewardship ecology that is rooted in the rural, and a new Vermont good life understanding of eco-friendliness that is rooted also in the rural, albeit an idealized rural, viewed through the imported lens of Burlingtonian urban romanticism. Sugaring often exists at a point where those two epistemologies converge in some measure. To be clear, I am not suggesting that these are mutually exclusive categories, or that farming is somehow "unfriendly" to the environment as a matter of course. The terminology is convenient shorthand based on vernacular usage, rather than definitional. As maple becomes more a trope in the culinary and economic worlds, it becomes more a public face of Vermont for visitors and incomers. At the same time, the narrative of being deeply rooted in the place with a sense of long history is part of maple's appeal to the foodie, which necessitates that the old story and the new culinary sensibility maintain each other. It is in this complicated mix that ecological meanings are made with maple.

So, how do all of these streams of influence come together for sugarmakers? What ecological meanings does Vermont make with sugaring? Is sugaring an environmentally threatening action, or is it the natural way of human/nonhuman interaction? Does it accord with the ecosystem, or violate it?

Interestingly, one of the major threads that came out of my conversations with sugarmakers was not so much that sugaring is or isn't a threat to the environment, but that the environment could be a threat to sugaring. Many of the sugarmakers who have spoken with me are very aware of climate change, particularly as it relates to the northern drift of climatic growing zones in North America. Every sugarmaker I know is keenly aware of the geographic boundedness of maple sugaring, and many spoke of a slow crawl northward of the southern and northern edges of the area where sugarable maples grow. While there are doubtless others who would do so, I heard only one sugarmaker who questioned the veracity of climate change science. The consensus among those who spoke about climate change with me was that it is a reality, and it is a threat to the long-term sustainability of sugaring in Vermont. My expectation that a general social libertarianism might lead to a wider suspicion of climate change science did not pan out in my experience. It was overridden by a stewardship sense for the trees specifically and the land in general, both of which are parts of sugaring's heritage. Because sugarmakers interact so intimately with the trees, the land, and the climate, they understand the complex webs of identity that are made among the different parts of an ecosystem. "If we want to know about environmental change, we need to know about the social worlds other species help to build."[133] Sugarmakers know those species and those worlds Anna Tsing mentions because they spend much of their daily and yearly routines in direct contact with them.

A form of ecological awareness spans the liminal space, the supposed divide between "old" and "new" Vermonters, then, drawing on traits of both ends of that spectrum. As the old Vermont agricultural sense of stewardship converges with the new Vermont sense of sustainability, the two systems of meaning start to resemble each other more and more. There are significant differences that remain, but in the case of sugaring, both mentalities share an analysis that sugaring (at least when done well) is a valid and sustainable form of human/nonhuman interaction. The sense of stewardship of the land is a strong theme in sugaring, and this comes as no surprise to anyone who has ever walked lines with a sugarmaker.

Walking lines is a constant ritual in sugaring. It means to walk through the sugarbush, following the tracks of the tubing that collects and centralizes the sap that is being drawn from the trees. Walking the lines before the season starts is a must, to catch any damage done to the lines by wind, snow, deer, squirrels, and so on. The need to keep an eye on the tubing does not stop when the sap starts flowing, either, as leaks in a tubing system can negatively affect vacuum pressure, or cause blockages due to freezing, loss of sap as it runs on the ground, and any number of other problems. Much of a sugarmaker's time is spent in the woods checking tubing. In these times, a most direct form of interaction with the land and trees is the norm. One man, who had experience in both sugaring and forestry, described why he likes to walk lines: "One of the things I like about sugaring is that, typically in forestry, you visit a tree maybe two or three times in its life, or in your life . . . with sugaring we visit every tree six, eight, ten times a year."[134] Because sugaring is an intensive year-round activity, each tree will become a very familiar entity to a conscientious sugarmaker. In the days of widespread collection on buckets, each tap had to be visited regularly during sugaring season, as each tap meant a solitary bucket whose contents would need collected, sometimes daily, sometimes more often in a heavy run. With tubing, the need to check each tree or each tap daily is no longer there, but the need to check tubing has replaced it. Because the maintenance of tubing systems can be spread out throughout the year, the number of visits to each tree has not necessarily decreased from the days of buckets—the visits have just been shifted from one intense period of about six weeks to whenever during the year the sugarmaker has time to get into their woods and inspect their lines. Some sugarmakers do these inspections late in winter, just before sugaring usually begins, while others get into their woods in the summer and fall, when the weather is often more conducive to spending time among the trees. Regardless of when it is done, every sugarmaker with tubing walks their lines.

Inspecting the tubing and inspecting the landscape go hand in hand. When sugarmakers are walking their lines, what they are really inspecting is not just the land, not just the tubing, and not just both. It is the intersection of the landscape (the natural) and the tubing system (the cultural) that is really being brought under the eye. It is the meeting of these two supposedly different worlds that is at the heart of sugaring, and a keen awareness of that intersection is fundamental to the identity of a sugarmaker. When walking their lines, sugarmakers are completely aware of the *oikos*, that place and everything that is in it, and they take into account and blend the ends of any dualisms they might hold.

This is not to say that sugarmakers do not see their land and trees as a separate entity. While I was walking the woods with them, many sugarmakers knew each of their trees individually and could tell me how much per tap each produced last year and the year before. A few even told me how much per tap a tree produced for their father and grandfather, as they were tapping it themselves now for another year. This long sense of time scale is strongly suggestive of the sustainability approach to eco-friendliness discussed above, with a sense of unfolding over time. Many sugarmakers are keenly aware of the health of their land, not just in terms of this year or even within their lifetime, but in terms of generations, giving a strong diachronic view to their understanding of their sugar woods.

The longer sense of time scale doubtless is related to the nature of sugaring as an agricultural process. Sugaring draws from trees, rather than reaping them. Even though sugarmakers talk about their maples, the product they are collecting from the field is not the plant itself, but the sap. A tree planted now will not be available for sugaring for many years, which makes the botanical life cycle with which a sugarmaker interacts one of decades, not a single year. This difference in scale made for a different negotiation of responsibility, according to one sugarmaker who explained the historic attitudes about the environment of past sugarmakers. "Those folks had a real stewardship ethic, and they realized that taking care of their woods was a long-term responsibility with a long-term, nice payback."[135] This fact lends itself well to a sustainability approach to ecology. Sugarmakers need to think far into the past and far down the road, because the trees' life spans are so long compared to other agricultural plants. Putting seed corn into the ground creates an expectation and hope of cutting a corn plant off that patch of ground in just a few months' time, but planting a maple creates an expectation and hope (with perhaps a greater percentage of hope in the mix in this case) that a descendant will tap that tree one day. Because sugaring is part of the heritage of the area, it is understood to have been passed down from, and to be capable of being passed onto, following generations. A diachronic view fits in well with these conditions, leading to both the sustainability model and the stewardship model.

Recent research and development out of the Proctor Maple Research Center may change this long-term view that sugaring engenders, though. In 2013, two research scientists at the University of Vermont, Abby van den Berg and Tim Perkins, happened upon a new method for extracting maple sap that involves much younger trees than is the norm.[136] It is still experimental and in need of further research, but this new approach is fundamentally different and worthy of attention here because it radically alters the ecological meanings that can be connected to sugaring. The method involves taking the entire crown off a young maple sapling, between five and ten years old, and placing the open, chest-high stump under vacuum pressure similar to that from the vacuum lines used by many sugarmakers in their tubing systems.

There are two very important differences in this system, compared to what is understood as usual sugaring. First, the age of the trees that provide the sap is much younger—a sugar maple should be a few decades old (forty years is an oft-quoted number) before it is tapped. Second, the younger trees can be purposefully spaced much more densely, in what the researchers describe as a plantation setup. With this new method, planting maples as a resource plant to be reaped by the planter becomes much more possible, as opposed to acquiring land that happened to have trees mature enough for tapping on it. This approach is little short of revolutionary. As one of the researchers, van den Berg, explains in a 2013 article from the

University of Vermont, "this changes the basic paradigm . . . we could deal with an entirely new framework" for sugaring.[137] An entirely new framework, a basic paradigm . . . what she is describing is not just a change in the mechanics of sugaring, but also in the epistemology of sugaring—the system of meaning making that one must use to understand this form of sugaring. The meanings that people can and will make, if this new method of sugaring becomes a reality and spreads, are going to change, not least on the ecological level.

The use of the term *plantation* to describe the potentially new form of sugaring points out another fundamental shift in ecological meaning. A plantation is a form of farm, and as such a form of farming. The sense of stewardship that comes from Vermont's agricultural past would seem to translate right over to this new form of sugaring, if it indeed ever comes into public production. However, the stewardship of the Vermont farmer is of a person over the land in a relatively close relationship, as discussed above. The term *plantation* brings to mind images of large-scale, orderly crops and more than a little power and hierarchy. In a US context, "plantation" is strongly connected with southern slavery, so the feelings of power and hierarchy are both more present and more insidious. The term carries similar meanings in the UK, where plantation agriculture was practiced in many of England's colonies, often with slave or immensely disempowered labor. However, even if one were to remove that part of the story, a plantation still suggests a more orderly and controlled form of farming, with a greater gap between the farmer and that which is being farmed. The space between the human and the nonhuman in plantation agriculture is conceptually wider and more difficult to transcend. Such a large gap simply does not fit with Vermont's version of agricultural or ecological identity.

Those images run counter to Vermont's sense of its farming identity because Vermont farming is paradigmatically small. Small farms, small workforces on each farm, and small scales of production are all impinged by the concept of a plantation. The plantation also violates the Vermont sense of ecological awareness that pervades both farming and the urban-ideal-based eco-friendliness of the state. A plantation is about humans ordering nature, even dominating nature. Vermont's ecological sensibilities run more toward peaceful interaction and coexistence as a part of the dynamic equilibrium, which makes the concept of a plantation seem very foreign and a bit jarring. Sugaring, with its paradigmatic place in Vermont at the intersection of the natural and the cultural, seems an especially egregious spot to put a plantation. The ecological meanings that that word, and that form of farming, tend to convey would at the very least necessitate a rethinking of what it means ecologically to sugar in Vermont.

In addition to the change in the meanings of power in this new flavor of sugaring, the sense of diachrony, while not disappearing entirely, alters radically. With sugaring as it's been practiced for generations, sugarmakers interact with trees that stretch back at least for decades, but the new plantation model uses trees less than a decade old. The biological life span that a sugarmaker interacts with changes from generational to a span of a few years, and the ecological meaning shifts from sustainability and stewardship to something closer to other forms of agriculture. For most farmed plants, the cycle unfolds usually over a single year from planting to reaping, while many animals are farmed on increments of at most a few years. The way sugaring is currently done more or less demands that a sugarmaker looks backward and forward for decades and across generations. The new method allows an individual to think of their ecological impact as occurring entirely within their life span. I do not want to indulge in any sort of ecological determinism here, thus my use of "demand" and "allow" in the two previous sentences. The ecological epistemology can promote and dissuade, provide possibilities and impossibilities, but it can never create wholly, so this new form of sugaring can strongly shape the way sugarmakers understand their craft, but never determine it. The ability to think in chronological terms as short as five or ten years is a departure from the longer time scale of sugaring as it has been practiced for a few generations in Vermont. Like the change in power dynamic, a new sense of time scale would be a huge change in ecological meaning.

The long time scale that marks sugaring as it is now practiced would also seem to conduce to an awareness of, and concern about, climate change. The looking back over generations of time and looking forward to generations with hope of continued sugaring make larger trends in weather more obvious a topic of consideration and perhaps concern. Even more, because sugaring is so dependent on the weather of a given season, many sugarmakers pay either explicit or implicit attention to changes and trends in weather over a span of years or even decades.[138] I visited more than one sugarhouse that had records of syrup production going back to grandparents. In at least a couple cases, these records were inscribed right onto the sugarhouse walls in more than one hand, suggesting that the recordkeeping act spread over generations along with the sugaring. Writing the memories of maple seasons past directly onto the walls of the sugarhouse is a form of capturing and chronicling the process. It is captured not just for the immediate moment, but preserved for posterity to recall and to add to as new sugaring seasons pass.

A couple sugarmakers showed me notes kept by ancestors of the weather conditions in seasons past. Even a simple recording of the start and end dates of sugaring is instructive, keeping in mind the fairly specific weather conditions involved. Barring the use of vacuum, temperature swings from below freezing overnight to above about 40° F in the day are needed to make a sap run worth sugaring, so recording the dates when sugaring occurs secondarily records when in the year those temperatures occur. To track the trends in when the season starts and when it ends is to pay attention to the weather year by year, and the climate over time. Seeing trends that indicate basic changes over time is recognizing changes in the climate. While "changes in the climate" and "climate change" may not be exactly the same, there is some overlap in those two terms. Sugarmakers are very used to paying attention to changes in weather over large spans of time.

In this way, sugaring is a sort of canary in the ecological coal mine. Because sugaring is so strongly tied to the state's identity, an ecological threat to sugaring such as climate change is felt very closely by many Vermonters, as a threat to themselves. While in some places, climate change is understood as a diffuse threat, perhaps specified only in general terms of an infringement on "our way of life," in Vermont, the threat is very immediate and very specific. Maple is an ecological thing in terms of both the trees themselves (the natural) and the process and product (the cultural). Regardless of how dualistic one's view or the understanding of the relationship one has, because maple is inherently ecological, an ecological threat is a threat to maple. Because maple and state identity are so inextricably linked in the Vermont imaginary, a threat to one is a threat to the other. To be Vermont is to be eco-*something*, at the very least. Climate change is a change to the *oikos*, and the threat of that resonates on a general "way of life" level throughout the state, much as it does in other places. Additionally, maple sugaring, which is so intimately tied to the state's identity, is understood to be very climate-sensitive, or more specifically weather-sensitive because of the direct roles swings in temperature play in the running of the sap. The trees and the syrup are dependent on the weather, and changes in the reliability of the patterns of weather are going to be felt as the potential loss of trees, syrup, or both. So, the ecological threat of climate change resonates on many other levels in Vermont, not only as some vague, diffuse threat to "our way of life."

Not all ecological awareness in the state is about threat and change, however. There are ecological understandings that are not about people threatening nature or nature threatening people. As is the case in many communities, the simple realities of the weather are a common topic of conversation on the streets and across the fences of Vermont. I am always amused and fascinated at the prevalence of conversations about the weather in places where I have done research. I'm especially intrigued by the standard tropes that I have heard over and over, such as "if you don't like the weather, wait ten minutes and it'll change." I've heard this one on four different continents, in at least five different languages. Vermont is no different in breaking out that old saw, but there is an understandable logic to it in the state because of the variations in the land and weather.

Because of the terrain, Vermont does not typically get a broad wash of one weather type or event that covers half the state. I grew up in western Ohio, where a weather event could easily cover an area of a dozen counties at a time. Moving to Vermont, where there are barely more than a dozen counties to begin with, the weather is in places variable valley by valley.[139] This pattern was a different experience for me, one more akin to my time in coastal Norway, where the close presence of the ocean and the many mountain ridges running perpendicular to the shore creates a series of small climate zones up and down the coast. Vermont is a small geographic area, but it is bounded by Lake Champlain on much of its west side and the Connecticut

River on its east, with the Green Mountain range running south and north right down the spine of the state. A thorough overview of Vermont's geography is maintained by St. Michael's College and the Vermont Geographic Alliance.[140] The Green Mountains have many ridges shooting off in various approximations of perpendicularity, providing a lot of elevation changes over such a small area of land. All of these features mean that the weather pattern in the state is one of many small, relatively localized weather areas. The running of maple sap is very weather-dependent, which is what confines the sugaring season to the beginning months of the year. The sap is made to run in quantity by internal fluid pressures in the tree, caused by a freeze-thaw cycle of a certain increment and length. This is why sugaring occurs when the overnight temperatures are below freezing, and the daytime temperatures are a bit above that level. That balance and swing of temperatures produces the freezing and thawing that creates the fluid pressures within the tree that cause sap to run in the vast quantities that a maple is capable of producing. Sugarmakers for millennia have tapped into that particular moment of pressure in the trees to claim an angel's share of the sap. Vacuum systems, attached to the tubing used to collect sap, are effective not, as is commonly thought, by sucking the sap out of the trees like a straw in a milkshake. Vacuum systems work by slightly lowering the external air pressure right at the taphole, thereby widening the narrow range of pressure change necessary to cause a strong sap flow from inside to out. So, sap will flow into a tubing system that is under vacuum with a less drastic swing in temperatures, thus increasing the overall sap yield.

As stated before, sugarmakers generally hold that the sap runs when the air temperature drops below freezing overnight and rises above about 40° F during the day. With all the micro-scale weather variances that occur across the state, it is easy to understand that the sap can be running well in some places and not in others, with little large-scale coherence to the map. Because this is true, sugarmakers' knowledge of their woods' local ecology extends to knowing which slopes will get morning sun, which ones tend to collect deeper snow pack, which ones hold runoff longer, and a host of other traits. The right combination of traits affects when that magic temperature swing occurs, all of which then affects when and how strongly the trees will produce. It is a simple enough thing to say that the sap runs between this temperature and that, but to know precisely when those conditions will occur at any given spot in a woods requires a whole other level of awareness of the local ecology. Such awareness of the physical environment is second nature to many sugarmakers. Their local ecology is immensely and intensely meaningful.

Those who sugar are aware of dependences beyond just the weather. Maples are closer to wild than cultivated, as very few people plant maples with an eye to sugaring them themselves, and most people think of a sugarbush as a thing that is there, rather than a thing to be created. This is not to say that the human involvement in a sugarbush is unknown or ignored, or as one sugarmaker expressed, "We don't actually plant the tree—that procedure takes care of itself—but without us, most of the trees might not make it . . . we tend that tree a lot."[141] But the awareness is always there that sugaring approaches pretty closely some perceived line between the natural and cultural worlds, more so even than other types of farming. The nearness of the approach makes the natural world a more immediate concern for sugarmakers. One told me that a sugarmaker is "totally at the mercy of the weather, or we stand to have real problems over it. Environmental things or global economy things like the Asian longhorn beetle could wipe us out in a couple years."[142]

The whole ecosystem is part of sugaring's awareness, and any part of the system that is off kilter is a cause for concern. The Asian longhorn beetle, for example, is an invasive insect species whose larvae feed on the inner bark of several species of tree, including maple.[143] Stopping the spread of the Asian longhorn beetle is an enormous concern for many people involved in sugaring, from the backyard sugarmaker to the Montpelier policymaker. The ecological meanings being made with this insect are along the lines of Hollywood disaster movies, where the asteroid or tidal wave threatens everything in its path. In the old wake of threats like Dutch elm disease, the potential danger to a whole species of trees does not seem hyperbolic, as Joe Cavey, insect expert inspector at the US government's Animal and Plant Health Inspection Service, says: "This is a bad animal."[144] So the Asian longhorn is a very meaningful bit of ecology for sugarmakers at the moment.

Because sugaring treads a path very close to the natural world, knowledge of the natural world and its potential interactions with the cultural world is very common among sugarmakers. There is a sense of intimacy with the woods that is widespread among those who sugar, which comes from being very involved in their woods. One Vermonter familiar with the forest ecology planning involved in sugaring explained that some people "seem to think that what they want to do is go in and treat the forest once, and not have to ever do it again. And of course that's not really understanding the forest because you can't set up a sugarbush once and never go back again."[145] The level of involvement necessary to run a sugaring operation means that the boundary between the natural and the cultural is almost nonexistent, if one works with that construct in the first place. By constantly being in and among the trees, working very closely on the landscape, sugarmakers build a familiarity that becomes an intimacy. The closeness of and to the natural world is both potential danger and source of comfort. In more than one instance, I have been taken aback by the easy, uncomplicated pleasure I have heard in the voices and seen in the strides of a sugarmaker while we walked through their woods. The sense of comfort was often greater, even, than when we were in the sugarhouse. Being in the woods and knowing the woods is part and parcel of the identity of many of the sugarmakers I have met.

In the same vein as knowing what surrounds their trees, knowing what is *under* them can shape a sugarmaker's expectation for their sap run as well. Just as with the small, interspersed climate zones, Vermont is a map of many small geomorphological zones.[146] Geomorphology is the study of the soil and land, what it is made of, how it is shaped, and the historical and geological processes that have resulted in that shape. The type of soil—clayey, loamy, sandy—as well as the characteristics of that soil—acidic or alkaline, high or low in certain minerals—can vary widely from one valley to the next in Vermont.

Sugarmakers who know their local area can and do read the land to gain understandings that they can apply to their sugaring process. "Ledge," for example, is the Vermont vernacular term for bedrock that is relatively near the soil surface. Because of the relatively thin soil strata in many parts of the state, ledge is often just beneath the surface, sometimes above. When it breaks the surface, its horizontal layers form natural shelves sticking out of hillsides or up from the ground (hence the name "ledge"). The presence of lenses of clay in otherwise more friable soils or the proximity of ledge are very unevenly and irregularly distributed around the state, and these soil characteristics have a strong effect on the vegetation that grows there. Sugarmakers all across the state are keenly aware of the importance of the soil to the syrup. One sugarmaker in the thick of the Green Mountains explained how much the underlayment shaped the syrup on his and his neighbors' properties: "you get into a specific syrup up and down the west side of the Green Mountains where the marble, limestone part of it. Even the guys over here in [another town], I can't make as light syrup as they do. We're stuck here on the slate muck, and slate doesn't produce the kind of light syrup that the marble does."[147] This man is a paradigm of "old-timer," so he is not one you might expect to embrace a French culinary concept like *terroir*, the idea that the physical characteristics of a place shape the culinary qualities of foods that come from that place. He's not evoking *terroir*, at least not as such. He is using a meaning-making system that Vermont sugarmakers have used for generations, applying an understanding of the soil to an understanding of the syrup. Even his syntax makes it clear how strong the connection is—slate doesn't produce light syrup, marble does. The rocks make the syrup what it is. The relationship between soil type and syrup is immediate, to the point that it doesn't even need to be discussed with the mediating steps of the trees or the sugarmaker. The soil type makes the syrup what it is, and other soils make other kinds of syrup.

Maples can occur among other species such as oak, birch, butternut, beech, or hemlock, and different species of maple like different conditions (Lovett and Mitchell 2004). Across the state, there are several different forest types, many of which include species of maple. Historically, the best forest type for sugaring is known as a northern hardwood forest, consisting of maples, birches, beeches, and ashes. Other types do include enough maples to make sugaring economically viable, though, even if those forests were not historically understood as the best bets for sugaring. Technologies such as vacuum and reverse osmosis have made sugaring on other stands of woods more feasible, which brings sugaring into lands that used to be marginal, according to one Vermonter. She told me how some forest stands "that are being tapped now are really not northern hardwood stands. They're hemlock hardwood, they're red maple swamps. There's a lot of things being tapped out there that would *never* have *ever* entered into the world of sugaring prior to [2005]."[148] In times past, a high concentration of sugar maples was necessary to make sugaring worthwhile because a sugarmaker needed a high percent of sugar in the sap to begin with. Sugar maples typically have at least 2 percent sugar, but can have as much as 7 percent, while other species often dip below 2 percent, making them less viable to tap without the assistance of vacuum (which increases the amount of sap drawn from a tree in a season) or RO (which concentrates the sugar in the sap before boiling begins). Both technologies mean a lower sap content out of the tree is still feasible for sugaring, which makes more stands of trees more capable of being tapped for syrup production. The knowledge of the trees directly influences how and where sugaring is done. Knowing what type of woods and what type of soil a sugarbush calls home can tell a sugarmaker quite a bit about what to expect from the trees when tapped. Between the air temperatures, the slope, the amount of limestone in the soil, and the sunshine, a sugarmaker certainly benefits by having an *oiko*-systemic understanding of the sugarbush.

Vermont's ecology, which is more friendly to sugar maples, helps make the state of central importance in the sugaring world. The predominance of the sugar or rock maple (*Acer saccharum*) is one of the reasons Vermont is understood as so central in sugaring. There are plenty of parts of the state where red maples (*Acer rubrum*) or silver maples (*Acer saccharinum*) dominate, but Vermont has more concentrations of sugar maple than many regions. In other places, different species of maple are more suited to the local ecology, which allows sugaring, but because sugar maples tend to have a higher concentration of sugar in their sap, it is easier and more cost-effective to sugar on sugar maples. Even a place as far away as Korea has species of maples that are tapped, especially *Acer mono*, which can have a sugar content over 2 percent, but the sap is generally consumed raw, rather than boiled down.[149] While the ideas of maple and sugaring are often used synonymously, Vermont's higher concentration of sugar maple due to its ecology make it very central in the maple sugaring world, if not necessarily the maple world in a botanical sense.

Many threads of information from many different realms feed into a sugarmaker's decision making. This depth and breadth of knowledge is necessary to sugaring because all of these varied factors shape not only the process, but also the product. Sugaring on a stand that is primarily north-facing slope will determine when one should be boiling, but it can also determine whether the syrup that ultimately results will tend lighter or darker, with a fruitier sweetness or a more molasses or caramel flavor. Just as sugarmakers pay attention to which stands and which trees are producing a lot of sap in a given year, they are also paying attention to what kind of syrup is being produced from each set of ecological conditions. Translating the conditions to the final product is sometimes straightforward, sometimes not. Knowing that a certain stand will begin producing earlier in a season might suggest that the resulting syrup will be lighter in color and possibly flavor. Knowing that a stand is in a low spot, and therefore full of more red maples than sugar maples, will suggest that the syrup might have a bit more mineral flavor. The species of maples tend to produce sap with flavor characteristics distinctive to the species. For example, the sugar maple (*Acer saccharum*, which gets its alternate name of "rock maple" because it likes to grow on dry ground, often where the ledge is very close to the surface) tends to produce the sap with the highest sugar concentration, hence the more common name, "sugar maple," although how much of that tendency is the species and how much is the terrain it prefers is a question. Red maple (*Acer rubrum*), on the other hand, can produce sap with a less sweet, more mineral flavor to it, depending on where it is growing. These are just tendencies, and as with all things in sugaring, the local conditions and situation can override tendency.

These connections between the soil, air, and other conditions and the end result product have been widely known and used among sugarmakers for generations. As discussed in my other chapter on the culinary meanings of maple, these connections are called *terroir*, the French culinary concept that dates back long in that culture. A fuller discussion of *terroir* is available in that chapter, but it is worth noting here that *terroir* is at least as much an ecological concept as it is a culinary one. Even though the word is entering the English-speaking world through its application to food, the real importance of the idea is the connection between a food item and all of the many variables that make up the ecosystem from which it comes. The definition of *terroir* quoted by Amy Trubek from *The Oxford Companion to Wine* captures the importance of the *oikos* in understanding *terroir*: "the total natural environment of any viticultural site ... climate as measured by temperature and rainfall; sunlight energy or insolation, received per unit of land surface area; relief (or topography or geomorphology), comprising altitude, slope and aspect; geology and pedology determining a soil's basic physical and chemical characteristics; hydrology, or soil-water relations."[150] This definition captures the importance of the natural environment and its many, varied traits in understanding *terroir*. Clearly, the ecology of a place can be understood as important, even vital, to understanding the flavors it produces. Sugarmakers have known of this relationship for quite some time, and it shows in the amount and kind of attention that they pay to the land, air, and water within which their maples exist. Even in far-flung Newfoundland, where maple sugaring exists as a backyard hobby at most, intense knowledge of local environmental conditions comes to the fore. I was talking with a couple who sugar in and around St. John's, which is about as far east as one can go in North America without falling into the Atlantic Ocean. This couple told me about how the presence of an iceberg in the St. John's harbor, a not infrequent occurrence in the springtime, makes the sap run at triple or quadruple the rate of a normal day. The harbor, which points more or less right at Greenland, catches icebergs that wander south from the Artic in the spring, and the changes in temperature, humidity, and barometric pressure that result when one floats into the harbor apparently have a noticeable effect on the local maples. It would be easy to dismiss such a statement as local color, but the fact that the sap runs are caused by fluctuations in the internal pressures of the trees makes it seem at least plausible. Even that far from the center of sugaring, a keen awareness of local conditions matters.

A *terroir* approach to sugaring fits nicely into that intersection of the stewardship and sustainability models. While *terroir* itself does not have much of a diachronic aspect to it, it does have a sense of holism, of taking into account as much as possible. The holism of that approach is reflected in the holistic parts of stewardship and sustainability, as well as the breadth of knowledge streams involved in all forms of farming. That analysis makes perfect sense, when one really stops to think about ecology. To have an understanding of ecology is to have an understanding of the ecosystem. I have already discussed the role of the eco-, the *oikos*, in ecosystemic understandings, but let's not forget about the other half of that word. An ecosystem is just that—a system. The stewardship and sustainability models both strive to take as much into account as possible. They attempt holism. As can be seen from the Robinson quotation above, *terroir* attempts to be holistic as well, to account for the household and everything in it. One step beyond that is to pay attention to how all the parts in the *oikos* interact and interrelate. That is the system of the ecosystem. The interrelationship suggests diachrony as well, as two things don't interact without the unfolding of some action between them, that is, they act on each other over time.

The difference between understanding something, and understanding that something unfolding over time, is huge and not to be underestimated. I am reminded of a passage from Book VII of Plato's *Republic*, wherein Glaucon and Socrates are talking about the education of philosophers. They are debating what subjects are the most important for a philosopher to know. The first three disciplines, they end up agreeing, are forms of math: numeracy, plane geometry, and solid geometry. The fourth is astronomy, which seems to be a departure from the first three, but in actuality isn't. If simple numeracy deals with that which has zero dimensions (abstract numbers and counting), plane geometry handles things with one and two dimensions (lines and shapes), and solid geometry covers the three-dimensional (solids), then astronomy deals with solid objects (planets, stars) that are *in motion relative to one another*. Motion is simply a change in position, understood as unfolding over time. The fourth dimension, commonly understood as time, is really duration, or a recognition of existence over a span of time. Astronomy is, in this way, just applied geometry with an eye for the diachronic. Having astronomy as the next in the series of disciplines recognizes both the connectedness and the important differences in paying attention to something and paying attention over time.

An ecosystemic understanding of sugaring, that sits between and combines the stewardship and sustainability approaches, takes a step toward a more fully cultural cultural ecology. The holism I discuss here takes into account not only the physical features of *terroir* as aspects of the natural environment, but also the lived experience of those aspects. The particular set of environmental phenomena from the ecology that become the food item are understood as experiences of people and given meaning by people. But doing so is indeed a choice. Often, it is a choice people make unconsciously or automatically because of our trained norms, but we make our ecology epiphenomenal when it suits our sensibilities and desires.

Vermont desires to make ecological meanings with maple. For people in the state, sugarmaker or no, maple is a phenomenon that is laden with symbolic properties, which are at least as important to the state as the mechanical properties of sugaring, such as the energy it takes or the money it makes. The ecology is a thing that is lived and experienced, indeed it is *made*, by people in their interactions with it. Maple sits at a very useful junction for all people in Vermont then, as it occupies a place of intersection between the natural and the cultural, and it is overtly *process*—maple is lived, done, and made by people *doing things over time*. So, sugaring functions nicely for both sugarmakers and non-sugarmakers in making a sense of Vermont. Ecology is understood as some sort of lived and living thing, perhaps as a system of lived and living things, and Vermont's green identity meshes well with the lived experience of sugaring. For sugarmakers, the lived experience is enacted every season when the sap runs and the sugarhouse fills with steam from the pan. For non-sugarmakers, the lived experience is all around them in various forms as well. In open sugarhouse weekends, locals and tourists both have a chance to visit a sugarhouse and be bathed in the steam from the pan as well. The widespread use of maple leaf logos on businesses, organizations, and other entities makes maple a constant part of living in or moving through Vermont. And every visitor to the state who isn't lactose-intolerant has been tempted by the ubiquitous maple creamee. A maple creamee is soft-serve ice cream that is flavored with maple syrup, a very popular treat with locals and visitors alike.

Even Vermonters who have never tapped a tree or drawn off a batch of syrup can lay claim to the ecological meaning of sugaring, as it deals explicitly with the whole ecosystem at the intersection of the human and the nonhuman. Maple is useful to make ecological meanings for insiders and outsiders alike—sugarmakers and non-sugarmakers, Vermonters and incomers—partly because the narrative of maple is so widespread and so evocative. As discussed in other chapters, the story of maple is used in manifold ways by various groups throughout the state, and because that story focused on a process that sits at that nexus of the human and the nonhuman, it makes for a powerful source of ecological meaning.

CHAPTER 5

The Agricultural Meaning of Maple

Depends on what part of it you're talking about, I guess, and if you talk to the IRS, they have their silly rules . . . if it's inside the sugarhouse, hell no it's not farming—it's manufacturing. If it's outside the sugarhouse, oh yeah, it's farming. From my point of view, it's all farming because it doesn't matter if you don't plant a tree if it's growing there. I mean, the grass grows wild too. You usually help the situation by restocking your fields and fertilizing and liming, but farming is just capitalizing on what grows. —Sugarmaker, 27 May 2010

The identity of sugarmaker and the identity of farmer are closely intertwined in Vermont. The history of sugaring has a lot to do with this connection, as sugaring was often one of the many processes that took place on the small hill farms of the state. Because most of the farms were small family holdings, and remain so right up into the present day, notions of monocropping and agribusiness are not part of farm identity in the state. So, farming has come to mean engaging in a wide variety of processes throughout a year, including sugaring, which one sugarmaker understood as "just part of what we do. It's part of the whole crop rotation. . . . Everybody did a little bit of every-thing. Sugaring is usually a part of any farm."[151] Maple is seen as a crop, just like apples or grain or any other produce of a farm. And it is widespread, being a feature of any farm, a thing that everybody did. Because of the predominance of rural areas and a long history of small-scale agriculture, farming plays a large role in the identity of Vermont, and because sugaring is viewed as an intrinsic part of farming, it is easy enough to see how maple becomes an important part of the identity of the place. The strong agricultural meaning that is given to sugaring dovetails nicely with the agricultural identity of Vermonters, regardless of whether they themselves farm or not.

The strong connection between sugaring and farming is not true of sugarmakers everywhere. At MapleRama 2014, hosted by Franklin County, I spoke with a young couple from Maine who were looking to expand their small, 150+ tap operation. This year was their first MapleRama and first time talking with sugarmakers in Vermont, and they were surprised at how closely sugaring was tied to farming there. In their understanding, Maine sugaring was more closely tied to forestry and logging, as another process that takes place in the woods, but is more important locally. Maine makes less meaning with agriculture when formulating its identity and more with logging and forestry, so it makes perfect sense for sugaring to be more closely associated with those processes there. This conversation brought home to me how interwoven Vermont's paradigmatic hill farms are with the hills and woods. The relatively small plots of land are dotted around and within stands of trees, making farming and woods parts of the same landscape, rather than separate landscapes. In Maine, where the woods are logged more than farmed, of course sugaring is going to belong in the logging realm. I hadn't thought about it until I met that young couple, as my default category of sugaring had been shaped by Vermont's farming culture. Hearing this different viewpoint made clear how important agriculture is to sugaring in Vermont.

The meaning of the word *agriculture* is based on an idea that there is a boundary between the natural world and the cultural world. Agriculture is a human activity that transforms the natural into the cultural, as indicated in the word itself: agri*culture*. Humans interact with the physical world outside of themselves in purposeful ways to extract sustenance and stability, what the sugarmaker at the head of this chapter describes as "capitalizing on what grows." In a sense, this capitalization brings parts of that world into their domain. A wild plant becomes domesticated, an organism becomes food. Anthropologists have complicated the simple understanding of a clean boundary between the natural and the cultural many times. Recently and enlighteningly, Atran and Medin have discussed the ways in which the very category of "nature" is culturally constructed.[152] Because the category is a cultural construction, it is culturally variable, and not a human universal; we would do well not to forget the complexity. However, a straightforward and strong division between nature and culture is an intellectual construct that many people, sugarmaker and otherwise, use in their everyday lives, so it is worth exploring as an epistemological tool, if nothing else. Anthropology is, at its core, concerned with the manifold ways people make and employ meanings, and anything that can be used as a meaning-making process is ripe for epistemological analysis. The boundary between nature and culture is a place of contact, what Anna Tsing calls in her book, *Friction*, a frontier, and therefore a place for negotiation of meanings—meanings of the human, the natural, and the cultural.[153]

Tsing's book discusses ecology and the botanical world as a particularly fruitful ground (pardon the pun) for negotiating meaning, as plants and plant environments are often understandable as liminal spaces, existing in the "weedy" areas between the human and the nonhuman, between different ways of making meaning. Laura Rival edited a volume that also delves usefully into the meanings made with plants, by exploring the varying ways in which a seemingly standard category like "tree" can range widely and be put to different uses in various cultures, demonstrating the power of the botanical to help the human make knowledge.[154] Much of that knowledge in the case of agriculture involves exploring and negotiating the boundary between the human and nonhuman worlds. Agriculture is an activity defined by the intersection of nature and culture, a place where that intersection is enacted and understood. Ironically, agriculture is in this sense a very weedy activity, in Tsing's terms. As such, it serves as a useful lens to make sense of sugaring—a process that involves humans interacting with trees, soil, sunshine, and snow. What can agricultural ideas tell us about the meanings of maple sugaring?

Agriculture is very important in Vermont. While a common image of the state is a rural, untouched wilderness, it is perhaps better described as pastoral (in both senses of the word), rather than rural and untouched. It is a pastoral place in that it has a reputation for quiet, rolling hills and small village greens that would be right at home on a postcard or a cheap couch-sized painting. To be sure, there are many places where one could stand and see just such a vista, but the notion that the whole of the state is covered in virgin forest, interrupted only by the periodic quaint village is more than a little overblown. Of course, the very notion of North American "virgin forest," untouched by human hands, is more an invention of the colonial mind than ever was true. The Abenaki have inhabited what is now Vermont for millennia, since before Europeans arrived, and their interactions with the landscape were and are both purposeful and effective. The myth of the untouched landscape is now well known within the social sciences, and even beyond to other disciplines. Foster and colleagues discuss the fallacy of the virgin forest idea in New England from a biogeographical point of view:

> The past changes and current composition of the region's fauna (and flora; cf. Bellemare et al., 2002; Gerhardt & Foster, 2002; Motzkin et al., 2002) are strongly influenced by human activity. Drawing this observation and the individualistic notion together, we can conclude that the seemingly natural appearance of the modern forest landscape, including its populations of coyotes, fishers, bears, moose, deer, and turkey, is culturally conditioned, even if not tightly directed, and is certainly only broadly analogous to pre-settlement conditions.[155]

What these biologists are saying in their technical vocabulary is that the current state of the natural parts of New England are not untouched, but rather very influenced by human activity. Further, the way the landscape looks and feels now is only similar to prehuman occupation in general terms. Even the reconstructed forest is not that similar to any untouched condition. Despite the widespread acceptance that the state is not untouched forest, Vermont is a pastoral idyll for many, with its rolling hills, wide swaths of green, and ambling rivers: "It's an image of hardworking men and women, of family enterprise, of pristine forests, lofty mountains clad with pine, birch, spruce, and abundant *maples*."[156] The idealization of the state includes both the natural and the cultural, the farm and the forest.

Vermonters are no more or less prone to this type of idealization and romanticism than any other group of people. And they are no less apt to balance their idealization and romanticism with a sense of practicality and the realities of modern economics. Idealized notions of a rural paradise exist in Vermont and elsewhere alongside an awareness of the hard work and small reward that farming often brings. Janice Harper explains how easily and powerfully a different forest landscape can become symbolic, almost mythological, in Madagascar, where for many Westerners, "tropical forests are near mythic landscapes, reflecting the natural history of non-human life. From the perspective of those who live in the forests, however, they reflect not natural history, but social history."[157] The people living in Vermont likewise simultaneously idealize their temperate forests as an agricultural idyll and recognize the harsh economic and physical realities of living in a place where nature is very close by. The landscape gets to be idyllic, but it is also lived, with a social history. The boundaries between the human realm and the nonhuman, which is the weedy, frontier place where agriculture occurs, are places where it is hard to disregard the realities of the social history on the landscape.

Those harsh realities do little to dampen the persistence of the idyllic narrative, though. In this way, contemporary Vermonters maintain a stance toward farming that has been around for some time: "While an agrarian way of life was idealized through most of the nineteenth century, Gilbert C. Fite (1981: 10) remarks that the proponents were usually people who had found some other occupation. Such admirers of farming encouraged everyone but their children to become farmers."[158] So the negotiation between idyllic postcard pasture and the realities of hard farmwork continues. The idealization of the rural by nonrural Vermonters is especially acute in what Fite points out as a hypocrisy, or at least a form of NIMBYism. Farms are wanted, even idealized, but many who want the farms don't want the farmwork to be done by themselves or those nearest them. I'm reminded of Jack Nicholson's role in the 1992 filmed version of *A Few Good Men*, when he testifies that "civilized" America wants him to defend it from its enemies, even while abhorring his existence. Vermont wants farmers on that wall; it needs them on that wall, maintaining the state's identity.

Vermont is also pastoral in the anthropological meaning of the word, in that much of the landscape is or has been used for pasture. The creation of a wool industry in the nineteenth century turned many acres into pasture for sheep, and when the market for Vermont wool dried up, the pastoral economy continued with other livestock, primarily dairy cattle.[159] Indeed, much of what is now the tree-covered landscape of Vermont is reclaimed forest, overgrown from earlier pastureland. As the sheep were moved off the sloping terrain, the forests reclaimed the hillsides and mountains, transforming the landscape from relatively open pastureland into thick woods. Much of the "primeval forest" that covers Vermont is not even a century old. An agricultural meaning has, in this case, been removed from the land, replaced with a narrative of virgin forest. Strangely, this new narrative actually feeds and supports the agricultural idyll that holds sway in the state. Vermont's paradigmatic farmer is a small holder who has carved out a steading from the hillside's supposedly virgin forest, and who runs a farm with a wide swath of crops and activities. The previous agricultural truth, a monocrop narrative of sheep grazing the hills mostly empty of trees, needs to be removed in order for that small holder to be situated in the idyllic forest.

The fictional and the fictive have merged into the contemporary understanding of Vermont as a pastoral place, with its economy driven by agriculture. To be sure, there is a very real agricultural identity in the state—Vermont farming constitutes a larger percentage of New England's agricultural economy than any other state in the region (*New England Agricultural Statistics 2009*, 5). Narratives aside, the real impacts of agriculture on the identity of Vermont cannot be overstated, with the black and white milk cow as much a viable symbol of the state as the moose or the maple leaf. As the NE Agricultural Statistics report states, the majority of dairy production is centered in the northern counties of Addison, Franklin, and Orleans, but the notion of Vermont dairy pervades the whole state's identity, as evidenced by Vern Grubinger, University of Vermont extension professor and agricultural essayist: "Agriculture holds a special place in the hearts and minds of Vermonters. We know it's important to our state, even if most of us aren't sure exactly why."[160]

The amount of importance of farming to Vermont's identity is obvious, and the lack of clarity as to why is not surprising either, given that farming "has shaped much of the world—its heritage, nations and cultures. Even in places where people do not farm, it echoes in the meaning to many homes of their gardens or, for those without gardens, their window boxes" (Brody 2000, 82). People make meaning with their landscape, especially in the human negotiation of the landscape. For those who farm or live among farming, the meaning is immediate, but even those who don't live among it attempt to make the meaning immediate by tending gardens and window boxes. Agriculture is a very common and very evident negotiation process all across Vermont.

Victor Turner, anthropologist of the mid-twentieth century, was well known for his examinations of the performance and symbolic interpretation of cultural tropes. As Turner puts forth in *Process, Performance, and Pilgrimage*, groups often set conceptual frames around certain parts of themselves or their behaviors, and use the bounded aspects to create or analyze their own identities. For Turner, ritual is one type of sacral space, a separate and bounded arena within which aspects of group identity can be scrutinized, shaped, and employed strategically as a set of symbols with which to communicate. Farming is a set of images and symbols that Vermont uses to construct its identity, and farmland functions as a sacralized space wherein Vermont can negotiate who and what it is as an entity. In short, it is in farming that Vermont performs itself. Grubinger is essentially extending Turner's idea when he states that "the value of agriculture [to Vermont] is not just economic. Farming's contribution to the region's appearance, culture, wildlife, and quality of life is something that statisticians will never be able to put an accurate number on. But it sure would be nice if they tried."[161] In short, agriculture is an epistemology, a set of ideas with which meanings that make up Vermont's identity are negotiated.

It is not only the large-scale, group identity of Vermont that is negotiated with the meanings that can be found in agriculture. Many of the small- to medium-sized sugarmakers of Vermont have farming as a part of their personal identity. Either they themselves are farmers, or their families farmed, sometimes for generations back. Farming as an economic activity is important to many Vermonters because, to a great degree, it is very personal. Vermonters often compare the state's small farms with large, industrial farms in the Midwest and the Plains, where factory farms of grain, meat, and dairy are more the norm. Despite the existence of small family farms in the Midwest and Plains states, the narrative in Vermont constructs the midwestern farm monolithically, as an enormous, anonymous enterprise, while the Vermont farm is a small operation, owned by a neighbor or a relative. In Vermont, "the farmer's shadow has got to strike the farm, and that's true in all of farming," according to one dairy farmer and sugarmaker in the north of the state.[162] In the dominant narrative, farming is done by the owners of the land, making the occupational identity of farming inextricably linked with regional, ethnic, and familial identities.

The primary source of agricultural income in Vermont is dairy farming, to a dominant degree. Not only is farming itself a major force in the construction of Vermont identity, but that farming is overwhelmingly dairy farming. Ever since cows replaced sheep as the main animal kept in Vermont fields, dairy has constituted 70–80 percent of the state's agricultural income, making Vermont the state most dependent on a single agricultural commodity.[163] Of all the states in New England, Vermont derives a greater share of its agricultural economy from dairy, and the numbers are not really close. In 2008, Vermont dairy made up 73 percent of its agricultural receipts, while the next closest state in New England was New Hampshire's relatively small 28 percent.[164] Being a farmer in Vermont is synonymous with being a *dairy* farmer, to a much greater degree than is the case in any other state in New England, indeed in any state in the country. Even in Wisconsin, "The Dairy State" (where I lived for a decade), being a farmer is not as thoroughly synonymous with being a dairy farmer. The dominance of dairy in the farming economy and culture of Vermont, combined with the dominance of farming in the state's identity for farmers and non-farmers alike, means that most sugar-makers, if they are removed from the dairy industry at all, are not all that far removed.

Sugarmaking and dairy production have many things in common, and it is perhaps natural that the two products fit neatly together for many Vermonters. Both maple and milk are liquid commodities that are gathered and processed in bulk, both products are essentially gathered from a raised and/or tended source, rather than the product being grown directly by the farmer, and both can be used in either a basic state or processed into many other edible and nonedible products. It is true that a farmer of any type needs to be a jack- or

THE AGRICULTURAL MEANING OF MAPLE

jill-of-all-trades, having some facility with a wide range of knowledge areas (mathematics, meteorology, biology, business, and many others), and they need to display the wide range of technical knowledge that James Fairhead saw among residents of Sub-Saharan Africa when he was exploring indigenous forms of natural resource management. Fairhead discusses how the local people there consistently "alter their practices to suit their diverse social and ecological circumstances," attributes that are of particular importance to dairy and maple as well.[165] Syrup and milk share some particular intellectual demands on those producing them, distinct from other forms of agriculture. Because maple and dairy both start with a liquid resource, for example, making either requires a healthy dose of the specialized knowledge of plumbing that is typically less necessary in other agricultural fields, and both are much more perishable than many other farm products.

Both commodities also require a sort of "all hands on deck" attitude, either the everyday slog of milking and processing or the immediacy of the sometimes long boiling schedule when the sap is running. While this attitude is prevalent in many forms of agriculture, the constant, almost pushy demands of milk and maple have a feel of their own. The Nearings, in their hugely influential book, *Living the Good Life*, discuss the intensive needs of sugaring, largely because of the fragility and perishability of maple sap once it has been extracted from the tree: "During the syrup making season we were extra careful to keep on schedule because so much depended on picking up the sap as soon as it was in the buckets and getting it into the evaporator before it began to ferment."[166] Making syrup, as they describe it, "asks for division of labor and a considerable degree of coordination of effort. . . . Gathering sap is one occupation, and boiling it down is another. These operations should be performed at the same time, especially in mild weather, so that the sap does not stand around and sour."[167] Modern maple production techniques mean that some of the practical facts the Nearings state are no longer true, although they were true in the not-too-distant past, according to one retired sugarmaker. She recalled that her mother was "the one that did all the boiling, and my father and I, we gathered the sap, and of course it was with horses then . . . I can't think of any other woman would do that."[168] This sugarmaker recalled the days of a strongly divided labor force, with her mother running the boil. Sugaring is generally a fairly strongly gendered activity, with men often being in charge of the gathering and the boiling both. Women's roles were traditionally relegated to other activities, such as finishing or canning the syrup, or secondary processing into candy, cream, and so forth. Women often served as support staff as well, handling the invisible work of the sugaring process. In the days of the all-night boil, they would bring food to the men in the sugarhouse who could not leave the constantly running evaporator. Gender divisions are still quite strong in many sugarhouses and woods, but, while women in more primary roles are still an exception, many more exceptions can be found today. For most operations, though, gathering and boiling are not separate processes in the same way because gathering is more often done with tubing, rather than the time-intensive emptying of buckets. Efficiencies in boiling also mean that the need for a division of labor within the sugarhouse is not as strong anymore. A well-organized sugaring system, even one of good size, can be operated by a single person today.

Helen and Scott Nearing did more with words to shape the identity of Vermont (for good or ill) than perhaps any two other people. The whole concept of "The Good Life," as embodied in the state in a back-to-the-land, simplified sort of human existence, takes its name from the Nearings' book. Ripples of their ideas are felt today in such ideas as vegetarianism, counting food miles, and the locavore movement, which encourages people to source the food they eat from as close a geographic area as they can. Vermont regularly tops the "Locavore Index," a ranking of states "in terms of their commitment to local food," although there are many ways such a thing as "commitment" can be measured.[169] The term "good lifer" has become a sometimes pejorative label applied by Vermonters with long history in the state to those who move there from outside the state, in an attempt to live an idealized version of the rural, pastoral idyll.

The Nearings' explanation of the demands of sugaring may not be as widely true anymore, but it is not completely gone either. When the sap runs, all attention still needs to be turned to processing it, even if the processing takes less time than it used to. There simply is not much flexibility in a system that necessitates boiling within twenty-four hours a substance whose appearance is neither regular nor terribly predictable in the long term. To be sure, some crops require a similar "all hands on deck" approach, especially at harvesttime for vegetables, for example, although that moment of harvesttime is more predictable. Itinerant farm labor depends on this condensed and immediate need for work to be done. Crops grown on a larger scale, such as grains, are harvestable on a more controlled schedule, partly because of the more intense use of large machinery in the process, but fruits or vegetables that are harvested by hand often have an urgency to their work similar to maple, as evidenced by one of the sugarmakers I interviewed, who explained that "most farm labor wants to work year-round, they don't want to work seasonally. That's ok for the dairy guys because they are working year-round, but with the crop people, like ourselves or the veggie guys, it's more of a seasonal operation."[170] Seasonality here implies short bursts of intense activity, rather than constant labor spread throughout a year. Sugaring and vegetable harvesting both work with these short bursts. In this way, the Vermont farm is again set in opposition to the factory grain farms of the Midwest. It is not simply agriculture that defines Vermont, it is small-scale agriculture, with implications of a greater dependence on human work, rather than giant machines and industrial processes.

Sugaring fits into this same conceptual niche, in that it demands human labor, not giant machines, and it demands that labor on its own schedule. To be sure, there are many machines involved in sugaring today, from vacuum to tubing to reverse osmosis machines, not to mention some evaporators that are bigger and more expensive than my car. The inclusion of these machines does not seem to encroach on the industrialized agriculture realm for many, mostly because there is still a known, named, individual sugarmaker running the operation. That individuality allows the identity of farmer to remain, even when that farmer is standing in front of a shiny stainless steel evaporator that stands twenty feet long and twelve feet high.

More than one sugarmaker told me that they will dump any sap that has stood for more than twenty-four hours, and a few had shorter windows. This one-day window seemed to be a norm across larger New England sugarmakers, at least in my experience, where sugaring is more widespread and engrained in the identity. In Newfoundland,

I encountered some backyard sugarmakers who would hold sap for up to two weeks before boiling, largely because of the amount needed to make a useful boil, and the low number of taps being collected. I can only imagine what some of the Vermont sugarmakers would have to say if presented with the two-week window. Having tasted plenty of syrup made in both ways, I can affirm that a longer window between gathering and boiling does indeed change the qualities of the syrup that results. The agricultural mentality of Vermont sugarmakers, which assigns a perishable agricultural meaning to the sap as soon as it is harvested, makes any period over a day seem like an unacceptable compromise. Much in the way that, when a cow needs milked, it must be milked, when the sap bucket or vat is full, it must be boiled. A recent visit to a sugarmaker in the center of the state demonstrated some of the changes and consistencies in boiling sap. As I arrived, he was preparing to boil several hundred gallons of sap that had run overnight and that morning. As he readied his new, oil-fired evaporator to boil, he compared this moment to the same event just a few years ago, when he boiled over wood chips. A big run of sap would have meant prepping the fire for a couple hours to get it up to temperature, boiling for a couple hours, and then tending the evaporator as the fire died back. This day, with his reverse osmosis rig, oil fire, and various other technological changes, he started the process by lighting his burner, and less than half an hour later, he shut it down, as the sap had been processed. The time scale changed. What didn't change, however, was his urgency in needing to boil that sap in that moment. Again, modern technology has changed the dynamics and time span of the boil itself a bit, but the sense of urgency because of the perishable sap remains.

The awareness of this immediacy is captured in an anecdote from the Nearings of some neighbors who were Seventh Day Adventists, whose belief system prevented them from working on Saturday, their holy day. Nevertheless, these neighbors "would milk and water their cattle on Saturday and perform other urgent chores," but refrain from other farm tasks.[171] These same neighbors had a crisis of conscience about sugaring, though, opting eventually to avoid gathering sap on their sabbath. While other farm chores could easily wait a day, sugaring and milking could not and still cannot. Rather than gather sap and

THE AGRICULTURAL MEANING OF MAPLE

leave it unprocessed, the Nearings' neighbors let the sap drain to the ground if it were running on Saturdays, but the fact that it was a point of discussion at all demonstrates how immediate the needs of sugaring are understood to be. My own interviewees echoed this recognition of the immediacy of sugaring, declaring that during sugaring season, they "make syrup all day, we work all day, we boil half the night, and this is a six-week-long procedure of actual boiling time and running time. We work on [other aspects of sugaring] year-round because of wind damage, squirrel damage and stuff, you have to be in the woods a lot more than that, but through that six weeks, it's not uncommon to have a neighbor stop at one o'clock in the morning or one-thirty in the morning, just to see how you're doing, like they're not tired enough to go home to bed."[172] This sugarmaker in northern Vermont discusses the need to work all day and half the night when the sap is running, to the point that people's schedules become shaped by the maple run. More than simply adjusting the agricultural calendar, a sap run alters the meanings of many parts of sugarmakers' lives. Visiting hours become distended because everyone knows that, when the sap is running, the sugarmakers are awake and working. There is no other option. It would be unusual and probably unseemly in September to drop in on a neighbor unannounced at one a.m., but to do so in early March during sugaring is a widely held norm because the assumption is that people are working late to process the sap.

Several sugarmakers told me that the standard of the all-day boil has become much less common, as boiling times have decreased with RO and other efficiencies, but late nights after work are still fairly common in late winter and early spring. As one young sugarmaker put it, "I've actually been working through since the '07 season, having a full-time job on the side."[173] This man's phrasing, having a "full-time job on the side," was intentional as a bit of a joke, but he is acknowledging a truth about his identity, that even with a regular profession, during sugaring season, he is primarily a sugarmaker because of the immediacy of the demands of sugaring. Several members of his larger family are also dairy farmers, making that immediacy of demand very familiar to him. Milk and maple have an urgency and an immediacy that many other farm products do not. Because of the prevalence of dairy in Vermont's farming identity, as discussed earlier, the immediacies inherent to both milk and maple sit comfortably, almost obviously, beside each other.

There are important differences between maple and dairy, though. Anyone who has ever worked on a dairy farm knows that the cows need milked every day of the year, usually (especially with the industrialized breeds of milk cattle prevalent in North America) twice a day. The relatively recent advent of completely automated, on-demand milking operations, with the cows entering a mechanized milking suite on their own schedule, provides a different understanding of the labor demands of dairy farming. Completely automated systems are still a minority in the state, though, so the dominant cultural norm for dairy is a year-round, twice-a-day demand on the farmers' time. Maple, on the other hand, is a strictly seasonal product in terms of production, with a short window of at most a few weeks in early spring when it is available for making. The long shelf life of real maple, once it is processed into syrup anyway, means that it is available to the consumer year-round, but it can only be made in that window of the year when the sap is running. The myriad forms of work involved in maple production are no longer confined to when the sap is running, though. As the interviewee earlier in this chapter makes clear, sap lines are strung and repaired in winter, often in deep snow. The equipment for gathering and boiling is also updated and maintained when not in use, and if a sugarmaker sells his or her own product, the marketing and selling of maple is done year-round.

In this way, maple more resembles grain crops, with a defined season of production and a rhythm of work that is married to the time of year, whereas dairy production is a year-round process with constant and consistent needs. Growing corn or rice is seasonally slightly variable, with the vagaries of temperature and rain shifting planting or harvesting a week or two up or back. However, within these parameters, the farmer determines what week to prepare, what week to plant, and what week to harvest. Sugarmakers have little of this type of foreseeability. Because the maple sap runs when the temperature swings from below freezing overnight to above about 40° during the day, when those conditions hit, sugaring needs to happen. In Vermont, such conditions can typically occur as early as the beginning of January, as late as the middle of May, and for any lengths of time in between. Sugaring seasons of six weeks are not uncommon, and seasons as short as one week have happened. There is relatively little ability to predict at any distance when a run will happen, and there is almost no ability to predict how long it will last, so the definition of "season" varies greatly whether you are talking about raising grain or making maple syrup. Wheat farmers know that, within a window of a couple weeks, they will be able to plant their crop at the end of spring or summer (depending on variety). Maple producers must have their equipment prepared, both in the woods and in the sugarhouse, at or near the beginning of the calendar year, and wait for a sugaring season of undetermined length to appear. The reliability of the payoff is considerably less with maple as well. In 2010, the maple season nationwide was nearly a week shorter than 2009 (twenty-three days, compared to twenty-eight the year before), while 2011 saw an average sugaring season of thirty-two days.[174] A few days may not seem that much on the surface, but in a season of less than thirty days, losing six has an enormous impact on the amount produced, and of course the resulting profit made. The equipment needs to be up and ready, so the labor costs to make one gallon of syrup aren't that far off of the labor costs to make a thousand gallons. The whims of yearly weather dictate terms to sugarmakers with much more impact than is true of other types of agriculture.

Maple is strongly influenced by the weather, both on the large scale of statewide temperature shifts and the smaller scale of micro-climatic differences between a north-facing slope and a valley floor. The awareness of local conditions is a norm among many farmers, and as Johan Pottier points out in his *Anthropology of Food*, "interaction between farmers, micro-environments and crops has been dynamic throughout history."[175] This is absolutely true of tapping maples as well, where production can depend "whether it's on a south or north side and all that, where you tap the trees, and you have to pay attention to all that. There's quite a trick to it."[176] This sugarmaker is being more than a little humble when she describes it as "a trick," as most sugarmakers, herself included, draw on a wealth of knowledge gained either from their ancestry or their own trial and error, and often some combination of the two, to perform their tricks.

A sugarmaker needs to pay attention to the yearly changes in the local weather, but they must also know the impacts of their specific property's terrain on the wind, sun exposure, rainfall, and snow cover. Changes in weather can impact the milk production of a cow, but the effects are not nearly as dramatic as those on maple, where a change of a few degrees in the overnight low temperature can mean the difference between a large sap run and no useful production at all. The liquid that results from each agricultural production process is different as well. Until recently in the United States and Canada, maple sap was almost never used in any quantity in its raw state, while milk is a usable product straight from the cow. Several sugarmakers discussed the health benefits of straight maple sap with me, including its vitamin and micronutrient content. In Korea, the sap from the gorosoe type of maple (*Acer mono*) is collected and drunk straight as a health tonic, said to be good for building the bones especially. While quite a few Vermont sugarmakers told me they periodically drank the sap raw, one enterprising sugarmaker discussed an idea to market the raw sap as an energy drink or vitamin water. His tone was half-serious, and I got the impression that he thought it was a good idea that would never come to fruition. This conversation took place in 2010, but by 2012, several outlets for commercial maple sap had been created or announced in North America.[177] I was offered samples of the straight sap by a few sugarmakers. The Vermont sap I tried tasted like water with faint hints of vegetal and mineral content, to my tongue very much like the store-bought "enhanced" water drinks that are currently very popular. Interestingly, when I tried a store-bought Seva brand maple water in Canada, its taste was different, and noticeably woodier. Perhaps the different trees were the cause, as this was sap from Quebec, or perhaps the Tetrapak container was lending a flavor. Either way, sales and distribution of straight sap as a drink seem to be increasing steadily, so the market is evidently there.

Both milk and sap can undergo a range of processes that alter them into a wide variety of other commodities, but even with the advent of maple water as a commodity, the vast majority of maple sap *must* be processed in some manner in order for it to be a widely salable, and therefore profitable, product. It should not be forgotten that maple and dairy are both businesses, as I discuss in my chapter on economic meanings. The ability to sell, and to make a profit on, maple and milk is a driving force behind their continued production.

The name for the activity, sugarmaking, carries the connotation of the processing involved as well. Sugar*making* entails taking something and making it into something else—transforming it from one form to another. (That it is called *sugar*making, rather than syrupmaking, is explained by the fact that most of it was boiled down into crystalized sugar in the past, rather than stopping at the point of liquid syrup.) There seems to be an implicit understanding that sugarmaking involves more than gathering, more than just collecting. To call the process sugar*growing* or sugar*raising* would make as little sense to sugarmakers in Vermont as it would to consumers in Florida who have never seen a sugar maple. I do not wish to lay out a psycholinguistic argument here, but the inclusion of the word "making" in the name of the activity surely speaks to some nod toward process. Corn is grown, milk is milked, but maple syrup is *made*, indicating a transformative process different from other agricultural products. Yes, corn is made into other goods, and milk is made into other goods, but in neither case is that making (of cheese, of corn syrup, etc.) a part of the agricultural process. Those are generally understood as an industrial process enacted on the agricultural commodity. With maple, however, the making is a fundamental and inseparable part of what it means to sugar. The quotation at the head of this chapter makes it very clear that, while the IRS may view maple sap gathering and maple syrup manufacturing as two separate processes, most sugarmakers do not. Gathering and boiling belong together, and they both belong on the agricultural side of the spectrum, as recognized by one sugarmaker who told me, "on the days when I'm feeling a little down about it, you know, I think we're everybody's poor stepchild, but I'd say we really hang out in the agriculture community more than the forestry community."[178] Both of these sugarmakers (quoted here, and at the top of this chapter) recognize that in some situations, sugaring is not understood as an agricultural process, and they both bemoan that fact in their own ways. For them, though, as for pretty much every sugarmaker in Vermont I spoke to, sugaring is unquestionably agriculture, with a straightforwardly agricultural meaning.

In this way, making maple is not the same as making corn or milk, where the agricultural meanings are confined to their being raised or grown. With maple, the manufacture (by definition, a human activity) is inextricably linked to the direct human/nature interaction that marks farming. Wheat can be understood as a natural plant that is brought into the cultural domain when it is planted and harvested. However, when wheat is ground to grain and baked into bread, it is understood as already firmly within the cultural sphere. Grinding or baking are parts of a manufacturing process. Maple, however, is only maple when it has undergone a manufacturing process. There is less of a separation between the manufacturing process and the agricultural process that occurs at the intersection of the natural and the cultural realms. For maple, manufacture is a part of the negotiation of that intersection.

Despite the differences, for nearly everyone I spoke with, maple is a straightforwardly agricultural product and process. I asked many of my interviewees whether they thought of maple as an agricultural thing. The most common response was that it was done by farmers, and it therefore was farming. Despite Amy Trubek's statement that "maple is really a wild food rather than a domesticated crop," for sugarmakers, it is farm produce.[179] Even when recognizing the aspects of sugaring that are more akin to gathering and forestry, maple is still understood as an agricultural product, not a gathered resource by sugarmakers. One sugarmaker from northern Vermont explained how maple is both a gathered and an agricultural resource, stating, "If you just go back to the real basics, why do we even do this, never mind the money part of it . . . the love of working in the forests, getting the sap from the trees, it's that first crop of the spring, of the season. I don't know, it's just in our blood."[180] This sugarmaker acknowledges that the maple comes from a woods, rather than a cultivated field, but the product that comes out is still a crop—an agricultural thing. Some sugarmakers were quick to point out that maple fits into the typical North American annual agricultural cycle, which helps it feel a part of the agricultural world. The refrain of maple being the first crop of the season, of it being part of the agricultural cycle and agricultural calendar, appears over and over, as with a sugarmaker who told me that maple is "actually our first crop of the crop season, and for us it represents much more than that. For me personally, it's evidence that winter is tail-ending. We do the sugaring in the spring of the year. Typically, winter for a lot of Vermonters gets to be long, drawn out, and so when we start moving toward sugaring, that means we're moving toward spring, new beginnings, new crop season."[181] Maple fits neatly into the agricultural calendar, and it carries a special meaning of being at the top of that calendar as the first crop of the year.

Winter, considered a dormant period in terms of growth and agricultural production, is symbolically marked in northern New England as ending with the first run of maple sap, and has been for centuries, as explained by a local Vermont author, who states, "The first crop of the year for an Abanaki [*sic*] farmer would likely have been maple," as it is today for Vermont farmers, Abenaki and non-Abenaki alike.[182] Many sugarmakers spoke to me almost wistfully about the first run of sap of the season. There is also special attention paid to the last run of the season, nicknamed "the frog run" because it generally occurs late in the season, when it is warm enough for frogs (locally called "peepers" because of the sounds they make) to begin appearing in the hills and woods. Both runs are spoken of with nostalgia—the frog run because it signals an end, and the first run because it marks a new beginning.

Interestingly, the degree of wistfulness does not seem to correspond to the time of year the conversation takes place. I have felt the same emotions attached to these symbolic first and last runs of sap at various times of year. One might expect a sugarmaker in the middle of September to be more nostalgic because of the long time elapsed since the last frog run, as well as the long time until the next first run. For the first run anyway, it seems the wistfulness is not a function of timing, but is somehow definitional. If mention of the first run elicits misty eyes in November, but not in May, it would be easy to understand the wistfulness as simply anticipation or nostalgia for that which is not immediate (i.e., sap running and maple season). However, because the first run seems to elicit strong emotion regardless of the time of year, it seems to imply that the first run itself is an evocative event, rather than an event more missed the further removed in time the speaker is. When I asked sugarmakers about this facet of the wistfulness, the explanations that followed were invariably that sugaring is the first process on the farm, or in the calendar year, that *produces*. Farmers are, by nature, people who want to produce something for consumption (it's not called the "produce section" in the market for nothing). As that first new crop of the crop season, maple is the first product in a calendar year that sugarmakers can produce from their land and their labor, and it marks the beginning of a new cycle. Awareness of cycles and the cyclical nature of the world is endemic to farmers, as made clear by one of my interviewees. He noted that many food consumers "have gotten away from knowing about seasons. They can go into a grocery store and buy a strawberry in February, or October, or any-time, and they forget about the fact that there's local seasons."[183] Maple feels especially agricultural when one takes into account the cyclical nature of it. All farming has cycles to it (even in climate zones without strong differentiation among seasons), and the deeply felt presence of the yearly cycle of winter's thaw, the night and day rhythm of the temperature swings that make the sap run, and the yearly rituals of walking lines all highlight the cyclical nature of sugaring and make it seem more obviously agricultural.

For many people who live in temperate climates, the arrival of spring is the marker of a new year of life and produce. The first sound of a robin's song or the first bloom of a crocus marks the beginning of spring and growth for many people. Because sugaring often takes place in Vermont with significant amounts of snow on the ground, the feel is decidedly not spring-like. The birds are not yet singing and the flowers are not yet blooming. Indeed, sap collecting is purposefully done before the trees start to bud, to avoid off-flavors in the syrup. The University of Vermont and the Vermont Agency of Agriculture have produced two charts that attempt to apply culinary tasting notes to maple syrup.

On page 10 of their report, they present a map of maple's off-flavors, including "buddy: chocolaty aroma and flavors, lingering aftertaste." Sap collected from trees that have set buds is often under-stood as marginal, if not outright useless, for producing syrup. Sap must be gathered earlier, when it is sweetest and most free of taint. The first sap run of the new year is described by many sugarmakers as the first productive activity of the spring. In essence, where sugaring is a part of the farming identity, the first run of maple sap usurps the role of harbinger of the new agricultural cycle that is elsewhere played

the map of maple

intensity →		
maple	maple	
toasted	baked apple, brioche, golden sugar, crème brûlée	toasted nuts, roasted marshmallow, burnt sugar, caramel, coffee
milky	fresh butter, condensed milk	melted butter, butterscotch
confectionary	light brown sugar, molasses	dark brown sugar, toffee
spice	vanilla, nutmeg	cinnamon, mixed spices
fruity	raisins, orange, peach, mango, raw nuts	prunes, grapefruit, apricot
floral	honey, floral blend	
earthy	grassy, oats, mushroom	hay
others	praline, bourbon, spiced meat, mineral notes	dark chocolate, soy sauce, leather

(aroma and flavor)

© University of Vermont

taste: sweetness • balance • maple intensity

mouthfeel: smooth ←→ mineral; thin, syrupy, thick

the map of maple: off-flavors

mother nature	sour sap	ropey appearance, citrus, soy sauce, fermented aromas, sour taste, thick, chunky mouthfeel
	metabolism	chocolaty, grassy aroma, lack of maple flavor, cardboard, popcorn, peanut butter flavors, dry mouthfeel
	buddy	chocolaty aroma and flavors, lingering aftertaste
defoamer	safflower and vegetable oils	vegetable aroma and flavor, oily, waxy mouthfeel
	canola oil	spicy, peppery flavors, walnut, pungent finish, astringent mouthfeel
processing (burnt)	scorch	burnt flavors (coffee, dark chocolate), thick body
(burnt)	niter	burnt flavors (coffee, dark chocolate), leathery, spicy meat flavor, chalky, gritty mouthfeel
(storage)	fermented	yeasty alcohol aroma, honey, fruity, spicy (soy sauce), vegetable flavors, thin body, foamy appearance (severe fermentation), effervescent mouthfeel
(storage)	metallic	tin can aroma, strong metallic flavor (affects back tongue and teeth)
chemicals	minerals / niter	fizzy, gritty mouthfeel
	chloride	salty taste
	acid / basic	acid or caustic odor (depending on chemical), pungent, burning sensations
others	musty / mold	moldy, yeasty, vegetable aromas and flavors, lingering finish (affects back tongue and throat)
	detergents	perfumy, floral aromas, soapy flavor
	lubricants / fuels	petroleum aroma and flavor, oily mouthfeel, astringent finish
	filters	these defects could stem from misuse or mishandling of syrup filters

Culinary tasting notes in maple syrup. *Images courtesy of University of Vermont, Vermont Agency of Agriculture.*

by that initial crocus or robin. Many people in Vermont talk about spring arriving with the first sap run. That is what marks the turn of the season, not a bird or a flower. Because maple starts the farming year, it is an important and inseparable part of the agricultural world for many sugarmakers.

There are some important aspects of sugaring that are very different from other farming processes, though. Defining maple simply as an agricultural product does not capture the whole story. Maple is a product garnered from trees, like pecans or oranges. However, unlike tree nuts or tree fruits, maple is not taken from planted orchards. A stand of maple woods (colloquially known as a "sugarbush") is very rarely the result of planned, planted clusters of trees. The length of time between the planting of a fruit tree and its first productive crop is at most five years, often much less. A maple tree cannot be a reliable producer of sugar sap for at least thirty (many standards say forty) years. It is economically unfeasible to formulate a business plan that requires the same person planting a maple tree to tap it when it is mature enough. Such a business plan would need to span generations, not a single lifetime.

The abundance of maples in Vermont, however, makes this amount of long-range planning unnecessary, and the idea is moot. There are plenty of maples occurring of their own accord, so the concept of a planned maple orchard or plantation is basically unheard of at the moment. However, it is important to note that sugarbushes, which may be unplanted, are anything but untended. Every sugarmaker I know is intimately familiar with her or his woods, and the vast majority takes at least some care in clearing and maintaining their woods, either for the economic benefit of cleared lumber, the health of their maples, or both. The Vermont Department of Forests, Parks and Recreation maintains information on forest management for maple stands at its site (http://bit.ly/2coCTA1) and consults with sugarmakers on maintaining and improving their stands with forestry practices. While the trees are managed, they are not planted, and the management is of something that has occurred more or less naturally—capitalizing on what's growing. In short, sugarmakers are removing the sap from a naturally occurring stand of trees, not reaping the produce of a planted field or orchard. In this way, sugaring is something akin to an extractive economic process, and not a straightforward agricultural process as understood by many. It is what Tsing calls "an intriguing nature-culture knot" in her recent and remarkable book, *The Mushroom at the End of the World*.[184]

Because of the above aspects of sugaring, a comparison of maple to foraging is tempting and in some ways appropriate, although generally foraged items like fiddleheads or mushrooms can be consumed immediately, while in North America, as discussed earlier in this chapter, most maple needs processing before it is the intended product. Some exploration of gathering as a food procurement activity will enlighten this conversation, though, and deepen the current understanding of the uncertain, weedy, liminal place maple holds between reaping corn from a planted row and gathering wild mushrooms from the forest floor. The difference between agriculturalists and hunter-gatherers is perhaps one of the first things every introductory anthropology class learns, and much anthropological ink has been spilled exploring that difference, refining the definitions, and understanding the transitions made by some historic groups from one economic activity to another, as the process is neither obligatory nor linear, and transitions in both directions have occurred.[185]

Ernest Schusky, in the introduction to his *Culture and Agriculture: An Ecological Introduction to Traditional and Modern Farming Systems*, discusses how meaningful the difference is by exploring the two ways of life as tropes in the Old Testament: "In the Garden of Eden the life of innocence is an easy one of food collecting. After gaining 'knowledge of evil,' or something like culture, humans are doomed to earn a living 'by the sweat of their brow,' obviously as farmers."[186] Leaving aside the obvious punch lines regarding the equating of the "knowledge of evil" with "culture," it is interesting to note that the idealized lifestyle here is hunting and gathering, not the pastoral idyll of the farm. Hunting and gathering is portrayed as the more "natural" way of being human, while farming is a transformation (in the biblical narrative, a corruption) of human activity. Schusky is describing a world where humans are intimately part of nature being turned into a world with a boundary between the natural and the cultural. The marker of that boundary is agriculture.

Departing from the strictly materialist and economic definitions of many anthropologists who count minutes and calories expended and gained, what really is the difference between hunting and gathering and agriculture? Hugh Brody suggests that "[h]unter-gatherer knowledge is dependent on the most intimate possible connection with the world and with the creatures that live in it."[187] This statement may be true enough, but can the same not be said of farming? The answer to my question may depend on one's definition of "most intimate possible connection," but it is at least a very arguable point with no easy universal answer. Brody's later assertion, that the "distinction between respect and control is of immense importance to an understanding of how agriculturalists approach hunter-gatherers. The skills of farmers are centred not on their relationship to the world but on their ability to change it" draws a clearer, if equally questionable, conceptual line between the two categories.[188] Hunter-gatherers can certainly be understood to change their environment as well, and Brody's analysis feels a little like the Noble Savage peeking its head above the horizon. Regardless, if we take for the sake of discussion that the goal of shaping the environment marks the agriculturalist, while a more mutual interaction with the environment is the goal of the hunter-gatherer, then sugaring, with its unplanned but tended stands of trees, sits somewhere between the two.

As stated above, sugarmakers do not plant their trees, and they do not harvest plants, at least not for the making of syrup. A maple tree can be harvested for timber or as part of woodland maintenance, but those are separate processes. Sugaring itself does not necessitate taking a tree down. The amount of control exerted over the natural world is less than the farmer who reaps rows of corn or soybeans. From a very simple visual standpoint, farmers of wheat make a more obvious mark on the wheat field than sugarmakers make on the maple stand. Over the course of a year, what looks like an empty plot of land becomes filled with uniform wheat plants and then cleared of those plants, while the maple stand remains more or less the same stand of trees, at least to the casual eye. Yes, plastic tubing runs between the trees and undesirable growth is often cleared out, but these changes are not seasonal. The amount of control and change exerted on a cultivated field is more evident than it is on a sugarbush. In this way, sugaring is a rough fit for the conceptual box marked "agriculture."

Discussions of land tenure are not much more helpful in determining the place of maple on a gathering/farming spectrum, either. As Tim Ingold makes clear, "It is indeed the case that in the apparently endless controversy over whether or not hunting and gathering bands 'own' the land they occupy, the object of such ownership has generally been conceived as a territory, whilst in accounts of agricultural societies this concept has more often been reserved to denote the wider domain of political sovereignty or jurisdiction rather than

THE AGRICULTURAL MEANING OF MAPLE

the particular blocks of cultivable land over which people may claim rights of use and disposal."[189] Ingold's differentiation between land as a piece of dirt and land tenure as the rights over that chunk of dirt may be useful from a distance, but the real difference he points out may be between less intensely and more intensely structured organizational systems, rather than just a different understanding of land tenure. In either case, the way sugarmakers talk about their sugarbushes can again be seen as a middle ground between gathering and farming. While every Vermont sugarmaker I've interviewed works with the legal system of the state, wherein land is owned, leased, and controlled according to an understanding of deeds and easements and such, conceptually, there are layers of meaning on top of the legal system that nuance the understanding of a sugarbush. Sugarmakers often tap trees on land that is not their own, in exchange for money or a share of the resultant sap or syrup, or share their equipment with others in informal relationships of family, neighbor, or simply friend. Terminology such as "my trees" and "their trees" or "my land" and "their land" are used without any consistency according to the legal definitions of ownership. For a sugarmaker, "my trees" may not be owned by the speaker or exist on land owned by the speaker, but tapping them gives some form of sovereignty over them. Such flexible usage implies that conceptually, the land and trees are strictly thought of neither as owned property, as territory, or as a set of enacted rights in the way Ingold discusses.[190] The relationship sugarmakers have with the landscape does not match easily the paradigms of either hunter-gatherers or agriculturalists. Ingold rightly warns us about ascribing overly simplistic analyses to the understandings of land tenure that we encounter ethnographically, and I take his warning to heart.

If land tenure is not helpful in determining whether sugarmaking belongs in the category of agriculture or not, then what are we left with? A lack of outside definition. This lack is only problematic, however, if we seek a definition in an ontological sense. If we try to decide what is fundamentally true about the nature of sugarmaking and its relationship to agriculture, the evidence, from cultural theory and ethnography both, seems to indicate we will chase our tails for some time. If, however, we look at sugarmaking from an epistemological point of view, to discover what it *means* to Vermonters in relationship to the agricultural identity of the state, then the task becomes not only feasible, but very clear.

Sugarmaking is understood by most Vermonters as an agricultural activity, whether they take part in it or not. This chapter has asked the degree to which sugaring is agricultural. As we have seen, digging into what defines agriculture makes the question more difficult to answer, at least in any clean, straightforward way. If we ask instead, in what ways do the meanings of sugarmaking intersect with the meanings of agriculture, then we can achieve some clarity. As discussed above, agriculture is very meaningful to Vermont. It is a basic part of the state's identity because Vermont's economy and history are more fully and exclusively tied into farming than any other state in New England. Maple can be described the same way. It is a process and product that is very meaningful to the state, and it plays a greater and more exclusive role in Vermont than it does in any other state in New England, indeed, any other state or province where sugaring is done.

However, it is not enough to say simply, agriculture is meaningful, and maple is meaningful, therefore they can easily be linked. Both maple and agriculture are not just cultural artifacts that we can view epistemologically, that is, as meaningful things. Maple and agriculture are not just epistemological; they are epistemologies themselves. Vermonters *use* maple and agriculture to make meaning, specifically, Vermont identity. Any identity can be understood as the result of an epistemological process. People construct their identities by assigning meaning to certain aspects of their lives and their environments. The identity that gets constructed is a set of meanings itself. Because both maple and agriculture are hugely important aspects of Vermont (economically, ecologically, historically), it is perhaps natural that they are used to make the set of meanings that is Vermont identity.

It is also logical that these two aspects are linked to each other. As discussed above, maple is a rough fit as an example of ontological, definitional understandings of agriculture because, while it is similar in many ways to other forms of agriculture, it is only similar up to a point. So, defining maple as agriculture is problematic. However, it is easy to see the linking of the two in the identity-making (the meaning-making) process of Vermont. Maple may not be agriculture is the

THE AGRICULTURAL MEANING OF MAPLE

strictest definitions of either anthropology's or the IRS's terms, but the similarities of the two categories are widespread and profound. The importance of both maple and agriculture to the state, combined with the overlap between so many aspects of the two processes, explains how the differences between making maple and farming can be comfortably elided. The meanings that come from both override the definitional differences, and maple takes on an agricultural meaning in the making of Vermont identity.

CHAPTER 6

The Heritage Meaning of Maple

It's more important than I think any job you're going to have because you don't really consider it a job. It's a way of life. It's what you were always raised to do. It's like a family tradition. To a family like us, the money you make from it's one thing, but it's really kind of a family thing, bringing people together and really just . . . I'm not going to say enjoying it because sometimes it's not that enjoyable when it's pouring rain or whatever else, but you know, it really—for those of us that are in it for the long haul, it means a lot to us. —Sugarmaker, 7 July 2011

Maple is property in Vermont, in more ways than one. The quotidian understandings of property as commodity are discussed in the chapter on economics, while in this chapter, I want to explore a different (if connectable) understanding. For many in Vermont, maple is not just a thing, an entity, but a thing that is capable of being passed from one person to the next, specifically from a person in one generation to a person in another. It is heritable, and once inherited, it is heritage. This may sound like linguistic tap-dancing of the worst academic kind, but the concepts of heritage and being inherited are closely and importantly linked, and the link is especially meaningful for Vermonters when talking with them about maple. Social anthropologist Noel Salazar talks about the dualistic nature of heritage, including both its tangible and intangible importance, stating that "sociocultural values are attached to heritage because it holds meaning for people or social groups due to its age, beauty, artistry. . . . On the other hand, heritage also has economic value, referring to the degree to which it is desired."[191] As Salazar makes clear, heritage is valued because it holds aesthetic and historic meaning, and also because it holds economic meaning. Maple is meaningful to Vermonters because it is viewed as something they have inherited from the past, but its very inheritability makes it a thing with economic meaning as well.

The trees themselves are understood as property in an economic and legal sense, so they can be inherited just as a house or a pocketwatch can. That does not necessarily make them heritage, though. One way to understand heritage is by combining the two parts of Salazar's description: that it is anything that is inherited *and* to which people attach a great deal of meaning (especially if that meaning includes their sense of identity). Different analyses of heritage have focused on its relationship to history (Hewison 1987), or more recently as a semiotic question (Waterton and Watson 2014), or as heritage and place intersect (Staiff, Bushell, and Watson 2013). As discussed in the introduction to Staiff, Bushell, and Watson, identity can be understood as a set of meanings that people make, maintain, and communicate to and about each other. So, for maple trees, products, or otherwise to be heritage, they need to be used as some meaningful part of the identity of the place or the people within it. If that is the criterion, then maple is most certainly an important part of the heritage of Vermont. The trees, the sugaring process, and the product of the syrup all are used to make a lot of meaning in the state, and to transmit the meanings internally and externally. As such, maple is a "communicative transaction" that conveys senses of heritage and identity.[192]

It is straightforward enough to see a sugarmaker think of the trees they tap as part of their heritage, especially if those trees were tapped, or even just owned, by an ancestor. They inherited the trees, and they make meaning with them. I ran into plenty of sugarmakers who have this kind of connection with their trees. The sense of inheritance translates into a feeling of responsibility, to themselves, the trees, and their ancestry, to take care of those trees. As discussed in the chapter on agriculture, to take care of the trees in this case means acting as their steward and interacting with them in ways that are proper for the relationship. Sugaring a maple is a very proper interaction in Vermont. Acting properly toward the trees is only important if the trees are meaningful beyond just their economic value. People do not steward something that is unimportant to them, or to put it another way, one does not care *for* that which one does not care *about*, as expressed by one Vermonter who works closely with sugarmakers in the forestry industry. She reminded me that sugaring is "a story of tradition, of family practices, of managing the forest for hundreds of years and passing it on to the next generation. It's a quality factor, just like all the other things that we make here that are known to have that Vermont brand. It's about quality, small, slow . . . not that any of that is necessarily true, but it is the story."[193] That narrative of Vermont identity is an important part of the heritage of those who sugar. The trees themselves are worthy of care, but in this case, the memory of the people from whom the trees came deserves tending as well. It doesn't matter as much whether the realities of the past or present match up with the ideal because the story makes the meaning, and that meaning is a legacy, an inheritance. So, if someone receives maple trees as part of their inheritance, taking care of them is only partly about taking care of the trees; it is also about taking care of the legacy they represent.

Very often, trees are not simply inherited. Because they are a commodity, and because the agricultural identity of the state instills a certain kind of practicality, often maples are bought and sold rather than just passed along, even within a family. If something is bought rather than inherited, can it carry the same amount of heritage meaning? The short answer is yes, and the evidence can be found in comparing instances when maples were sold within a family to those when they were sold between people who were comparative strangers. I talked to sugarmakers for whom each was true, and in both cases, the sense of stewardship and responsibility for acting properly toward the trees was the same whether they knew the seller intimately as family or not at all. If the feeling of connection and responsibility are not coming from a shared identity with the seller, then from where does it come? The trick here is that there is a sense of shared identity with the seller—the identity of sugarmaker. It matters less for an understanding of heritage that a person is blood relation than that they also sugar.

This attitude makes perfect sense if we stop thinking about maples as the possession of an individual or even a family. Yes, the trees and land are owned by individuals, but the sense of heritage and responsibility is often not to an individual ancestor or family member, but to Vermont, or at least a particular version of Vermont. This Vermont is of the distant (although sometimes not-too-distant) past, where the state was covered with verdant forests and rustic hill farms. There is an abstraction of the state, a romanticizing process that makes the state the possession of all, at least all who have a forebear in that distant past. Individual ownership becomes blended into a shared participation in the past of the state. Pieces of Vermont become lost in an evenly distributed "Vermont" that is under the care and watch of all who are properly Vermonters. Even while an individual tree or sugarbush is owned by some individual person, the trees as a concept belong to Vermonters, and anyone coming into possession of those trees bears a responsibility to Vermonters for their care and proper treatment.

Definition becomes very important here, in terms of who counts as a Vermonter. As suggested above, some versions of Vermonter depend on an ancestral connection to the state's past. History and heritage are seen to merge and become nearly synonymous. This authentication process of who counts as insider is common enough in a lot of parts of the world, where being in a place for a longer period of time gives one a claim on it, either legally or conceptually. Of course, this kind of authentication is often used very selectively, as any colonized group of people can tell you.[194] In sugaring especially, while the origin of the process with Native Americans (in Vermont, particularly the Abenaki) is widely acknowledged, the implications of indigeneity on the ownership of the land and trees is rarely complicated by that part of the story. One old sugarmaker explained, "You can go back and look at history. I've looked at stories out in Michigan, and the Michigan people have their own story, a certain Indian discovered [sugaring], did whatever-whatever-whatever. Same thing here in the northeast, and it don't really matter who discovered it, the Native Americans *did* make maple syrup of sorts before the white man got involved, in effect showed the white man."[195] Despite this sugarmaker's at-times archaic terminology, the point of his story is clear—sugaring was known to the indigenous people of what is now Vermont long ago, and they taught the European incomers about sugaring, in effect, helping create one of the things that defines Vermont and Vermonter to the present day.

THE HERITAGE MEANING OF MAPLE

There is widely used terminology in Vermont that creates strong definitional divisions between Vermonters, who are termed "woodchucks," and outsiders, who are referred to as "flatlanders." These terms are used to differentiate insiders and outsiders to the state's identity, and some sugarmakers use these terms as well. The separation between the two groups falls along many different lines, as one sugarmaker whose family has long roots in the state explains when discussing people who have moved to Vermont more recently and started sugaring: "I don't know if they carry a lot of the culture of it either. I mean, these guys are IBMers or 9-to-5 jobs, and they happen to have a nice house with some property in the country, and they know they can pay some of the tax bill with trees that are already growing there. And so I think it's a dollars-and-cents incentive, very much more so. If you could go back in time with the same dwellers and have to gather with a horse and sled with three feet of snow, regardless of the economics, they probably wouldn't do it."[196]

The term "IBMer" is sugaring shorthand for someone who comes to Vermont from outside for some non-sugaring occupation, especially one that pays comparatively well, and takes up sugaring as a hobby or sideline project. The term comes from an IBM chip production facility that opened in Essex Junction in 1958, creating an influx of well-paid incomers. It's not a term of endearment. There are certainly class differences in what is described as an insider/outsider identification, but in this man's explanation, the important difference is in cultural identity. IBMers do not have sugaring in their blood and bones, rooted in a family past of gathering on buckets in deep snow. That connection to the past is hugely important in these conversations, as made evident by another sugarmaker who responded to my question about what tradition means in sugaring. It means "family. I mean, it's passed down from generation to generation here, and to work with your father, with your family on a nice spring day in the woods, I don't think there's anything any better than that. . . . It's nice to tap some of the trees that your father did or your grandfather did."[197] The connection to the past is made synonymous with sugaring and Vermont identity. A violation of one invalidates the other two, so someone without a long history has a much steeper climb to be understood as a proper sugarmaker and a Vermonter, although as this same man stated just a short time later, it is possible for an outsider to come in and become a good, proper sugarmaker: "Everybody needs to start somewhere, . . . there's room for everybody."[198] What is more important is that the properness of sugaring is maintained, by either new blood or old.

Economic realities of real estate in Vermont mean that those who get the opportunity to sugar on any large scale have some wealth at their disposal, either through an IBMer-type job that provides a comparatively large income, or commonly, a family connection that allows for ownership of land and trees, because to sugar, "you either have to own a lot of land, or you have to lease it, and so a lot of people that sugar probably were farmers . . . and that's often a family, you know."[199] A family that has been in the state for many generations has a better chance of having accrued the land necessary to sugar, so there is a connection between long ancestry and sugaring. While many people talked to me about heritage and history, I heard just as many sugarmakers who either did not make a distinction between incomer and Vermonter or did not care about the distinction when it came to sugaring. The sentiment seemed to be that a flatlander was potentially just as proper a steward of the maples, as long as they sugared the right way. The stewardship was more important than who was doing the stewarding, or whether the owner was born in the state or not, according to many sugarmakers such as this one: "I think stewardship is a much higher aspiration than ownership, you know, because ownership is very temporal, but stewardship can go on forever."[200]

Interestingly enough, in this analysis, a long sense of time is still important, but time's arrow points forward here instead of backward. The justification for propriety is sugaring in a way that makes it sustainable far into the future, rather than a history of sugaring that extends far into the past. Either way, personal ownership is nearly irrelevant. This approach, expressed by a sugarmaker here, seems to suggest that the trees do not belong so much to Vermont or Vermonters, but to some sense of proper Vermontiness that includes caring for the maples, and for maple.

> In its basest form, it's really about "this land is mine, and I don't want any threat to it, or to take away what I perceive to be either my rights or my heritage," and that's one sentiment that I

don't find so healthy. . . . You can't really look at land ownership in the sense of "me me me" because if you're really in it for the long term, in the way you want to manage a woodland, it isn't going to be yours forever. So that whole property rights thing strikes me as sort of odd because it doesn't reflect the true values that most of us are after if we're in this maple business for generations.[201]

In this man's construction, the "true values" of Vermonters and sugarmakers disallow someone from making strong distinctions based solely on class lines or insider/outsider identities. The very sense of properness that is a trait of sugaring demands that properness be the differentiator, rather than birthplace or occupation. If someone sugars well, with an eye to a longtime line (forward or backward), they are proper.

The term *flatlander* for an outsider has been explained to me a couple different ways. The first is that Vermont is the land of green mountains (it is right there in the name, after all), and to be an outsider is to come from somewhere flat, outside the mountains. The other story I've heard is more intriguing in the context of the current conversation, though, because it deals with how to do things properly. The first waves of European immigrants who came into Vermont and settled did so on the sides of the hills, carving out small hill farms for themselves in the process. When Vermont became a Europeanized place with its own identity, this is where the farmers lived. Later waves of immigration settled the land in the flats and bottoms, rather than the hillsides, either out of preference for that land and that form of farming, or simply because the upland was more or less all claimed by earlier immigrants. So, "flatlander" became a term for the people who farmed the low-lying areas, as opposed to the hill farms of the first wave. Regardless of which story is true—and every good folklorist will tell you what every good historian should, that to ask which story is true is to ask the wrong question—the meanings contained in both stories are very similar. Both versions of the story convey a sense of what Steve Watson calls "the rural-historic," a trope of real history being situated in the countryside.[202] A flatlander is a person who is not part of the proper rural history, and therefore not properly Vermonty. They lack properness either because they come from somewhere outside the lines on the map called Vermont, or they are not proper because they farm the wrong part of the landscape. In the second narrative explanation, living in Vermont and even having generations in the state are not important. What is important is the sense of propriety, of doing things the way they ought to be done. That sense pervades sugaring, with its ideal of stewardship of the land and trees.

Propriety in sugaring walks through a potentially tricky minefield of history and that sense of responsibility to the trees and the past. It is an easy line to cross between respecting the past and being beholden to it, and in an activity as rooted in a time and place as much as sugaring is, it would be very easy to understand "doing it properly" as "doing it the way we always have." The red-checked coats, horses, and buckets of the maple bottle imagery speaks of "the way we've always done it," and that narrative is constantly reinforced in many marketing and other communications between sugaring and the public. However, relatively few sugarmakers with operations of significant size gather on buckets with a horse-drawn sledge, opting instead for other processes that increase efficiency. The question is, how much change from the traditional way of sugaring can the process accept, and still be understood as sugaring properly?

This question is not an easy one, or one with a universal answer. A ready example of the complexities and variations in people's answer can be found in the technology of reverse osmosis, a process of removing particulates from liquid by forcing the liquid through filters under pressure. In sugaring, RO systems are used to remove water and concentrate the sugars in the sap before putting over the boil. Sugarmakers typically talk about the RO process in their sugaring in terms of what percent they run their sap to, that is, what percentage of sugar concentration do they aim for at the end of reverse osmosis. The sap comes from the tree at anywhere from 0.5 percent sugar (for a bad run and/or a marginal species of maple) to perhaps 3 percent sugar (for a sugar maple, *Acer saccharum*, in good soil) or higher if conditions are favorable. Simple logic will tell you that the higher concentration of sugar in the sap before you start boiling, the less time and fuel you will have to expend boiling the sap into syrup, which legally becomes syrup at around 67 percent sugar concentration.[203] So, if a sugarmaker runs some sap through reverse osmosis and concentrates the sugars further than the, say, 2 percent the trees give out, that sugarmaker is going to save even more time and money in the boil. How far (to what percent) to run the RO is a topic of much discussion, with a wide range of opinions. Among sugarmakers who use RO rigs, I have heard concentrations from a low of 4 percent up to 24 percent, with rationales for every number along the way. One sugarmaker told me of someone who ran his RO up to 35 percent, and there was more than a little suspicion in his voice when he mentioned that number to me.

What difference does it make what percent a sugarmaker runs their RO to before boiling? The end goal is to remove water molecules from the sap, so does the method used to remove the water matter, or how much water gets removed by which method? A refrain I heard over and over, from sugarmakers from all over the sugaring world, was that real maple syrup had only two ingredients: sap and heat. As long as those two ingredients were present, then the resulting product could legitimately be called maple syrup. As one sugarmaker explained, "sap comes from the tree. Nothing's added, nothing's removed. We essentially make our syrup by boiling it and removing the water."[204] Another sugarmaker echoed the same sentiment by discussing the process of boiling, rather than focusing on the sap. There is something inviolable about putting sap over heat and boiling it to remove water. Without those two factors, maple isn't maple and sugaring isn't sugaring, as they are the most necessary, most fundamental parts of sugaring. You can't sugar without pure sap, and the "boiling process would be one that hasn't changed, one of the few. It's getting more efficient, but the actual process of putting [sap] in the pans and over a fire, that's probably one of the few things that hasn't changed."[205] Again and again, I heard some version of that statement. There was always an essentiality to the sap and the boil. From a legal standpoint, maple syrup made in the United States must be made exclusively by concentrating maple sap, although how that concentration occurs is not specified. The sap is a legal requirement, while the heat is a cultural norm within the sugaring community. It is a cultural norm that is very deeply engrained, though. "You have to cook it, for sure," as one sugarmaker definitively told me.[206]

There are other methods available for concentrating the sugar and/or removing the water from maple sap. The process of reverse osmosis is discussed more thoroughly in just a bit, but there is a much older technology that can remove water from maple sap. I was told by a handful of sugarmakers of this other concentrating process, whereby the sap is left out overnight to freeze. The frozen portion will be mostly purer water, while the inclusions in the sap, particularly the sugars, will precipitate out and remain in the liquid portion. The ice can then simply be removed to leave a liquid with a higher concentration of sugar than before the freeze. Repeated freezing and removal of the ice can supposedly concentrate the sap down to a fairly high percentage of sugar. I know of no one using this method to make maple products, and the lack of boiling in this method would make it suspect, at the very least, as a proper sugaring technique because, for sugarmakers, boiling sap over heat is a necessary process to make maple.

Within that framework, though, there is room for discussion and debate (and a bit of disagreement) as to how much heat needs to be part of the system. No one I spoke with said that boiling at all was unnecessary. The heating process was understood to create flavor notes in the syrup that could not be replicated without boiling, although explanations of how these flavors developed varied. Some sugarmakers told me that the smoke of the wood fire perfumed the syrup, which would leave those boiling over oil or electric in a bind. Others explained that processes of caramelization, similar to the Maillard reaction, occurred in the boil, and that this irreplaceable process helped make both the color and the flavor that we understand maple to have.

Funnily enough, you will not find further discussion of the Maillard reaction in the chapter on culinary meanings earlier in this book. The food science and chemistry of maple tells us that Maillard browning does indeed occur in maple syrup during the boil, provided the sucrose in the sap is broken into fructose and glucose. However, this book is not about the chemistry of maple. Those topics have been written about elsewhere, but here I am exploring the *meanings* people make with maple.[207] The truth or falseness of the presence of Maillard browning in boiling maple is of less importance than the fact that this particular bit of science is a part of some sugarmakers' narratives, and that they make meaning with Maillard in their discussion of the proper maple-making process.

Regardless of where the flavor comes from in boiling, the boil is vital to proper sugaring according to every sugarmaker I've met. Sap and heat. Those two ingredients are the only inviolable aspects of making maple, and they are also the only two aspects that are inviolable in making meaning with maple. The evaporator is central, therefore, and it serves as a sort of nexus point, a node of meaning in sugaring. This is not terribly surprising, as the evaporator is also a nexus point of the physical process as well—all the sap has to go through the evaporator at some point to become syrup. The machine's centrality, explained by a sugarmaker here, is perhaps helped by the constant presence it has had in sugaring. The normal evaporator "that we still use today was created in the late 1800s, so you had a unit here that's been relatively simple for a hundred years."[208] Sugarmakers recognize that, even with the incorporation of various peripheral technologies, the evaporator has been a fundamental part of sugaring for quite some time, and it has remained, at its core, fundamentally simple, fundamentally the same. Sap and heat. The oldest technologies for bringing maple sap to a boil—fire and heated stones—have been joined by other methods of getting heat into the sap, including firing over oil burners and electric elements. Oil and wood (along with its relative methods, wood chips, wood pellets, even gasification, etc.) seem to have a more or less equal footing in terms of meaning, in that some form of combustion occurs right under the sap. These direct-combustion methods of burning wood or oil mean roughly the same thing and amount in sugaring, although not necessarily to those outside of sugaring. A sugarmaker who has boiled over both wood and oil explained the potential for different meanings to me, explaining that "we used to have a wood-fired evaporator, and we switched to oil years back. One of the expectations, or what [tourists] are thinking about coming to see is that quaint old sugarhouse with a wood-fired evaporator and the old Vermont farmer with the checkered shirt on."[209] The stereotyped image of sugaring is of a wood-fired evaporator, an image that is perpetuated on bottles of syrup and advertisements all over the place. Sugarmakers, nevertheless, while utilizing that imagery, know the realities of modern collection and evaporation technology, and that a wide variety of heat sources is possible and even common. The disjuncture between what sugarmakers know and what tourists and consumers expect is sometimes problematic, especially for the sugar-maker above who fires on oil.

The imagery of the wood-fired evaporator is not always a prob-lem, though, even for this sugarmaker who understands the gulf between reality and the tourist/consumer narrative. If tourists "have a little vision of it, something to do with horses and buckets and steam [rising from the boiling sap], that's fine. The fact is, the basic physiology that produces sap flow isn't going to change, and that's what makes us so unique."[210] Even sugarmakers who acknowledge that boiling over a wood fire is more traditional generally accept that oil is a common enough fuel in sugaring. And if the outsider has a different understanding, that's fine because the narrative of sugaring is part of the heritage, and the heritage is part of the narra-tive. The image of steam rising from the sap is part of the narrative, and a part that can be both seen and felt. A visit to a sugarhouse during the season will often include a multisensory immersion (so to speak) in the boiling sap, with the sight of the bubbles, the sound of the roiling liquid, and the feel of the moisture evaporating out and up all complemented by the rich, sweet smell of the nascent syrup. Waterton and Watson delve into the various aesthetic aspects of a heritage tourism experience, in order to make sense of how and why such experiences are so often so meaningful. They state that "while the visual appears to predominate in representations, we have to consider other forms of practice and experience, and we must con-sider these both within, and as a part of the contexts of meaning, the semiotic landscapes of heritage tourism."[211] The story in the minds of tourists and consumers places emphasis on such displays, even when they depart from the realities of sugaring, but that is not a problem, as sugarmakers know the line between the story and the actuality, the inner frame and the outer face.[212] Again, the essential nature of sap and heat is evoked by the sugarmaker above—the trees produce sap for the same reasons, and it is boiled, so everything else, such as whether a sugarmaker boils on wood or oil, is incidental. Electric evaporators, which work along the lines of a scaled-up electric tea kettle, tend to be more for the smaller producer and are generally not widespread in commercial sugaring, so their meaning is mini-mal in terms of maple being communicated across a wide range. The two dominant forms of heating sap are oil and some version of wood (cut timber, wood chips, etc.)

Steam evaporators are another technology for boiling that make a slightly different meaning. Steam is gaining some popularity in the commercial sugaring world, albeit slowly. The steam referred to in the anecdote above is the steam that rises from any open pan of boiling sap, and that steam is understood as a necessary part of all sugaring. A steam evaporator is a different beast entirely, and one whose wide-spread approval is tentative at best. As one sugarmaker told me, "It was gaining a mixed reaction, of course. I mean, change doesn't come easy around here, but it had everybody's curiosity."[213] Steam evaporation is, in essence, a giant double-boiler, where steam is generated from water by another apparatus and piped over to the evaporator, where that steam is used to heat the sap. The boiling point of sap is a little above the boiling point of water, so the steam has to be pressurized to achieve the desired temperatures for evaporation. One of the immediate advantages to steam evaporation is that it makes it impossible to burn on. Burning on is when the maple sap burns to the bottom of the evaporator pan, forming a dark and stubborn crust that could, in addition to creating a cleaning problem, taint the flavor of a batch of syrup, or worse, ruin a boiling pan by warping it. Burning on has been the bane of many a sugarmaker, as one explained to me that there are "a lot of exaggerators and liars in the maple industry too. Show me somebody that says they never burned their front pan, and I'll show you a liar."[214]

Steam evaporation, however, eliminates that danger because of the gentle, moist heat it provides. The gentle, moist heat of a double-boiler is precisely why this method of heating is used for various temperamental cooking tasks, such as heating dairy products, which can scorch or split easily, or melting chocolate, which can burn in a heart-beat (there is more than one reason that the purposeful heating and cooling of chocolate is called "tempering"). The precision involved in hitting the relatively small window of concentration required of syrup, that magical 66–68 percent sugar solution, makes maple a pretty temperamental cooking job as well. Boiling on steam takes some small portion of temperament out of the equation. A sugarmaker who wants to boil on steam takes on the task of learning how to be a steamfitter and how to run a steam engine, but making use of another realm of knowledge is nothing new to a sugarmaker. Because steam evaporation creates no smoke or combustion products though, at least not in the place where the sap is being boiled, it has raised an eyebrow on more than one sugarmaker. Does the lack of the products of combustion make the syrup different? Does it lose that ineffable something that boiling over a fire gives to the maple?

Steam boilers do just that—they boil. So, the essential ingredient of heat is there, even if steam evaporation does not have the same widespread level of trust that wood firing does. The question of properness comes into play because steam boiling encroaches on the outer boundary of the core of sugaring. It sits closer to the margin between proper sugaring and improper sugaring, making steam mean something different from oil or wood-fired evaporation. Fire seems to be the key. While many sugarmakers expressed the essential aspects of sugaring to me as sap and *heat*, perhaps for some, the real essentials are sap and *fire*. Whether it is a wood fire or oil fire matters less because those two fuels are accorded roughly equal status, but steam, with its fire physically removed and at a distance from the sap, comprises a different meaning to the essential two ingredients.

The concentrating process that occurs over the heat is one thing, but most commercial and some smaller-scale sugarmakers begin the concentration process in their sap well before it hits the back pan, through the use of reverse osmosis. So, what does it mean to run RO up to 24 percent? Concentrating the sugar without fire may be marginal for some sugarmakers, but concentrating the sugar without heat at all is really stepping toward an edge. How close to that edge one goes is determined by what that percentage number of RO concentration means to them, in terms of sugaring properly. For some sugarmakers, 24 percent means cost savings and an edge of economic efficiency that keeps their operation in business from one year to the next. In this case, a sugarmaker is making a very economic meaning with reverse osmosis. For another sugarmaker, though, 24 percent may be too high, and some ineffable quality of the syrup may be lost by concentrating to that percentage before boiling, in the same way that steam's remote combustion raises doubt in some. For that sugarmaker, a heritage meaning is being made with RO, such that using too much RO, and by association, not using enough boiling, presents a threat to the heritage of maple, to doing it properly.

The threat to heritage is a diffuse threat to "the way we do/did things," but it is also a more material threat to the trees, landscape, and inherited property. The state and its resources are wealth, held commonly by all Vermonters (although not politically organized as a commonwealth, such as Kentucky or Pennsylvania), and just as the idea of propriety needs guarding, so too does the land as material possession. Tim Cresswell argues in his book *Place: A Short Introduction* that "people, things and practices were often strongly linked to particular places and that when this link was broken—when people acted 'out of place'—they were deemed to have committed a 'transgression.' . . . place does not have meanings that are natural and obvious but ones that are created by some people with more power than others to define what is and is not appropriate."[215]

For some sugarmakers, running RO up to 24 percent is a transgression, not just against maple syrup, but against the inherited land and landscape of maples, people, and the process of sugaring. Others negotiate the meaning of appropriate and transgressive differently, and their acceptable percentage is settled on a different number. Who gets to decide is based on things like connection to the land, personal and family history in Vermont, and sense of doing things the proper way, often conceived as *our* way. As the journalist Alexander Wolff states, "Vermonters fetishize a sense of community and apartness."[216] So you end up with different sugarmakers making different meanings by applying different understandings of appropriateness and transgression, all by deciding where to stop concentrating their sap through their RO rigs.

Both meanings are being made with RO, and these two meanings, contradictory though they may be, work together to show how important the tightrope walk between notions of old and notions of new can be in sugaring. Reverse osmosis is very, very widespread in sugaring operations of any size. RO rigs are expensive, so, although there are homemade RO setups that backyarders can try, incorporating a proper RO rig into an operation suggests economic investment beyond the backyard hobbyist stage. As discussed in the introduction, this book is about sugarmakers who work at a level above the home hobbyist because it is at that level that the publicly negotiated meanings of maple begin to become important. At that level of sugaring, RO is almost as common as tubing systems. The question is not, does using RO hurt the heritage of maple? The question is, how much RO can the heritage of maple handle?

The tightrope walk of any technology (and there are a good few) in sugaring is a balance of perceived authenticity, which is a fraught and problematic notion. Regina Bendix's *In Search of Authenticity* enlighteningly delves into what authenticity is and what it isn't. One of the major things authenticity is, is overused. I often ask students to delve into what they actually mean when they make a claim of authenticity, and where they are situating the authority that makes something authentic. A simple response whenever one of my students claims something to be authentic is to ask, authentically what? Ethnic restaurants provide a good example. If one walks into a Chinese restaurant in Cleveland, what will determine whether the food is authentic? Is it whether the dish is something Chinese people eat? If so, then Subway is authentically Chinese because I know there are people who are ancestrally and ethnically Chinese in Cleveland who eat at Subway. Is it whether a Chinese person made the food? If so, then is a Chinese employee working at Subway making authentic Chinese food? Is it a matter of whether the food in the Cleveland restaurant is eaten in China? Well, Subway has nearly five hundred locations in China, so. . . . You get the picture. Whether any technology is seen as a threat to the authenticity of sugaring is largely based on where one seats authenticity, and the seating arrangements are by no means clear or easy when it comes to being authentic. The shibboleth for sugaring seems to be that sense of propriety. If something is going to maintain the authenticity of maple, it is going to do so because it is "proper sugaring."

In addition to RO and steam evaporation, many other technologies have been invented for, or assumed into, sugaring over the years. Looking at each one to see how they balance between maintaining propriety and pushing sugaring forward is instructive to what really is fundamental and unalterable to sugaring, and what is peripheral to that core and therefore malleable. The evaporator itself is just a fancy setup that puts a pan over a fire, so it may not raise too many flags. All the evaporator does is standardize and make more efficient something that has been understood as basic to sugaring for ages—the placing of a vessel for sap over a heat source. Innovations in that system, such as the arch and the flue pan, are just variations on that theme, so they seem fairly innocent as well. I have yet to hear a sugarmaker express suspicion of a boiling pan that has flues in it, as opposed to a flat-bottomed pan, and no one has questioned the validity of an arch to contain the firebox, rather than setting the pan over an open fire.

However, other pieces of equipment that can be attached to the evaporator, such as an air injection system or a steam away, change the boiling process in a more basic way.[217] Air injection systems pump air into the boiling sap in either the front pan or the back pan (or both), and they are generally thought to help a sugarmaker produce lighter-colored syrup. A steam away is conceptually similar to a turbocharger on a car engine, in that it takes a side product of evaporation (steam) and cycles it back into the system. In this case, the goal is to use the steam to preheat the sap before it enters the pans, thus decreasing the time needed to bring it to the boil. Neither of these systems raises much of an eyebrow, though I did hear a couple sugarmakers scoff gently at air injection. The scoffing seemed less about air injection being a violation of proper sugaring, and more an implication that some sugarmakers needed some artificial help making Fancy, the lightest grade of syrup. The ability to make Fancy, especially to be able to make it regularly and reliably, has long been seen as a mark of skill and expertise as a sugarmaker. Neither of the sugarmakers who scoffed at the use of air injection used it in their own rigs, and their response fell more on the side of a brotherly ribbing than a scornful reproach toward someone sugaring improperly.

Technological innovations outside the sugarhouse were also a little more varied in their reception and perceived level of threat to sugaring properly, although none was rejected, and all had achieved a wide acceptance after a sort of probationary period. Usually, a handful of sugarmakers act as early adopters, and others wait to see their results and reactions to each new piece of technology. Check valves, plastic tubing, and wet and dry vacuum systems all came into sugaring in stages, with some sugarmakers suspicious of either the impact on their bottom line (an economic meaning) or the threat to sugaring properly (a heritage meaning). Some of these technologies really needed a probationary period, as they were fine tuned to work with the other parts of sugaring. Tubing, for example, was not immediately accepted or successful when it debuted in the late 1950s, as explained by a sugarmaker who is widely regarded as a source for good historical information on sugaring. Tubing was initially "an experiment, that's really what it was. A lot of the tubing three years later was laying out behind the sugarhouse somewhere, it just wasn't doing the job. It took fifteen more years of science, by '75, tubing was then working, but it wasn't doing it in 1960."[218] The first tubing systems were rigid metal affairs, with many joints and little flexibility—a noble idea that outran the capabilities of the available materials of the time. A technology that is today nearly ubiquitous in commercial sugaring went through some awkward growing pains before becoming widely accepted as a part of proper sugaring.

At MapleRama 2014, hosted by Franklin County, the latest technology that was in that probationary period was Tap Track, a system for monitoring the amount of vacuum pressure in the lines that drain and collect the sap from the trees. Any sugarmaker with a vacuum setup will tell you that loss of pressure or worse, loss of sap, due to leaks or other flaws in the system is a constant threat and struggle. Knowing the layout of the lines and how each set of lines performs usually involves the sugarmaker regularly walking the woods, checking the integrity of the system.[219] Tap Track is a set of remote, wireless sensors that attach to the vacuum tubing system and measure the amount of pressure in the lines to which they are attached. Properly distributed, a set of Tap Track sensors is able to monitor the many branches and connections of lines running through a sugarbush, and then relay that information to any smart device (tablet, computer, even a smart phone) that the sugarmaker wants. So, instead of walking the lines regularly to check for leaks, all a sugarmaker with Tap Track has to do is open an app on their phone and check if any of the lines on the graphic is flashing red or orange.

Several sugarmakers who opened their sugarhouses for MapleRama in 2014 had Tap Track, and it was very much the latest-and-greatest thing on display for that season. The reception was generally positive, and more than a few literal oohs and ahhs were heard as Tap Track was being demonstrated. There is genuine good reason for the oohing and ahhing, as this system directly addresses one of the more time-consuming and, frankly, tedious parts of being a sugarmaker—the constant walking of the lines to check for damage. Time and timing are everything in sugaring, from knowing when to start the boil, to regulating the flow of sap from the back pan to the front, to knowing how much sap to run into the RO and how quickly the RO will feed the evaporator, to how to keep the heat at the constant perfect temperature, sugaring involves coordinating the timing of many different, interacting systems. The constant tweaking of the various systems to get peak flow makes not only good economic sense, but also represents the height of sugaring properly. Anything that can save a sugarmaker *time*, allowing them to devote themselves more fully to perfecting their *timing*, is going to be given an attentive reception.

While those demonstrating Tap Track were already converts and therefore enthusiastic about its potential, some of the sugarmakers on the tour at that MapleRama in 2014 were hesitant about this new innovation. As we rode the bus from a sugarhouse where Tap Track was on display to the next stop on the tour, I spoke with a sugarmaker about what we had just seen. I did not know him, and I don't recall where he was from, but he did not have any of the stereotypical New England accents, and he did not present himself as a multigenerational Vermonter. In any case, he did not strike me as an old-timer, either chronologically or conceptually. Still, he spoke in guarded terms about his enthusiasm for Tap Track. He told me he would worry about a sugarmaker who was not regularly in the woods, relying instead on a machine to indicate whether things were working properly out there. Echoes of conversations from other contexts, about students' inability to do long division since the advent of the calculator or the loss of map reading skills due to GPS, rang in my head as this man explained his fears to me. And I understood and sympathized with his argument—I still prefer maps to GPS when driving. He seemed worried that the loss of intimacy with the woods would be a violation of the proper-ness with which sugaring ought to be done. In addition to the recipe of sap and heat, this sugarmaker was suggesting that an immediacy with the woods and trees was an irreducible need for proper sugaring. Now, to be sure, I got no indication from any sugarmaker that they would ever consider abandoning their woods and leaving the lines to the machines, and I don't think this sugarmaker on the bus with me was seeing that scenario as an immediate threat either. However, Tap Track seemed to him to at least have the potential to be a thin end of a wedge he was not completely comfortable seeing driven into sugaring. For this man, and for many other sugarmakers, the woods is just as vital a location of maple as the sugarhouse. The field of sugaring includes both, and in some cases other locations as well, into a semiotic landscape that, taken together, conveys the heritage meanings of sugaring.[220]

So, authenticity means propriety in sugaring. To honor the heritage of maple is to make heritage a *meaningful* meaning, to use heritage as a rationale for ensuring integrity in the way one sugars. To maintain the integrity of maple as process and maple as product, one must enact the process properly, which means guarding the essential qualities (widely held to be that "sap plus heat" recipe, although we have seen nuance to the equation) and altering at the edges only in ways that do not threaten the core. People often negotiate their sense of authenticity in a food item in terms of a traditional referent. That traditionality forms a necessary part of the sense of authenticity.[221] The appeal to tradition, to "the way we used to do it," sets a standard or widely accepted set of practices that embodies proper sugaring. If a sugarmaker meets the standards of the forebears by acknowledging and orienting herself to the accepted reference point, then that sugarmaker can claim propriety, and therefore authenticity.

Mind, though, that "the way we used to do it" is not understood as completely static. The reference point is not just technological or methodological, beyond some adherence to the "sap plus heat" model. More important is attending to the spirit of sugaring properly, not just the method. Merely adhering to old ways of *doing* is far too simplistic an understanding of the authenticity that inhabits sugaring, as is made evident by the constant flow of new technologies and innovative changes into sugaring, only some of which are discussed here. Perhaps because of the many changes to the process that have come to be accepted, sugarmakers rarely talk in terms of authenticity itself. The idea is there, but it is negotiated in terms of sugaring properly or sugaring well, both of which can be done while including newer technological changes, such as RO or tubing. In so doing, sugarmakers subvert a simplistic narrative of authenticity that Bella Dicks explains "suggests the existence of an original, pristine cultural identity, existing in isolation from influences brought in" from the outside.[222] Influences from outside the traditional methods of sugaring have often been blended into what is considered proper sugaring. Indeed, to sugar properly has come to demand newer technologies in some cases. Using equipment made with lead solder used to be the norm, but now, to do so is widely viewed as bad, improper sugaring. It is also illegal, which helps reinforce the sense of impropriety.

The language of propriety shifts the focus away from a sense of the past that authenticity often clings to, and puts attention more squarely on the present, on how to sugar right here, right now. Propriety has a sort of built in flexibility, allowing what counts as proper to change with the times, where authenticity, with its common rooting in the past, is beholden to that past in a way that would make innovation more difficult. Sugaring has a reference point that is rooted in the past, but the past is not in itself meaningful in terms of heritage. The story communicated outwardly reflects authenticity in terms of methods, with the imagery of buckets and horses, which is a common enough process in many places and with many food items, such as wine, as scholars Claude Chapuis and Benoît Lecat discuss in France, where some grape growers "entertained regular customers, visitors, and tourists who were passing through. They conveyed the image of humble, warm, cheerful country people sticking to the good old methods."[223]

The outward display of authenticity rooted in past methods is the same in both cases, whether in the French countryside or on a bottle of syrup. Sugarmakers themselves, though, make meaning with the more flexible notion of propriety. Their heritage, what they have inherited from the past, is not the methods of making syrup, but a sense of responsibility for making it well. Certain methodological constraints remain, but if sap is boiled over heat, then the form of authenticity that is internally meaningful to sugarmakers is maintained.

Folklorists such as Henry Glassie (1992, 1993) and Handler and Linnekin (1984) will tell you that an understanding of authenticity that is simplistically rooted in exact reflection of the past is hugely flawed. Folklorists are correct. Every tradition one cares to throw on the table as an example very likely includes some innovation in the way it is enacted now, compared to its original form(s). That is the very nature of tradition, as it is a lived thing. Various phrases such as "oral-formulaic" or "living tradition" indicate the balance between static form and variable process involved in most cultural activities. I am not talking in this chapter about the folklorist's understanding of authenticity, however. What I mean here is the sense of authenticity that is generally employed by the public (including sugarmakers), and that sense of authenticity is very often justified by the non-sugaring public with a sense of rootedness in the past and a rejection of changes in the present. Sugarmakers root it in propriety, while often simultaneously reinforcing the rooted-in-past narrative with marketing materials and other communications of sugaring's process.

Who decides what is proper, though, and who decides whether a new innovation maintains properness in sugaring? It might be instructive to look at how sugaring in Vermont is regulated in a legal sense. I am not pretending that senses of propriety are controlled at a governmental level; in fact they quite often act extra-judicially and even contra-judicially.[224] However, in this case of sugaring, the same epistemology is behind both who determines properness and who regulates the industry. There are certainly governmental rules about maple, such as the Code of Vermont Rules "CVR 20-011-002," 2013, that hold sway in Vermont, at both the state and the federal level.[225] Like any other process understood as agricultural, sugaring has its share of regulations that shape how it should be done. Local, less top-down meanings of "should be done" are layered onto those governmental regulations, and every once in a while stand in contradiction to one of those many rules handed down by the government. One of the rules most frequently quoted to me as one that can be broken while maintaining propriety deals with the sugarhouse floor. Governmental rules state that the floor of the sugarhouse needs to be easily cleanable, for health and safety reasons. I have been in more than a few sugarhouses that had floors made of dirt, gravel, or other materials that a government inspector might not deem "easily cleanable." I have happily enjoyed the syrup produced in those sugarhouses just as much as any.

Technically, the FDA and USDA could inspect sugarhouses to ensure adherence to the rules, but in reality, this is a rare occurrence.

THE HERITAGE MEANING OF MAPLE

This fact is not an example of poor government oversight; in fact, quite the contrary. Sugarmakers (in Vermont especially) have a long-standing reputation of policing themselves and making sure that their product is pure. Many sugarmakers could tell me stories of other sugarmakers who were not sugaring properly, who were "out there making syrup, some of it got so bad you could wind it up on a spool, that's how bad it was, you know. We didn't need that kind of stuff."[226] What this man is describing is syrup that is "ropey." Ropey syrup is too thick and has a viscosity that evokes strings or fibers, making the syrup feel wrong in the mouth and not pour properly. Ropey syrup also tends to have a lot of off-flavors, sometimes tasting overcooked, sometimes having a taste too heavy in mineral flavors. Regardless, it is syrup that no Vermont sugarmaker wants being bought and consumed, as it taints the reputation of all maple to have such an inferior product out there. Sugarmakers tend to be very protective of their syrup, by which I mean *all* syrup that is made properly, not just the syrup they themselves make. The state's Agency of Agriculture and the Vermont Maple Sugar Makers Association have lobbied with a good deal of success to allow sugarmakers in the state to keep watch over themselves. As such, sugarmakers determine to a large degree the enforcement of the regulations, if not determining the regulations themselves.

Many sugarmakers, from the smallest producers to the largest operations, take the responsibility for enforcement seriously. A standard refrain is that one bad batch of syrup from one bad sugarmaker (i.e., someone who is sugaring improperly) would hurt everyone who makes maple. A customer lost could easily become a narrative tainted, and the story of Vermont's purity distilled into the bottle of syrup could be transformed into a story of violated expectations and another customer sticking with the now perceived safety and ease of other options from Log Cabin or Aunt Jemima. A rising tide lifts all boats, but the lowering tide of a bad batch of syrup being sold could sink all sugarmakers. Here, the economic meaning and the heritage meaning are so closely intertwined as to nearly become one. I was told a couple stories about a sugarmaker "from around the hill" (always somewhere that was definably *not here*) who either purposefully tainted his syrup by cutting it with corn syrup or caused some misdeed through negligent practice. In both cases, what is being violated is a sense of propriety. Either the maple was not the proper product, or the process of sugaring was not enacted properly. In all versions of this story, local sugarmakers got wind of the issue and some form of mob justice was enforced. I am not talking about someone sending "a couple'a boys" around to the offender's sugarhouse with pillowcases full of doorknobs, but the offender and the offender's syrup were both made known to governmental authorities so that the syrup and the faulty practice could both be removed from the system as quickly and as thoroughly as possible.

Another narrative I was given by several sugarmakers was about the maple producer who was sent to jail for a period of some years for selling maple that had been blended with beet sugar. One sugarmaker told me that the story occurred "before your time—he's actually out of jail now—there was a maple candy producer that actually went to jail because he was doctoring his maple sugar with beet sugar. You can't tell the difference between beet sugar and maple sugar in maple sugar candy. Of course, it's much cheaper, and so he would use a little bit of maple and a whole lot of beet sugar and was marketing it as pure. And they caught him at it, and he went to jail for quite a while. How many states would do that?"[227] Sometimes, emphasis was put on the role other sugarmakers played in ferreting out the bad seed, while other tellings stressed that this could only happen in Vermont. The thrust of the story was always that the purity and propriety of sugaring had to be maintained, and that such maintenance meant more in Vermont than elsewhere. An infraction that would draw a fine at most in another state resulted in significant jail time in Vermont.

Given that sugarmakers have taken and enacted this much responsibility for overseeing the legal purity and validity of maple, it is not surprising then to know that what gets called proper in a less legalistic sense is negotiated on a fairly informal basis as well. Sugarmakers as a whole allow a new technology, such as a check valve or a steam evaporator, to be taken in and called proper by common assent. Common does not always mean unanimous, of course, and it does not always mean permanent. Check valves, for example, are designed to disallow sap from flowing back into the tree once it has left and entered the tubing system. Sap reentering the tree can be problematic for a couple reasons. Sap returned to the tree is sap lost, so there is an economic meaning being applied, while sap flowing back into the tree can carry bacteria from the tubing system, potentially harming the tree (an agricultural meaning) or, a more common explanation, causing the tree to shut down the sap flow by beginning the process of healing the wound that is the taphole (another economic meaning).

There was a time when formaldehyde pellets were used toward a similar end in sugaring, preventing a tree from healing a taphole too early, but their use has been illegal in both the United States and Canada since the 1990s. More important, every sugarmaker who spoke of formaldehyde told me that it is bad for the tree, and therefore bad for sugaring. It is considered a violation of proper sugaring. No one knew of anyone who still used formaldehyde pellets, and more than one sugarmaker made it clear to me that anyone using them would very likely be subject to the sugaring version of "a couple'a boys" coming around to their woods. The rationale given, that formaldehyde is bad for the trees and therefore bad for sugaring, draws heavily on the stewardship identity of sugarmakers, employing both an ecological and an agricultural meaning.

Heritage is a complicated concept, involving senses of property ownership and properness of action toward it. Because maple is very often constructed as heritage in Vermont, many sugarmakers there apply an enormous feeling of responsibility to themselves and others to sugar well. They are beholden to many different entities by this responsibility: themselves, their trees, their neighbors, their ancestors, the Vermont way of life. Perhaps the most important sense of responsibility is to sugaring itself. These categories are nothing close to mutually exclusive, of course. Indeed, the responsibility to sugaring itself encompasses the people from the past (genetic ancestor or not) who sugared, as well as the land and trees on which one sugars. A duty to protect sugaring by doing it well and helping/reinforcing others to do it well carries many layers of meaning with it. In addition to serving the responsibility of heritage, protecting sugaring also protects the economic, ecological, and other meanings that sugaring has. Every kind of meaning that is made with sugaring, whether it is granted a chapter title in this book or not, is overseen and protected by Vermont sugarmakers' sense of propriety and responsibility toward sugaring's heritage. Heritage is a very meaningful meaning, and in Vermont, sugaring plays a hugely important role in the state's heritage, for both those who sugar and those who don't. It seems only logical then, that heritage meanings are vital to understanding sugaring in Vermont.

Epilogue
Identity

It's kind of like a little bit of a disease. It just keeps getting worse. You never quite make enough syrup, you always want to make a little bit more each year. And that's the nature of a sugar-maker. —Sugarmaker, 30 June 2010

Maple carries a lot of meaning, and a lot of different meanings, for Vermonters. The syrup is an exportable symbol of the state, literally distilled into jars and bottles and shipped around the world. The state's identity goes along with the syrup, in the form of narratives of the place and the sugaring process. Externally, maple acts as vehicle for the state's identity. Internally it serves the same purpose, or nearly the same purpose, as maple is used by Vermonters to communicate to and among themselves who they are. The internal narratives of greenness, simplicity, and a more "authentic" way of life are easily attached to sugaring, with its historic imagery of an open pan in the woods over a log fire. Those images, of the wood fire, the sap buckets, and the boiling taking place within nature, resonate with people in the state. Even for a longtime sugarmaker, "The aesthetic quality of the buckets is cool to me," evoking something simpler, something from the past that still gets to occur in Vermont.[228] Appreciating these images emphasizes for Vermonters that such tropes are fundamental to the place and the way the people are there.

The images that evoke a past are obviously placing priority on history, or at least precedent, for a sense of legitimacy. Sugaring has been done here before, therefore sugaring is a valid part of our identity. Sugaring has been done in this particular way before, so aspects of that way of sugaring are part of what validates our identity. Thinking of the past as a thing that has been handed down to the present turns history into heritage, with all the senses of entitlement and responsibility that come along with it. Sugaring means heritage in Vermont, so many Vermonters are protective of maple, thinking it more "ours" than "yours," and of decisions about what is proper for maple to be more validly made here than there. The distance between proper and property is not very far at all.

That sense of ownership appears in all manner of situations, from the idea that people who really know sugaring prefer Fancy syrup, while the darker grades are for tourists and foodies (both outsiders), to the notion of sugaring's spiritual home being in a state that makes less than a fifth of the world's total supply. Another sense of ownership comes in the form of stewardship, watching over the land and the trees by sugaring on them well. Because Vermont owns the identity of sugaring, there is a responsibility to walk that border of human and non-human as well as possible. The sometimes murky boundary between those two categories is where farming often exists, and maple pushes a little further conceptually, as a farming process that moves a little further within nature than most. All of these meanings root maple in Vermont, making the geography of immense and intense importance.

It is easy to discern the performance of rural idealism on a syrup bottle that shows a horse-drawn sledge and buckets hanging from trees. Less obvious may be how a sugarmaker walking their lines is performing part of their identity, or how labeling syrup with a new grading system that includes mention of taste is a fundamentally different performance. But they are, just the same. Every cultural act performs because every act that is culturally meaningful sends out signals that can be interpreted by others. On a syrup jar, the signal of the horses and buckets is meant to be interpreted, meant to communicate a certain meaning of rurality and tradition to the viewer. But the grading system that calls the syrup "Golden with Delicate Taste" instead of "Fancy" also sends out signals, some of them similar, some not. Golden and delicate are more objectively descriptive than fancy, which has more of a value judgment involved, but all three adjectives are communicating the same thing—that the stuff inside is extra-special and worthy of special attention. "Golden with Delicate Taste" also sends a signal that the consumer needs more information about the syrup inside the container. Fancy connotes, while golden and delicate denote. Fancy requires more knowledge beforehand to be interpreted properly, while golden and delicate are more broadly understandable and give more types of information. Fancy signals to the knowing audience, but golden and delicate signal to any audience. Even if the signals are the same, the assumed audiences are not.

When a sugarmaker labels their syrup "Pure Vermont" and emphasizes their geographic location, they are performing any number of identities by sending out signals—Vermont-iness, perhaps Franklin County-ness, maybe even *Not*-Quebec-iness. All of these things communicate and send meanings out to be received and interpreted, in this case to a consumer, but some signals go to other sugarmakers. Every time a sugarmaker talks about how much they make per tap, or describes how they clean their lines, or mentions the size of their RO, they are performing, sending out signals. They are communicating to other sugarmakers that they are proper, or that their operation is impressive and worthy not just of attention, but admiration because of its properness. These signals are rarely loud or showy; as one sugarmaker humbly and simply put it, "there are people in this state who know how to make syrup," but everyone I spoke to balances pride with humility, or at least caginess.[229] Good sugarmakers are not rare in Vermont. Rare is the sugarmaker, regardless of skill, who crows about how good they are.

All of these signals get sent out, some to specific audiences, others just to the wide world, where they are interpreted. Sugarmakers are like anyone else in relying on enough of a shared set of experiences and meanings with whoever receives their signals that the intended meaning comes across. The intended meaning that is almost always in the mix, consciously or unconsciously, is identity. A signal sent out that says, "this is what I do" or "this is how I do it" can just as easily be understood as saying, "*I am a person who* does this, in this way." There is a construction and communication of self at play here, which is true of pretty much any human action. Because sugaring has been used so long and so consistently in the construction and communication of Vermont and Vermonters, it has become the paradigmatic symbol of the state. The people who live there live among maples, even when they live nowhere near an actual maple tree themselves. They do so because maple trees, maple syrup, maple sugaring, and maple tropes are constantly present and used to convey the place or some trait the place is supposed to have. Maple is a constant symbol, carrying many and varied meanings internally and externally. Vermonters live among maples because maples are extremely meaningful there. Perhaps it is just as accurate to say that Vermonters live among *maple*.

NOTES

1. *A Taste of Spring*, n.d.
2. Interview with a sugarmaker, 13 June 2011.
3. Ritzer and Galli, *Food and Drink*, 58.
4. Interview with a sugarmaker, 21 July 2010.
5. Interview with a sugarmaker, 7 June 2010.
6. Wilk and Cliggett, *Economies and Cultures*, 66.
7. Johnston and Baumann, *Foodies*, 76.
8. Weil, "Virtual Antiquities," 231.
9. Flagg, *The Vermont Syrup Rush*, 14–15.
10. Interview with a sugarmaker, 30 June 2010.
11. "Organization," n.d.
12. Interview with a sugarmaker, 13 June 2011.
13. Interview with a sugarmaker, 13 June 2011.
14. Interview with a sugarmaker, 13 June 2011.
15. Wilk and Cliggett, *Economies and Cultures*, 66.
16. Hann and Hart, *Economic Anthropology*, 4.
17. Pollan, *The Omnivore's Dilemma*, 59.
18. Pollan, *The Omnivore's Dilemma*, 63.
19. Pollan, *The Omnivore's Dilemma*, 58.
20. Pollan, *The Omnivore's Dilemma*, 61.
21. Evaporators are often labeled by the size of the pan—the container in which the sap itself is boiled. An evaporator with a pan four feet by fourteen feet is a fairly large unit by most standards. To have two of this size running simultaneously is a considerable operation. More pointedly, running five RO rigs is a sign of a huge operation.
22. Nickerson, "Why Vt. Maple Producers Are Afraid of This Company."
23. Johnston and Baumann, *Foodies*, 79.
24. Interview with a sugarmaker, 15 June 2011.
25. Peterson, *Being Human*, 4-5.
26. Interview with a sugarmaker, 23 October 2010.
27. Lange, *The Norwegian Scots*, 199.
28. "Forestry and Timber Law," n.d.
29. There are layers of complexity to capitalism beyond this analysis, of course. For a further understanding, one should start with Smith's work itself, particularly *The Theory of Moral Sentiments* and *The Wealth of Nations*.
30. The imagery is nearly always male. Female figures are not absent from maple containers, but they are depicted very, very seldom. On the infrequent occasions when they do appear, they are always in the company of men, usually in red-checked coats. Sugaring itself is a gendered activity, with the physical spaces involved (woods, sugarhouse, evaporator) having roles understood as more appropriate to one gender.

31. Such an interpretation relies on a very limited definition of technology, of course. To think of plastic tubing and vacuum systems as technology and buckets as not technology, or to put them on a spectrum from "more technological" to "less technological," is a very chauvinistic and self-centered mindset. If McLuhan (*Understanding Media*) taught us nothing else, he showed us that technology is a thing with which people can make more or less meaning, but is not usefully differentiated as more or less validly technological.

32. Sugarhill Containers, which bills itself as "the most widely recognized plastic Pure Maple Syrup container in the industry" (http://bit.ly/2bWi4Hs), provides the iconic plastic bottles and a range of standard and customized labels to maple producers throughout North America.

33. Interview with a sugarmaker, 20 July 2010.

34. Cleave, "Sugar in Tourism," 159.

35. Interview with a sugarmaker, 9 June 2011.

36. Dicks, *Culture on Display*, 122.

37. Interview with a sugarmaker, 7 June 2010.

38. Lange, *The Norwegian Scots*, 249–50.

39. Interview with a sugarmaker, 13 June 2011.

40. Interview with a sugarmaker, 13 June 2011.

41. Harris, *Good to Eat*, 13.

42. Hawkins, "Food Ethics," 72.

43. Wilk, *Home Cooking in the Global Village*, 14.

44. Mintz, *Tasting Food, Tasting Freedom*, 3.

45. Mintz, *Tasting Food, Tasting Freedom*, 3.

46. Mintz, *Tasting Food, Tasting Freedom*, 12.

47. Collings et al., "Human Taste Response."

48. Understandings of whether this fruit-derived sweetness is primarily sweetness, or merely fruitiness that carries sweetness along with it, vary widely. Many fruits in Brazil, for example, are understood primarily as fruits that happen to be sweet, rather than as sources of sweetness first and foremost, an interpretation suggested by the wide availability of tropical fruit drinks from food carts (Wisniewski, pers. comm.). The flavors and liquid nature of the offerings are important parts of the meanings being made, not just sugar content or sweetness as a taste. Certain fruits have become more widely used in industrialized food production to provide a generic sweetness or fruitiness that is not identifiably a specific fruit. Acerola and apple juice, for example, are frequent components of juice blends that serve more as sweetness than as the flavor of fruit they are. They provide a relatively inexpensive "fruit/sweet" quality that can then carry other flavors, such as blueberry or pomegranate, the juices of which are more expensive.

49. *USDA Census*, Table 1, page 8.

50. Interview with a sugarmaker, 7 January 2011.

51. Morse, *Golden Times*, 151.

52. Johnston and Baumann, *Foodies*, 26.

53. Johnston and Baumann, *Foodies*, 70, italics in original.

54. Johnston and Baumann, *Foodies*, 55–56.

55. Interview with Amy Trubek, 27 May 2009.

56. Harris, *Good to Eat*, 13–15.

57. Johnston and Baumann, *Foodies*, 69.

58. Johnston and Baumann, *Foodies*, 73.

59. West, *From Modern Production to Imagined Primitive*, 18.

60. To be sure, there is a powerful draw in having "inside knowledge" of an ingredient, restaurant, or the like before anyone else does. Part of being a foodie is being in the know, which only matters if there are others who are identifiably not in the know.

61. West, *From Modern Production*, 18.

62. There is such a thing as "urban sugaring," however. There are people tapping trees within cities and boiling what comes out. These tappers are only tangentially a part of the sugaring world, though, being more akin to people who raise chickens in their urban backyards than to even a small sugaring operation in rural Vermont. By the same token, the urban chicken raiser is probably more alike an urban maple tapper than to a rural farmer who raises chickens.

63. Wilk, *Home Cooking in the Global Village*, 123.

64. Interview with a sugarmaker, 13 June 2011.

65. Johnston and Baumann, *Foodies*, 73.

66. Spend five minutes watching a food-oriented cable television network (or a travel-oriented one, as seen with *Bizarre Foods*), and you will see the degree to which foodie identity has shaped the way food is presented, visually, auditorily, and conceptually.

67. Farrell, *The Sugarmaker's Companion*, 118.

68. Farrell, *The Sugarmaker's Companion*, 118.

69. Much of the foodie lifestyle is communicated and spread in mass media (television cooking shows and lifestyle shows) and the Internet (blogs, vlogs, and the like). The rise of the foodie coincided with the popularization of social media, which is certainly not a coincidence.

70. Callaway, "Maple Syrup Grades."

71. Interview with a sugarmaker, 9 June 2011.

72. Interview with a sugarmaker, 9 June 2011.

73. Technically, Grade C in the old system was not legally supposed to be sold to the public, but it could be obtained with a wink and a nudge if you knew someone. Many sugarmakers were not happy about producing Grade C, which was considered lower in quality, the syrup equivalent of the "trash meat" discussed previously. Like offal, Grade C has been brought out of the shadows and more prominently onto the dinner table as culinary norms have changed over time.

74. "Maple Production," n.d.

75. Each year, a set of standards was made available to sugarmakers that depicted the color norm for each grade. In true capitalist fashion, these grade standard sets become a tourist commodity themselves; four bottles were packaged together, each containing a small measure of syrup (or in the case of the really cheap version of this tourist item, a small measure of colored liquid) reflective of one of the four grades.

76. Interview with a sugarmaker, 12 June 2012.

77. McWilliams, *Just Food*, 37.

78. Interview with Amy Trubek, 27 May 2009.

79. Johnston and Baumann, *Foodies*, 85.

80. Trubek, *The Taste of Place*, 208.

81. Johnston and Baumann, *Foodies*, 85.

82. Interview with a sugarmaker, 27 May 2010.

83. Wilson, "Selling Culture," 155–56, italics in original.

84. Davenport and Staats, "Maple Syrup Production for the Beginner," 2015.

85. Farrell, *The Sugarmaker's Companion*, 104-105.

86. Interview with a sugarmaker, 23 October 2010.

87. Morse, *Golden Times*, 151.

88. Cresswell, *Place*, 31.

89. Strathern and Stewart, "Epilogue," 236.

90. "USDA National Agricultural Statistics Service News Release: Maple Syrup Production."

91. *USDA Census of Agriculture: Vermont State and County Data.*

92. Interview with a sugarmaker, 21 July 2010.

93. Cresswell, *Place*, 24.

94. Gray, "Open Spaces and Dwelling Places," 225.

95. Ryden, *Landscape with Figures.*

96. Interview with a sugarmaker, 13 June 2011.

97. Trubek, *The Taste of Place*, 215–22.

98. Interview with a sugarmaker, 7 June 2010.

99. Agnew, "The Devaluation of Place in Social Science," 10.

100. Tye, "A Poor Man's Meal."

101. Farrell, *The Sugarmaker's Companion*, 28.

102. Sugar-on-snow is a sort of quick candy made by heating up maple syrup to a strong boil, then pouring it over clean snow (or, in the case of something like Maple Fest, over shaved ice). Rapid stirring and the cold of the snow pull the syrup into a denser, taffy-like consistency.

103. This phenomenon could have something to do with a geographic quirk of many parts of New England, wherein placenames are not consistently displayed at the place they name. Many street intersections in several New England towns lack street signs, for example, the assumption being that one already knows where they are or where they are going. The lesser emphasis on the city name here may be influenced by the New England lack of urgency in displaying placenames.

104. Interview with a sugarmaker, 7 June 2010.

105. http://bit.ly/2c4Md8p.

106. Interview with a sugarmaker, 5 July 2011.

107. Interview with a sugarmaker, 11 June 2010.

108. Marshall, "Quebec," 15.

109. The word itself speaks of this shaping. Landscape derives from Old Norse *land skap*, literally, "the shape of the land," but implying in its modern use both the shape and the shaping of the land. The word part—*skap*—is used in modern Norwegian, Swedish, and Danish to denote an essential quality of something, similarly to the English word parts -ness or -ship. Norwegian *vennskap* = friendship. The shape of the land in "landscape" is about more than its shape, it is about the essential qualities that make and cause that shape.

110. Basso, *Wisdom Sits in Places*, 60.

111. Morse, *Golden Times*, 151.

112. Lange, *The Norwegian Scots*, 153.

113. Morse, *Golden Times*, 156.

114. Basso, *Wisdom Sits in Places*, xiv.

115. Interview with a sugarmaker, 23 October 2010.

116. Anderson, *Mahogany*, 11.

117. The maple leaf is used more in sugaring, but that symbol does not communicate much in the way of geographic meanings.

118. Picard, "How '802' Went Viral."

119. Of course, a map can and should be understood as a technology as well. I am not using "technology" in the Marshall McLuhan sense of medium (*Understanding Media*, for example), but in the simpler, more popular usage. In this construction, things that were first made or used closer to the date of speaking are thought to be more technological or more validly technology.

120. Tsing, *Friction*.

121. Hastrup, "Nature," 1.

122. Senécal, "The Name Vermont," 8.

123. Interview with a sugarmaker, 27 May 2009.

124. Haraway, *When Species Meet*, 10.

125. Interview with a sugarmaker, 3 June 2010.

126. Ellingson, *The Myth of the Noble Savage*.

127. Tsing, "More-than-Human Sociality," 33.

128. Interview with a sugarmaker, 3 June 2010.

129. Ingold, "Designing Environments for Life," 233.

130. Argyrou, *The Logic of Environmentalism*, 16.

131. Ingold, "Designing Environments for Life," 233.

132. FitzPatrick, "The Environment We Create," 67.

133. Tsing, "More-than-Human Sociality," 33.

134. Interview with a sugarmaker, 13 June 2011.

135. Interview with a sugarmaker, 13 June 2011.

136. Brown, "Remaking Maple."

137. Brown, "Remaking Maple."

138. Siccama, "Vegetation, Soil, and Climate."

139. Siccama, "Vegetation, Soil, and Climate," 329–30.

140. http://bit.ly/2coCyxy.

141. Interview with a sugarmaker, 21 July 2010.

142. Interview with a sugarmaker, 27 May 2010.

143. Milius, "Son of Long-Horned Beetles."

144. Milius, "Son of Long-Horned Beetles," 380.

145. Interview with a sugarmaker, 5 July 2011.

146. Siccama, "Vegetation, Soil, and Climate."

147. Interview with a sugarmaker, 7 June 2010.

148. Interview with a sugarmaker, 5 July 2011.

149. Choong-Mo, Du-Le, and Hwa-Joong, "A Study on the Ingredients," 481.

150. Robinson, *The Oxford Companion to Wine*, 700, quoted in Trubek, *The Taste of Place*, 65.

151. Interview with a sugarmaker, 9 June 2011.

152. Atran and Medin, *The Native Mind*.

153. Tsing, *Friction*.

154. Rival, *The Social Life of Trees*.

155. Foster et al., "Wildlife Dynamics."

156. Lockhart, *Maple Sugarin' in Vermont*, 17, italics in original.

157. Harper, "Memories of Ancestry in the Forests of Madagascar," 89.

158. Schusky, *Culture and Agriculture*, 106.

159. Klyza and Trombulak, *The Story of Vermont*, 85–86.

160. Grubinger, *With an Ear to the Ground*, 57.

161. Grubinger, *With and Ear to the Ground*, 113.

162. Interview with a sugarmaker, 13 June 2011.

163. Parsons, "Vermont's Dairy Sector," 1.

164. *New England Cash Receipts 2008*.

165. Fairhead, "Indigenous Technical Knowledge," 14.

166. Nearing and Nearing, *Living the Good Life*, 163.

167. Nearing and Nearing, *Living the Good Life*, 164.

168. Interview with a sugarmaker, 12 June 2012.

169. http://bit.ly/1a3BpNh.

170. Interview with a sugarmaker, 9 June 2011.

171. Nearing and Nearing, *Living the Good Life*, 164.

172. Interview with a sugarmaker, 21 July 2010.

173. Interview with a sugarmaker, 7 July 2011.

174. *New England Agricultural Statistics 2010* and *New England Agricultural Statistics 2011*.

175. Pottier, *Anthropology of Food*, 123.

176. Interview with a sugarmaker, 12 June 2012.

177. Farrell, *The Sugarmaker's Companion*, 225–26.

178. Interview with a sugarmaker, 13 June 2011.

179. Trubek, *The Taste of Place*, 216.

180. Interview with a sugarmaker, 3 June 2010.

181. Interview with a sugarmaker, 11 June 2010.

182. Lockhart, *Maple Sugarin' in Vermont*, 25.

183. Interview with a sugarmaker, 9 June 2011.

184. Tsing, *Mushroom*, 52.

185. Panter-Brick, Layton, and Rowley-Conwy, *Hunter-Gatherers*; Bettinger, Garvey, and Tushingham, *Hunter-Gatherers*.

186. Schusky, *Culture and Agriculture*, ix.

187. Brody, *The Other Side of Eden*, 254.

188. Brody, *The Other Side of Eden*, 255.

189. Ingold, *The Appropriation of Nature*, 130.

190. Ingold goes on to explain that "[e]thnographers who have attributed two-dimensional tenure to hunters and gatherers have generally done so in one of two ways. Either they have confused it with the demarcation of territories for practical purposes, or they have assumed that holding particular sites or paths is necessarily derived from possession of a determinate surface area around or on each side of them. Both approaches have created rather more problems of interpretation than they have solved" (*The Appropriation of Nature*, 148). In essence, Ingold is talking about a different meaning of land tenure, involving a different system of

map, land, and territory (see Basso, *Wisdom Sits in Places*, for further exploration of these complicated relationships).

191. Salazar, "Shifting Values and Meanings," 24.

192. Staiff, Watson, and Bushell, *Heritage and Tourism*, 1.

193. Interview with a sugarmaker, 5 July 2011.

194. Naithan, *The Story-Time of the British Empire*.

195. Interview with a sugarmaker, 7 June 2010.

196. Interview with a sugarmaker, 11 June 2010.

197. Interview with a sugarmaker, 21 July 2010.

198. Interview with a sugarmaker, 21 July 2010.

199. Interview with a sugarmaker, 15 June 2011.

200. Interview with a sugarmaker, 13 June 2011.

201. Interview with a sugarmaker, 13 June 2011.

202. Staiff, Bushell, and Watson, *Heritage and Tourism*, 103.

203. Regulations vary slightly from state to state and province to province, but they all range from 66 to 68 percent concentration to be sold as maple syrup. In the United States and Canada, the legal minimum standard is 66 percent. Vermont and New Hampshire set their own minimum at 66.9 percent, just a tad bit sweeter.

204. Interview with a sugarmaker, 15 June 2011.

205. Interview with a sugarmaker, 21 July 2010.

206. Interview with a sugarmaker, 7 July 2011.

207. For a deeper discussion of the chemistry of sugaring, see Leavitt and Long, "Stable-Carbon Isotopic Composition"; Tyree, "Maple Sap Uptake"; Johnson, Tyree, and Dixon, "A Requirement for Sucrose"; and Warner, *Sweet Stuff*.

208. Interview with a sugarmaker, 7 June 2010.

209. Interview with a sugarmaker, 9 June 2011.

210. Interview with a sugarmaker, 13 June 2011.

211. Waterton and Watson, *The Semiotics of Heritage Tourism*, 36-37.

212. Goffman, *The Presentation of Self in Everyday Life*.

213. Interview with a sugarmaker, 21 July 2010.

214. Interview with a sugarmaker, 20 July 2010.

215. Cresswell, *Place*, 27.

216. Wolff, "We Bought a Team."

217. Steam-Away is actually a trade name for the version of this apparatus sold by Leader Evaporator, but like the term Kleenex, it has become popularized and coopted a bit, so that any rig that does the same job is referred to in a generic sense as a "steam away."

218. Interview with a sugarmaker, 7 June 2010.

219. Interestingly, walking the lines involves an awareness of the natural space (the landscape and trees) as well as the cultural space (the tubing system). Walking the woods is an inspection of both, and more importantly, of the intersection of the natural and the cultural.

220. Waterton and Watson, *The Semiotics of Heritage Tourism*, 32.

221. Johnston and Baumann, *Foodies*, 88.

222. Dicks, *Culture on Display*, 55.

223. Chapuis and Lecat, "Embedding Food and Drink Cultures," 118.

224. Kathleen Stokker's *Folklore Fights the Nazis* makes this point in clear and entertaining detail.

225. http://bit.ly/2cqRLce.

226. Interview with a sugarmaker, 7 June 2010.

227. Interview with a sugarmaker, 7 January 2011.

228. Interview with a sugarmaker, 23 October 2010.

229. Interview with a sugarmaker, 23 October 2010.

BIBLIOGRAPHY

Agnew, John. "The Devaluation of Place in Social Science." In *The Power of Place: Bringing Together Geographical and Sociological Imaginations*, edited by John Agnew and James Duncan. London: Unwin Hyman, 1989.

Agnew, John, and James Duncan, eds. *The Power of Place: Bringing Together Geographical and Sociological Imaginations*. London: Unwin Hyman, 1989.

Anderson, Jennifer L. *Mahogany: The Costs of Luxury in Early America*. Cambridge, MA: Harvard University Press, 2012.

Appadurai, Arjun, ed. *The Social Life of Things: Commodities in Cultural Perspective*. New York: Cambridge University Press, 1986.

Argyrou, Vassos. *The Logic of Environmentalism: Anthropology, Ecology, and Postcoloniality*. New York: Berghahn Book, 2005.

Arnott, Nancy. *The US Market for Ethnic Foods*. 3 vols. New York: Packaged Facts, 2003.

Atran, Scott, and Douglas Medin. *The Native Mind and the Cultural Construction of Nature*. Cambridge, MA: MIT Press, 2008.

Basso, Keith. *Wisdom Sits in Places*. Albuquerque: University of New Mexico Press, 1996.

Bendix, Regina. *In Search of Authenticity*. Madison: University of Wisconsin Press, 1997.

Bettinger, Robert L., Raven Garvey, and Shannon Tushingham. *Hunter-Gatherers: Archaeological and Evolutionary Theory*. New York: Springer, 2015.

Boglioli, Marc. *A Matter of Life and Death: Hunting in Contemporary Vermont*. Amherst: University of Massachusetts Press, 2009.

Bourdieu, Pierre. *Outline of a Theory of Practice*, translated by Richard Nice. Cambridge: Cambridge University Press, 1977.

Bower, Anne. *Recipes for Reading*. Amherst: University of Massachusetts Press, 1997.

Breidenbach, Joana, and Pál Nyíri. *Seeing Culture Everywhere: From Genocide to Consumer Habits*. Seattle: University of Washington Press, 2009.

Brody, Hugh. *The Other Side of Eden: Hunters, Farmers and the Shaping of the World*. Toronto: Douglas and McIntyre, 2000.

Brown, Joshua. "Remaking Maple." University of Vermont, University Communications. http://bit.ly/2c4NQCM, accessed 19 February 2015.

Caldaro, Niccolo Leo. *The Anthropology of Complex Economic Systems: Inequality, Stability, and Cycles of Crisis*. Lanham, MA: Lexington Books, 2014.

Callaway, Nina. "Maple Syrup Grades: Sometimes B Stands for Better." http://bit.ly/2c6ScvT, accessed 14 January 2015.

Chapuis, Claude, and Benoît Lecat. "Embedding Food and Drink Cultures: The Case of Burgundy." In *Food and Drink: The Cultural Context*, edited by Donald Sloan, 114–33. Oxford: Goodfellow Publishers, 2013.

Chibnik, Michael. *Anthropology, Economics, and Choice*. Austin: University of Texas Press, 2011.

Childs, Stephen. "Chemistry of Maple Syrup." Cornell Maple Bulletin 202. Cornell University College of Agriculture and Life Sciences: Cornell Maple Program, 2007.

Choong-Mo Kim, Du-Le Jung, and Hwa-Joong Sheo. "A Study on the Ingredients in the Sap of *Acer mono MAX.* and *Betula costata T.* in Mt. Jiri Area—On the Components of Mineral and Sugar." *Journal of the Korean Society of Food Science and Nutrition* 20, no. 5 (1991): 479–82.

Cleave, Paul. "Sugar in Tourism: 'Wrapped in Devonshire Sunshine.'" In *Sugar Heritage and Tourism in Transition*, edited by Lee Jolliffe. Toronto: Channel View Publications, 2013.

Coleman, Simon, and Peter Collins, eds. *Locating the Field: Space, Place, and Context in Anthropology*. New York: Berg, 2006.

Collings, Virginia, et al. "Human Taste Response as a Function of Locus of Stimulation on the Tongue and Soft Palate." *Perception & Psychophysics* 16 (1974): 169.

Cresswell, Tim. *Place: A Short Introduction*. Malden, MA: Blackwell Publishing, 2004.

Cruikshank, Julie. *Do Glaciers Listen? Local Knowledge, Colonial Encounters, and Social Imagination*. Vancouver: University of British Columbia Press, 2005.

Davenport, Anni L., and Lewis J. Staats. "Maple Syrup Production for the Beginner." http://bit.ly/2crqhpE, accessed 5 February 2015.

Deerr, Noel. *The History of Sugar, Vol. 2*. London: Chapman and Hall, 1950.

Descola, Phillipe, and Gisli Palsson, eds. *Nature and Society: Anthropological Perspectives*. London: Routledge, 1996.

Dicks, Bella. *Culture on Display: The Production of Contemporary Visitability*. Maidenhead: Open University Press, 2003.

Dupont, Jean-Claude. *Le Sucre du Pays*. Ottawa: Lemeac, 1975.

Ellingson, Ter. *The Myth of the Noble Savage*. Berkeley: University of California Press, 2001.

Fairhead, James. "Indigenous Technical Knowledge and Natural Resources Management in Sub-Saharan Africa." Paper commissioned by the Social Science Council, New York, 1992.

Farrell, Michael. *The Sugarmaker's Companion: An Integrated Approach to Producing Syrup from Maple, Birch, and Walnut Trees*. White River Junction, VT: Chelsea Green Publishing, 2013.

Feld, Steven, and Keith Basso, eds. *Senses of Place*. Santa Fe: School of American Research Press, 1996.

Fite, Gilbert C. *American Farmers: The New Minority*. Bloomington: Indiana University Press, 1981.

FitzPatrick, Malcolm S. "The Environment We Create." *Canadian Journal of Public Health / Revue Canadienne de Santé Publique* 76, no. 1 (May/ June 1985): 67–68.

Flagg, Kathryn. "The Vermont Syrup Rush Is On, but Is Big Maple a Boon or a Bubble?" *Seven Days* (May 8–14, 2013), 18, no. 36 (2013): 14–15.

"Forestry and Timber Law: The Maple Tap Act." http://bit.ly/2crrH3u, accessed 28 June 2016.

Foster, David R., Glenn Motzkin, Debra Bernardos, and James Cardoza. "Wildlife Dynamics in the Changing New England Landscape." *Journal of Biogeography* 29, no. 10/11 (2002): 1337–57.

Geertz, Clifford. *Works and Lives: The Anthropologist as Author*. Stanford: Stanford University Press, 1988.

Gingrich, Andre. "Establishing a 'Third Space'? Anthropology and the Potentials of Transcending a Great Divide." In *Anthropology and Nature*, edited by Kirsten Hastrup. New York: Routledge, 2014.

Glassie, Henry. *Passing the Time in Ballymenone*. Philadelphia: University of Pennsylvania Press, 1982.

———. "The Moral Lore of Folklore." *Folklore Forum* 16 (1983): 123–52.

Goffman, Erving. *The Presentation of Self in Everyday Life*. New York: Overlook Press, 1973.

Gray, John. "Open Spaces and Dwelling Places: Being at Home on Hill Farms in the Scottish Borders." In *The Anthropology of Space and Place: Locating Culture*, edited by Setha Low and Denise Lawrence-Zúñiga. Malden, MA: Blackwell Publishing, 2003.

Grubinger, Vern. *With an Ear to the Ground: Essays on Sustainable Agriculture*. Burlington, VT: Northeast Region Sustainable Agriculture Research and Education, 2004.

Handler, Richard, and Jocelyn Linnekin. "Tradition, Genuine or Spurious." *Journal of American Folklore* 97, no. 385 (1984): 273–90.

Hann, Chris, and Keith Hart. *Economic Anthropology: History, Ethnography, Critique*. Malden, MA: Polity Press, 2011.

Haraway, Donna J. *When Species Meet*. Minneapolis: University of Minnesota Press, 2007.

Harper, Janice. "Memories of Ancestry in the Forests of Madagascar." In *Landscape, Memory, and History: Anthropological Perspectives*, edited by Pamela J. Stewart and Andrew Strathern. London: Pluto Press, 2003.

Harris, Marvin. *Good to Eat: Riddles of Food and Culture*. New York: Simon and Schuster, 1985.

Hastrup, Kirsten, ed. *Anthropology and Nature*. New York: Routledge, 2014.

———. "Nature: Anthropology on the Edge." In *Anthropology and Nature*, edited by Kirsten Hastrup. New York: Routledge, 2014.

Hawkins, Rebecca. "Food Ethics." In *Food and Drink: The Cultural Context*, edited by Donald Sloan, 72–97. Oxford: Goodfellow Publishers, 2013.

Heiligmann, Randall. *North American Maple Syrup Producers Manual*, 2nd ed. Columbus: The Ohio State University, 2006.

Hobsbawm, Eric, and Terence Ranger, eds. *The Invention of Tradition*. Cambridge: University of Cambridge Press, 1983.

Hugill, Peter. "Home and Class among an American Landed Elite." In *The Power of Place: Bringing Together Geographical and Sociological Imaginations*, edited by John Agnew and James Duncan. London: Unwin Hyman, 1989.

Ingold, Tim. *The Appropriation of Nature: Essays on Human Ecology and Social Relations*. Iowa City: University of Iowa Press, 1987.

———. "Designing Environments for Life." In *Anthropology and Nature*, edited by Kirsten Hastrup. New York: Routledge, 2014.

Interview with Amy Trubek, 27 May 2009.

Interview with Burr Morse, 27 May 2010.

Interviews with Jon Branon, 11 June 2010, and 15 December 2010.

Johnson, Robert W., Melvin T. Tyree, and Michael A. Dixon. "A Requirement for Sucrose in Xylem Sap Flow from Dormant Maple Trees." *Plant Physiology* 84, no. 2 (June 1987): 495–500.

Johnston, Josée, and Shyon Baumann. *Foodies: Democracy and Distinction in the Gourmet Food Landscape*. New York: Routledge, 2010.

Jolliffe, Lee. *Sugar Heritage and Tourism in Transition*. Toronto: Channel View Publications, 2013.

———. "Connecting Sugar Heritage and Tourism." In *Sugar Heritage and Tourism in Transition*, edited by Lee Jolliffe. Toronto: Channel View Publications, 2013.

Klara, Robert. "Look Out Coconut Water." *Adweek*, July 22, 2015. http://bit.ly/1TS3Fem, accessed 28 June 2016.

Klyza, Christopher McGrory, and Stephen C. Trombulak. *The Story of Vermont: A Natural and Cultural History*, 2nd ed. Hanover: University Press of New England, 2015.

Krupp, Ron. *Lifting the Yoke: Local Solutions to America's Farm and Food Crisis*. Brattleboro, VT: Whetstone Books, 2009.

Lange, Michael A. *The Norwegian Scots*. Lampeter, Wales: Edwin Mellen Press, 2007.

———. "Sweet Bedfellows: Continuity, Change, and *Terroir* in Maple Syrup." *Digest: A Journal of Foodways and Culture* 1, no. 1: (Fall 2012).

Lavin, Chad. *Eating Anxiety: The Perils of Food Politics*. Minneapolis: University of Minnesota Press, 2013.

Leavitt, Steven W., and Austin Long. "Stable-Carbon Isotopic Composition of Maple Sap and Foliage." *Plant Physiology* 78, no. 2: (June 1985): 427–29.

Lockhart, Betty Ann. *Maple Sugarin' in Vermont*. Charleston, SC: The History Press, 2008.

Lovett, Gary M., and Myron J. Mitchell. "Sugar Maple and Nitrogen Cycling in the Forests of Eastern North America." *Frontiers in Ecology and the Environment* 2, no. 2 (March 2004): 81–88.

Low, Setha, and Denise Lawrence-Zúñiga, eds. *The Anthropology of Space and Place: Locating Culture*. Malden, MA: Blackwell Publishing, 2003.

Lyon, Sarah, and E. Christian Wells, eds. *Global Tourism: Cultural Heritage and Economic Encounters*. Lanham, MA: Alta Mira Press, 2012.

"Maple Production." http://bit.ly/2bQi4Ka, accessed 29 June 2016.

Marshall, Peter. "Quebec: After the English Conquest." *North American Review* 256, no. 3 (1971): 10–23.

McLuhan, Marshall. *Understanding Media: The Extensions of Man*. Cambridge, MA: MIT Press, 1964.

McWilliams, James. *Just Food: Where Locavores Get It Wrong and How We Can Truly Eat Responsibly*. New York: Back Bay Books, 2009.

Medeiros, Tracey. *Dishing Up Vermont*. North Adams, MA: Storey Publishing, 2008.

Milius, Susan. "Son of Long-Horned Beetles." *Science News* 155, no. 24 (June 12, 1999): 380–82.

Mintz, Sidney. *Sweetness and Power*. New York: Penguin, 1986.

——. *Tasting Food, Tasting Freedom*. Boston: Beacon Press, 1996.

Monaghan, Leila, and Jane E. Goodman. *A Cultural Approach to Interpersonal Communication*. Malden, MA: Blackwell Publishing, 2007.

Morse, Burr. *Golden Times: Tales through a Sugarhouse Window*. Poultney, VT: Historical Pages, 2008.

——. *Sugar Words: Musings from an Old Vermonter*. Montpelier, VT: Morse Farm Maple Sugarworks, 2012.

Naithani, Sadhana. *The Story-Time of the British Empire*. Jackson: University Press of Mississippi, 2010.

Nearing, Helen and Scott. *Living the Good Life*. New York: Schocken Books, 1954.

Nickerson, Colin. "Why Vt. Maple Producers Are Afraid of This Company." *Boston Globe Online*, April 18, 2016. http://bit.ly/2cA8fmg, accessed 28 June 2016.

Official Vermont Maple Cookbook, The. 3rd ed. South Royalton, VT: Vermont Maple Foundation, [n.d.].

"Organization." http://bit.ly/2c6T6si, accessed 28 June 2016.

Palsson, Gisli. "Life at the Border: Nim Chimpsky et al." In *Anthropology and Nature*, edited by Kirsten Hastrup. New York: Routledge, 2014.

Panter-Brick, Catherine, Robert H. Layton, and Peter Rowley-Conwy, eds. *Hunter-Gatherers: An Interdisciplinary Perspective*. Cambridge: Cambridge University Press, 2001.

Parsons, Bob. "Vermont's Dairy Sector." Center for Rural Studies, University of Vermont, Food System Research Collaborative: Opportunities for Agriculture Working Paper Series. http://bit.ly/2bMNoLo, accessed 4 September 2016.

Peterson, Anna. *Being Human: Ethics, Environment, and Our Place in the World*. Berkeley, CA: University of California Press, 2001.

Peterson, Richard, and Roger Kern. "Changing Highbrow Taste: From Snob to Omnivore." *American Sociological Review* 61, no. 5 (1996): 900–907.

Picard, Ken. "How '802' Went Viral and Became Vermont Shorthand for Cool." *Seven Days* online, July 31, 2013. http://bit.ly/2c6SAu2, accessed 30 March 2015.

Pollan, Michael. *The Omnivore's Dilemma: A Natural History of Four Meals*. New York: Penguin Press, 2006.

Pottier, Johan. *Anthropology of Food*. Cambridge: Polity Press, 1999.

"Production and Value of Honey and Maple Products," Statistics Canada: http://bit.ly/2c6Shzx, accessed 28 June 2016.

Ritzer, George, and Anya Galli. "Food and Drink: The Declining Importance of Cultural Context?" In *Food and Drink: The Cultural Context*, edited by Donald Sloan, 51–71. Oxford: Goodfellow Publishers, 2013.

Rival, Laura. *The Social Life of Trees: Anthropological Perspectives on Tree Symbolism*. Oxford: Berg, 1998.

Robinson, Jancis, ed. *The Oxford Companion to Wine*, 2nd ed. Oxford: Oxford University Press, 1999.

Ross, Anne, Kathleen Pickering Sherman, Jeffrey Snodgrass, Henry Delcore, and Richard Sherman. *Indigenous Peoples and the Collaborative Stewardship of Nature: Knowledge Binds and Institutional Conflicts*. Walnut Creek, CA: Left Coast Press, 2011.

Ryden, Kent. *Landscape with Figures: Nature and Culture in New England*. Iowa City: University of Iowa Press, 2001.

Salazar, Noel. "Shifting Values and Meanings of Heritage." In *Global Tourism: Cultural Heritage and Economic Encounters*, edited by Sarah Lyon and E. Christian Wells. Lanham, MA: Alta Mira Press, 2012.

Schusky, Ernest L. *Culture and Agriculture: An Ecological Introduction to Traditional and Modern Farming Systems*. New York: Bergin and Garvey Publishers, 1989.

Senécal, J.-André. "The Name Vermont." *Journal of the Vermont French-Canadian Genealogical Society* 1, no. 1 (Fall 1996): 8–15.

Siccama, Thomas G. "Vegetation, Soil, and Climate on the Green Mountains of Vermont." *Ecological Monographs* 44, no. 3 (Summer 1974): 325–49.

Sloan, Donald, ed. *Food and Drink: The Cultural Context*. Oxford: Goodfellow Publishers, 2013.

Staiff, Russell, Robyn Bushell, and Steve Watson, eds. *Heritage and Tourism: Place, Encounter, Engagement*. New York: Routledge, 2013.

Staiff, Russell, Steve Watson, and Robyn Bushell. "Introduction—Place, Encounter, Engagement: Context and Themes." In *Heritage and Tourism: Place, Encounter, Engagement*, edited by Russell Staiff, Robyn Bushell, and Steve Watson. New York: Routledge, 2013.

Stewart, Pamela J., and Andrew Strathern, eds. *Landscape, Memory, and History: Anthropological Perspectives*. London: Pluto Press, 2003.

Story of Maple Time in Vermont, The. South Royalton, VT: Vermont Maple Sugar Makers' Association, published in cooperation with the Vermont Agency of Agriculture, Food, and Markets; the University of Vermont Extension; and Perceptions, Inc., [n.d.].

Strathern, Andrew, and Pamela J. Stewart. "Epilogue." In *Landscape, Memory, and History: Anthropological Perspectives*, edited by Pamela J. Stewart and Andrew Strathern. London: Pluto Press, 2003.

Taste of Spring, A: Maple-Sugaring in Canada, A Guide Book Containing Information for Teachers and Suggested Related Activities, Group and Individual, for Students. The Curriculum Services Branch, The Board of Education for the Borough of Etobicoke, 1974.

Taylor, Charles. *The Ethics of Authenticity*. Cambridge, MA: Harvard University Press, 1992.

Taylor, Morgan. "Why Maple Water Is Better than Coconut Water." *Spoon University*, 23 February 2016. http://bit.ly/2c4H6G5, accessed 28 June 2016.

Thomas, Matthew, Kelly Jackson, and Marcus Guthrie. *An Archaeological Overview of Native American Maple Sugaring and Historic Sugarbushes of the Lac du Flambeau Band of Lake Superior Chippewa*

Indians. State Historical Society of Wisconsin, Lad du Flambeau Tribal Historic Preservation Office, and George W. Brown Jr. Ojibwe Museum and Cultural Center. Report for Planning Grant #55-98-13157-2, 1999.

Trubek, Amy. *The Taste of Place*. Berkeley: University of California Press, 2008.

Tsing, Anna Lowenaupt. *Friction: An Ethnography of Global Connection*. Princeton, NJ: Princeton University Press, 2005.

———. "More-than-Human Sociality: A Call for Critical Description." In *Anthropology and Nature*, edited by Kirsten Hastrup. New York: Routledge, 2014.

———. *The Mushroom at the End of the World: On the Possibility of Life in Capitalist Ruins*. Princeton, NJ: Princeton University Press, 2015.

Turner, Victor. *Process, Performance, and Pilgrimage*. New Delhi: Concept Publishing Company, 1979.

Tye, Diane. "A Poor Man's Meal: Molasses in Atlantic Canada." *Food, Culture & Society: An International Journal of Multidisciplinary Research* 11, no. 3 (2008): 335–53.

Tyree, Melvin T. "Maple Sap Uptake, Exudation, and Pressure Changes Correlated with Freezing Exotherms and Thawing Endotherms." *Plant Physiology* 73, no. 2 (October 1983): 277–85.

Urry, John. *The Tourist Gaze*, 2nd ed. London: Sage Publications, 2002.

USDA Census of Agriculture: Vermont State and County Data, Volume 1, Geographic Area Series, Part 45. USDA National Agricultural Statistics Service, Washington, DC, 2009 and 2014. http://bit.ly/2c6Shzx.

"USDA National Agricultural Statistics Service: Milk Cows and Milk Production." http://bit.ly/2c4Md8p, accessed 1 July 2016.

"USDA National Agricultural Statistics Service News Release: Maple Syrup Production." USDA Northeastern Regional Office: Harrisburg, PA, 2014.

Varriano, John. *Wine: A Cultural History*. London: Reaktion Books, 2010.

Warner, Deborah Jean. *Sweet Stuff: An American History of Sweeteners from Sugar to Sucralose*. Washington, DC: Smithsonian Institution Scholarly Press, 2011.

Waterton, Emma, and Steve Watson. *The Semiotics of Heritage Tourism*. Toronto: Channel View Publications, 2014.

Weil, Jim. "Virtual Antiquities, Consumption Values, and the Cultural Heritage Economy in a Costa Rican Artisan Community." In *Values and Valuables: From the Sacred to the Symbolic*, edited by Cynthia Warner and Duran Bell. Walnut Creek, CA: Alta Mira Press, 2004.

Werner, Cynthia, and Duran Bell, eds. *Values and Valuables: From the Sacred to the Symbolic*. Walnut Creek, CA: Alta Mira Press, 2004.

West, Paige. *From Modern Production to Imagined Primitive: The Social World of Coffee from Papua New Guinea*. Durham, NC: Duke University Press, 2012.

Wilk, Richard. *Home Cooking in the Global Village*. Oxford: Berg, 2006.

Wilk, Richard, and Lisa Cliggett. *Economies and Cultures: Foundations of Economic Anthropology*. Boulder, CO: Westview Press, 2007.

Willits, C. O., and Claude Hills. *Maple Sirup Producers Manual*. Washington, DC: USDA Agricultural Research Service, 1976.

Wilson, Damien. 2013. "Selling Culture: The Growth of Wine Tourism." In *Food and Drink: The Cultural Context*, edited by Donald Sloan, 154–74. Oxford: Goodfellow Publishers, 2013.

Wisniewski, Kent. Personal Communication, 2006.

Wittstock, Laura Waterman. *Ininatig's Gift of Sugar: Traditional Native Sugarmaking*. Minneapolis: Lerner Publications, 1993.

Wolff, Alexander. "We Bought a Team." *SI.com Longform*. Retrieved from http://on.si.com/2crraOP, accessed 4 September 2016.

INDEX

Abenaki. *See* Native Americans
Acer (maple genus), 62, 109–10, 130, 150
April's Maple, 29
authenticity, 1, 3, 26–28, 39, 45, 54, 55, 146,
 158, 162, 163
backyard sugaring, xxxvi, 66, 68
Betula (birch genus), 62
branding, 3, 4, 51–54, 145
buckets, xix, xxiii, xxix, 2, 14, 16, 20, 98, 150
bulk packers, 6, 7–11, 13, 65–66
Butternut Mountain Farm, 7, 12–13, 14
Canadian maple, 11–12, 27–28, 50, 55, 62, 71
chemistry, xxvii, 38, 152
climate change, 97, 103
craft specialization, 8–9, 12
corn syrup. *See* pancake syrup
eco-. *See* oikos
epistemology, 34, 36, 77, 81, 87, 92, 117, 120,
 139
ethnicity, 44
evaporator, xxx, 23, 59, 126, 153–155, 158–59
exchange value, 19–20, 22–23, 32
exoticism, 40–43, 45
family, xix, xxii, 147, 148
farming: calendar, xviii, 127, 132, 134; dairy,
 xvii, xxxvii, 15, 71, 115, 120–123, 125,
 127–28
Federation of Quebec Maple Syrup
 Producers (*Fédération des Producteurs
 Acéricoles du Québec*), 7, 19, 50, 55
foodie, 5, 39–46, 54, 56
forestry, xxvii, 98, 108–09, 131, 136
Franklin County, VT, xvi, 11, 62–65, 160
gender, 123–124
geographic limitations of production, 3, 40,
 62, 66, 72, 85, 97
good lifers, 90–92, 96, 124
grading system. *See* syrup grades
Green Mountain Mainlines, 12–15, 32
horse teams, xix, 2, 20, 150
humor, 16, 52, 63, 89, 91–92, 127
imitation maple syrup. *See* pancake syrup
income, xxvii, 6, 16–17; farm income, xxiii,
 xxxvi, 1
international marketing, 4, 6, 11, 28
Juglans (walnut genus), 62
landscape knowledge, xxiii–xv, 61, 99,
 106–07
locavore, 43, 124
Maine, xxxvii–xxxviii, 63, 116

map of Vermont, 75–78
Maple Fest, 68–69
maple leaf symbolism, 72–74
maple water, 31–32, 109, 130
MapleRama, xxxv, 66, 68–71, 80, 160
Native Americans, xxix, 118, 133, 146
Newfoundland, 11–12, 66–67, 111
noble savage, 92, 138
oikos, 95, 99, 104, 109, 111
Orkney, 17, 26, 76
pancake syrup, xv, xxxvi, 4, 39, 45, 46, 165
Proctor Maple Research Center, 100–101
reverse osmosis (RO), xx, xxxii, 17–19, 57,
 108, 109, 150–51, 156–57
St. Albans, VT, xxvi, 69
stewardship, 93, 96, 99–100, 144, 148
sugar: as sweetness, 35–37, 40; beets, 37;
 sugarcane, 37–38; molasses, 67;
 percentage in sap, xxx, 109, 150–51;
 percentage in syrup xxx, xxxiii, 150, 155
sugarhouse: cooking in the, 57–58;
 description, xxx, 23, 25, 59, 103; location,
 xxi, 22–23
Sweet Tree Holdings, 13, 32
sweetness. *See* sugar
syrup grades, xxxiii, 46, 170–71; Grade B,
 xxxiv, 47–48; Grade C, xxxiv, 30, 48;
 Fancy, xxxiv, 46–47, 170–71; new grading
 system, xxxv, 3, 46–50, 170–71
table syrup. *See* pancake syrup
taphole maple wood, 78–81
tapping, xxix, 75, 78–80, 95
tasting notes, 51, 53, 56, 134–35
technological change, xx, 20, 84, 126, 158,
 166–67
temperature for sap run, xiii, 103, 105, 128
terroir, 51–55, 108, 110–11
tourism, 24, 25, 46, 154
traditional imagery, 2, 20, 24, 29, 69, 84, 150,
 163
tubing, xvii, xxiv, xxix, 98–99, 128, 159, 160
University of Vermont, xxxiv–xxxv, 99–100,
 134–35
use value, 19–20, 22–23, 32
vacuum, xxi, 17, 105, 108, 109, 159, 160
Vermont Agency of Agriculture, xxxiv–xxxv,
 5, 134–35, 165
Vermont Maple Sugar Makers Association
 (VMSMA), 5, 49, 55, 165
walking lines, 98, 161